GBC

The world of sub-central ~~~~~~~~~~~~~~~~~~~~~~~~ including local authorities, quas~~~~~~~~~~~~~~~~~~ ~~~~~s and the agencies
of public-private partnerships – has seen massive changes in recent
years and is at the heart of the current restructuring of gov-
ernement in the United Kingdom and other Western democracies.

The intention of the *Government Beyond the Centre* series is to
bring the study of this often-neglected world into the mainstream
of social science research, applying the spotlight of critical analysis
to what has traditionally been the preserve of institutional public
administration approaches.

Its focus is on the agenda of change currently being faced by
sub-central government, the economic, political and ideological
forces that underlie it, and the structures of power and influence
that are emerging. Its objective is to provide up-to-date and
informative accounts of the new forms of government, management and administration that are emerging.

The series will be of interest to students and practitioners of
politics, public and social administration, and all those interested
in the reshaping of the governmental institutions which have a
daily and major impact on our lives.

GOVERNMENT BEYOND THE CENTRE

SERIES EDITORS: GERRY STOKER & STEVE LEACH

Published

Wendy Ball and John Solomos (eds)
Race and Local Politics

Richard Batley and Gerry Stoker (eds)
Local Government in Europe

John Stewart and Gerry Stoker (eds)
The Future of Local Government

Forthcoming

Clive Gray
Government Beyond the Centre

John Gyford
Citizens, Consumers and Councils

Steve Leach, John Stewart and Kieron Walsh
The Changing Organisation and Management of Local Government

Yvonne Rydin
The British Planning System

David Wilson and Chris Game
An Introduction to Local Government

Local Government in Europe

Trends and Developments

Edited by
Richard Batley
and
Gerry Stoker

MACMILLAN

Selection and editorial matter © Richard Batley and Gerry Stoker 1991
Foreword © Robin Hacking 1991
Individual chapters © T. J. Barrington, Richard Batley, Hans A. G. M. Bekke, Philip Blair, Bruno Dente, Dieter Grunow, Agne Gustafsson, Peter John, Petter Lodden, Dominique Lorrain, Juan Ferrer Mateo, Ove Nissen, Alan Norton, Armando Pereira, Gerry Stoker 1991

First published 1991

1064674 4

Published by
MACMILLAN EDUCATION LTD
Houndmills, Basingstoke, Hampshire RG21 2XS
and London
Companies and representatives
throughout the world

Edited and typeset by Povey/Edmondson
Okehampton and Rochdale, England

Printed in Hong Kong

British Library Cataloguing in Publication Data
Local government in Europe: trends and developments.
1. Europe. Western Europe. Local Government
I. Batley, Richard 1942–   II. Stoker, Gerry 1955–   III. Series
352.04
ISBN 0–333–55479–5 (hardcover)
ISBN 0–333–55480–9 (paperback)

Contents

List of Tables and Figures

Tables

Figures

Notes on the Contributors

T. J. Barrington is a former civil servant, who served mainly in the Irish Department of Local Government (now Environment). He was a founder and first editor of the journal *Administration* (Dublin), a founder and first director of the Irish Institute of Public Administration, and a founder of the European Group of Public Administration. He writes, lectures and agitates extensively on problems of Irish government and of local government in particular.

Richard Batley is a Senior Lecturer in the Development Administration Group of the Institute of Local Government Studies at the University of Birmingham. He has conducted research and consultancy on the politics and administration of urban policy in several Latin American, Asian and African countries as well as in Britain. He was previously employed at the Universities of Sussex, Leeds and Durham and in the British civil service.

Hans A. G. M. Bekke undertook his studies in organisational sociology at Erasmus University, Rotterdam. Since 1968 he has been working as a management consultant for governmental organisations. He was a member of the Dutch National Committee for Administrative Reform (1979–81) at the local level. He was Professor of Public Administration at the University of Nymegen until 1989, when he moved to Leyden University.

Philip Blair has since 1977 been an international civil servant with the Council of Europe, where, after a period in the secretariat of the Standing Conference of Local and Regional Authorities of Europe, he is currently secretary of the intergovernmental Steering Committee on Local and Regional Authorities and responsible for organising the conferences of Ministers responsible for local government. He was previously a Lecturer in government and politics at the University of Kent.

Bruno Dente is Associate Professor of Public Administration, University of Bologna, and Research Director in Policy Studies, Institute of Social Research, Milan. He is the author of several pulications on local government in Western democracies.

Dieter Grunow has been Professor of Political Science and Public Administration at the University of Duisberg since 1986. He has undertaken research on German public institutions since 1971, his main focus being on the relationship between citizens and public institutions. During recent years he has participated in the development and evaluation of local health services. On the basis of these research activities he has been a consultant to local governments, to the Ministry of Interior (Bonn), to the OECD, and to voluntary organisations.

Agne Gustafsson is Assistant Professor in the Department of Political Science at the University of Lund, where he has worked since the 1950s. He has published several books on constitutional and political subjects and has held many local government appointments. He has also served as a permanent member or expert adviser on constitutional subjects in several government inquiries concerning local government.

Peter John is a Research Officer at the Policy Studies Institute, London. He was formerly a research officer at Nuffield College, Oxford, working on regional government in Western Europe. He represents the Local and Central Government Relations Research Committee of the Joseph Rowntree Memorial Trust. He is the author of a study of the community charge in Scotland.

Petter Lodden is a political scientist. Since 1986 he has been coordinator of the Norwegian experiments with 'free local government'. Previously he worked with urban renewal policy and he was specifically engaged in developing strategies, through experimental programmes, for the improvement of post-war housing areas.

Dominique Lorrain has been a full-time researcher for the Centre National de Recherche Scientifique in Paris since 1980. He has undertaken extensive research on local policies and politics, and more particularly: assessment of local economic policies, research into urban utilities, studies on decentralisation, the history and role of municipalities in the French political system, and the socio-economics of local civil services. Since 1973 he has been a member of a consulting society – the Fondation des Villes – working both for the state and the municipalities.

Juan Ferrer Mateo joined the Valencian Regional administration in 1982 as an industrial economist after a few years working in computing in the private sector. In 1986 he joined the European Commission as Industrial Economist. He is still an official in the EEC but has returned to Spain as General Director of Organisation and Information Systems in the Generalitat of Valencia.

Ove Nissen, a lawyer, has since 1978 been Director of Planning and Environment with the Association of County Councils in Denmark, where he is also international relations officer and legal adviser to the Board. Before entering the Danish regional government association he was in state service in the Danish Ministries of Cultural Affairs and the Environment.

Alan Norton is a Senior Lecturer at the Institute of Local Government Studies; he was previously an educational administrator in Nigeria and Yorkshire. He has undertaken studies of the management of local government, local authority amalgamation, inter-service collaboration, and government of metropolitan areas internationally. He is currently undertaking a study of the role of the local government chief executive and completing an extensive comparative work on advanced local government systems.

Armando Pereira is an economist who has worked for the Portuguese Ministry of Planning and Territorial Administration in Oporto since 1976. He took his postgraduate degrees in Public Administration and Public Policy at the University of Southern California, Los Angeles (1981) and the London School of Economics and Political Science (1988). At present he teaches public administration and has responsibility for developing organisational and training projects for local authorities in Portugal.

Gerry Stoker is Lecturer in Government at the University of Essex. He was previously employed at the Institute of Local Government Studies, University of Birmingham and at Leicester Polytechnic. He is the author and editor of several books on local government and planning in the United Kingdom. He has undertaken a range of work for the Local Government Training Board and provided seminars and consultancy advice for a wide range of local authorities.

Foreword

The role of local government within the European Community is bound to become increasingly important. As the legal and social framework of the EC comes to provide democratic guarantees and common standards for the individual throughout Europe, local government will be seen as the only deliverer of services which reflects regional identity and which is differentiated by local democratic choice. The themes of this book are therefore crucial.

Whilst the responsibilities of local government in all European countries are changing in response to national legislation, they are also increasingly having to reflect the common effects of the single European act, of pan-European demographic change and of growing consumer demand for better services and more consumer involvement.

Local authorities will have to face the social and economic impact of 1992; comparisons of performance and efficiency will operate increasingly on a pan European basis. A better understanding of local government systems across Europe will be of advantage to a local authority competing to attract economic activity and jobs. On the other hand, some local authorities will need to cooperate with counterparts across national boundaries as transfrontier regions grow in importance and processes are harmonised. There is also clear scope for a sharing of experience in issues, such as environmental protection and the care of the elderly, where substantial increases in public expenditure will be required and local government will play a leading role. New approaches to service delivery are being developed across Europe, as customers demand more and better services while local authorities are faced with decreasing financial resources. As this book shows, local government in all countries is assuming the role of enabler as services are contracted out to the private or semi-private sectors.

So I see a great deal of common ground for local authorities in Europe. The significant variance between Great Britain and the rest of Europe is in the area of central–local relations. This book explores and illustrates the differing interactions between levels of government and the ways in which differences of interest between the levels are resolved.

The conference on which this book is based demonstrated to me, and no doubt many of the other participants, the vital importance of sharing and exploiting the common ground that exists. In supporting the conference, I am pleased that ICL has been able to make a gesture to reflect its status as a major supplier of information systems in Europe and to local government in Great Britain. From those two perspectives I hope that this book will inspire many others to adopt an increasingly European outlook on the development of local government.

ROBIN HACKING

Director
Local Government and Health Business
ICL (UK) Ltd

Acknowledgements

The contributors to this book, who come from most of the countries of Western Europe, were among the participants at the Conference organised by the Institute of Local Government Studies to mark its 25th Anniversary in October 1989. For publication in this book we asked contributors to revise and rework their papers substantially. We are grateful to them for their rapid rewriting. We also commissioned a further chapter from Alan Norton as well as providing additional chapters ourselves.

We were fortunate to find a sponsor, ICL Ltd, who not only made it possible to run the conference and to bring our participants to Britain, but who also contributed to the development of ideas while leaving us free to establish our own direction. We would like to thank particularly Robin Hacking, Director, Local Government and Health Business; Brian Sellers, European Sales Director; Paul Vevers and Helen Salah.

Colleagues contributed their time and ideas to the discussions which led to this book, particularly Ken Davey, Ken Young, John Stewart, Kieron Walsh and Malcolm Wallis. Others were helpful and tolerant administrators and secretaries who made it possible to run the conference efficiently and to bring out this book rapidly: Caroline Raine, Lorraine Doherty, Amanda Williams, Kathy Bonehill, Mary Furamera, Vikki Casstles and Ann Westover. Finally we would like to thank Steven Kennedy of the publishers for his helpful suggestions and comments on the project and Keith Povey for his careful editorial advice.

RICHARD BATLEY
GERRY STOKER

1 Introduction: Trends in European Local Government

Gerry Stoker

Local government is a key element in the political systems of Europe's liberal democracies. Local government organisations provide a range of services – education, welfare, housing and transport to name but a few – which are central to the social and economic well-being of their citizens. They are large-scale spenders of public money and major sources both directly and indirectly of employment. But local government is about more than the delivery of services. It is the level of government closest to the citizen and has a role in representing the concerns and views of the locality. Local government provides an opportunity for political participation and expression that can have a pivotal role in a democratic political system.

Given the profound political changes in Eastern Europe it is interesting to note that in Poland, Hungary and other former 'communist' countries those seeking to remake the structure of their societies have placed a strong emphasis on the development of a viable and effective system of local government. In Poland, for example, local self-government is seen to have a vital role in dismantling the power of the central state apparatus and local party bureaucrats (see Department of the Environment, 1990). More generally the establishment of viable local government in Eastern Europe is seen as central to the establishment and maintenance of a democratic process. It is also seen as an appropriate level for effective government intervention to meet welfare needs and stimulate economic efficiency.

1

The development of new local government systems in Eastern Europe, however, is not the prime focus of this book. Our concern is with the local government organisations of the Western European democracies. We recognise, however, that those established Western systems provide a vital learning base and a source of models for those in Eastern Europe seeking to remake their systems. The developments in Eastern Europe will provide a major source of future research interest and insight for those concerned with local government.

The driving force for the book is a concern to examine how the systems of local government in Western Europe are changing and developing. We cannot offer a comprehensive description of local government structures and functions (see Norton, 1991). Our purpose is to capture developments and trends and give an idea of the diverse and shared directions in which different local government systems are going.

There are several reasons why it is particularly appropriate to examine in a comparative way developments in local government systems. First, the continuing development of 'a single European market' and interest in greater political unity suggests that greater mutual understanding is essential for all European countries. On the one hand it might be argued that it is useful to know more about your competitors, their infrastructure and support systems in the opening market. On the other hand there is an increased desire for cooperation and a concern to learn from the experience of others in dealing with both the social and the economic challenges faced by localities. A feature of the late 1980s and the beginning of the 1990s has been the rise of a number of ad hoc groupings of European cities and municipalities. Meetings, conferences and workshops are arranged to exchange experience, views and ideas. These ad hoc organisations are in addition to the more formal gatherings organised under the auspices of the Council of Europe or the International Union of Local Authorities.

A second broad argument for examining developments in Europe is that the last two decades have thrown up a number of new challenges for local government. Post-war growth in public spending, especially associated with the expansion of the welfare state, led to increased service provision and activity by local government. But the more difficult economic climate from the mid-1970s onwards led to a concern with public spending restraint. Spending by local government and its taxation powers became the subject of sharper scrutiny; although, as we shall see, the pace and direction of policy response varied throughout Europe.

The challenge facing local government, however, is broader than that posed by the 'fiscal crisis'. A wider pattern of social and economic change has had a profound impact on the environment in which local government is operating. A full discussion of these changes will not be attempted here (see Stoker, 1989, 1991) but a few key trends can be identified.

The pattern of industry has shifted with an increased emphasis on using computers, robotics and information technology to control and direct production. There is a growing role for service industry. With these changes have come shifts in the demand for labour and the structure of the labour market. In this changing economy local government has had to deal with the decline of old industries and the growth of new economic activities. Its ability to recruit and employ staff has been affected and it has increasingly found private sector service industries willing to compete for and provide publicly-funded services on contract. Accompanying these shifts in economic activity have been changes in culture and ideology. The consumers of goods and services in both private and public sectors show signs of being more demanding, expecting higher quality services tailored to their needs. Within private management thinking a 'new wave' of ideas has come to the fore, critical of over-centralised, bureaucratic and hierarchical forms of organisation. The new wave emphasises strategic planning to give direction, but devolved management structures and systems to maximise flexibility in a changing environment. Within the public sector, too, traditional bureaucratic forms of organisation have increasingly been seen as problematic, lacking flexibility and with a tendency to be remote from the public. The challenge facing local government is to find more responsive and effective organisational forms. Add in the growing concern with ecological and environmental matters and it is clear that local government faces a range of sharp challenges in both its service delivery and its wider governmental role.

This book explores the way that local government in Europe has been responding to the challenges it faces. The comparative light we throw onto the subject confirms one broad message; there are alternative routes to making local government more open, responsive and effective. This basic insight is valuable in challenging the established assumptions and ideological certainties of different local government systems.

The remainder of this introductory chapter is divided into three parts. First, a framework for comparative analysis is established, identifying three broad themes which guide the discussion in the book. Second, the background to a sub-plot for the book is outlined. The issue is whether Britain is out of step with the rest of Europe in terms of the development of its local government system. A third section highlights some of the key points from the single country studies that occupy the bulk of the book.

A framework for comparative analysis

The comparative analysis of social and political systems is fraught with difficulties. A key problem in comparative studies is that of finding the correct balance between description and analysis. It is necessary 'to decide both what to compare and how to compare as well as gathering enough descriptive material to make comparison possible' (Higgins, 1981, p 1). Our approach in this book is guided by a concern to capture trends and developments in the local government systems of Western Europe. The themes for discussion are:

- the changing status of local government in respect of its powers and relationship with other levels of government
- changes in the organisation of local service delivery
- developments in the political management of local government and the future of local democracy.

These three themes capture a shared agenda of change in the local government systems of Western Europe.

A factor in choosing these themes is that they relate not only to the concerns of academics but also to those of practitioners. In short we are seeking to contribute not only to understanding but also to the development of policy and management practice.

We wish to explore whether lessons can be learnt through the experience of comparison. We recognise the difficulties involved in simply transplanting a successful method or initiative from one country to another. What makes it 'work' in that country is a reflection of its integration into a particular set of relations, interests and culture, and taken out of that context the approach may have little value. Yet few would wish to deny the potential value of learning from and adapting the successful schemes of other countries. Equally it is difficult to ignore the virtue of examining the commonplace assumptions and burning issues of one country's local political system against that of other countries. The practice of comparing can contribute by opening the mind to alternative approaches and by providing a critical back-cloth against which to assess the strengths and weaknesses of one's own system.

Before exploring in more detail the particular themes which provide a focus for the comparative study contained in this book, it is appropriate to indicate our response to the second half of the problem of comparative studies posed at the beginning of this section. We have suggested what and how we intend to compare but can we achieve an adequate descriptive base for our comparisons? The chapters on the experiences of particular countries do provide some information and analysis but it is Chapter 2 that provides key background on the structure and operation of Western Europe's diverse local government systems.

Norton's chapter sketches the main features of the various local government systems in terms of their structure, functions, spending, size and position within a wider governmental framework. It is by no means a comprehensive account but it provides an essential backcloth for the discussion in the remainder of the book.

Chapters 3 and 15 are the only other chapters which have an explicitly comparative character. It is possible to explore some of their findings and provide a useful framework for the single-country studies which occupy the bulk of the book by examining in slightly more detail the three themes identified above.

The changing status of local government

A key element in the discussions presented in this book is an examination of the changing nature of central-local relations. In order to guide debate and facilitate comparison three models of the relationship between central and local government can be presented (adapted from Clarke and Stewart, 1989).

1. The relative autonomy model

This model gives an independence to local authorities while not denying the reality of the nation state. The emphasis is on giving freedom of action to local authorities within a defined framework of powers and duties. Central government relations with local authorities are therefore determined largely by legislation. Controls are limited. Local authorities raise most of their revenue through direct taxation. Within the relative autonomy model local authorities may pursue policies which they share with central government or which differ from those advocated by central government.

2. The agency model

This is the model in which local authorities are seen mainly as agencies for carrying out central government's policies. This is ensured by detailed specification in legislation, the development of regulations and the operation of controls. There is therefore little need or justification for significant local taxation. Grants or other non-local funding make up the bulk of the local authority income.

3. The interaction model

In this model it is difficult to define the spheres of action of central and local government, because they are involved in a complex pattern of relationships, in which the emphasis is on mutual influence. The political processes of central and local government are closely inter-related – possibly through the dual mandate – with issues often being resolved by mutual discussion. The officers of both levels are closely involved in joint discussion of projects and plans. In this model it is difficult to define responsibilities, since the emphasis is on working together. Local government finance will involve both taxes and grants, but taxes may be shared and grant levels protected.

Plainly no country can be simply described in terms of one model. The pattern may vary between activities or service areas. Other dimensions of central-local relation might also be brought into play. For example, whether supervision and representation of local government is the responsibility of one department or several within central government. The models, however, do suggest alternative stances in central-local relations and provide a base against which to assess trends.

Several of the single country chapters seek to place their systems within the framework of competing models. In terms of a broad trend the message that overwhelmingly emerges is that most of Europe is moving down the path of greater decentralisation.

The establishment of a viable local democracy is seen as vital in Spain and Portugal. France and Italy have undertaken decentralisation measures. The Scandinavian countries have, in the context of already decentralised systems, introduced experiments in 'free local government', aimed at further promoting local autonomy and initiative. Britain in contrast (as Batley suggests and John demonstrates) is moving in the opposite direction towards a more centralised system and even towards an agency status for local government.

It is perhaps an overstatement to suggest that the well-resourced and organised local authorities of Britain have become mere agents of the centre. Readers will note the absence of any local tax powers in Italy (although a system of user charges appears to have gained in importance) and the very heavy reliance on central government grant support in the Dutch case. Moreover the local councils of Southern Europe may have independent status but, as Blair points out, are limited in their ability to undertake effective action by lack of financial and staff resources. Further it may be noted that in Denmark, in attempting to restrain local spending, central government has cut back on the block grant, introduced penalties and launched an ultimately unsuccessful attempt to abolish the county tier of local government.

It would be unwise to try and draw general conclusions about the degree of autonomy available to different local government systems on the back of the contributions made to this book. A sustained and detailed analysis is required to deal with the issue fully but what we can identify is the changing direction and concerns of central-local relations. Issues of local government spending have driven much of the agenda. But central government has also sought to reinvigorate local government's capacity for service delivery and its relationship with its citizens.

What is clear is that in Britain the degree of conflict and intensity of central government interventions against local government has been greater than elsewhere in Europe. Blair comments in Chapter 3 that the concern of the British government with controlling local government expenditure finds only a partial echo on the continent. This reflects the fact that in some countries local revenue-raising capacity is limited but it also reflects the fact that spending restraint has been promoted more through negotiation than legislation and within a realistic appreciation of the pressures on local government. Blair comments in particular that the narrow focus on the financial accountability of local councils to their electors is not to be found elsewhere in Europe. He comments that community charge is generally 'regarded as rather exotic, and has certainly found no imitators'.

The issue of the status of local government is wider than the matter of central-local relations; it is an issue of the esteem and support given to local government by the public. Here Blair suggests three factors to consider in assessing different local government systems. The first is the issue of general competence powers. Briefly the position is that while in most of continental Europe local authorities have a general power to act on behalf of the citizens of their locality, in Britain they do not but rather are given a series of powers to undertake particular activities. In practice this may not have overly constrained British local authorities (i.e. they have found legislative support for most of activities they have wished to undertake), but it does diminish the status of British local government compared to that elsewhere in Europe.

A second factor identified by Blair is the presence of a separate and identifiable political executive to provide a focus for public attention and leadership within a locality. Here the situation varies from country to country. Undoubtedly in France the mayor is a focal point for the local electorate and a key participant in the political system. The committee systems which combine executive and representative functions – such as those which dominate in Sweden and Britain for example – do not throw up a natural focal point. In particular few local politicians in Britain could claim to be as well-known as or carry as much prestige as many French mayors. A further factor in considering the relationship with the public is the size of the local authorities. Here there is a difficult balance to be drawn between authorities which are large enough to have the necessary technical competence and expertise to carry out complex governmental tasks and authorities which are so large that it is difficult for the local population to identify with their local government. It might be suggested that Britain scores highly in terms of its professional competence but the large size of its local government units makes it more difficult for the public to identify with it. On the other hand local councils in, for example, Southern Europe may be very close to their public but lack the expertise and organisational strength to take effective action.

The issue of service delivery

The second theme of the book is concerned with how to improve both the efficiency and the responsiveness to the public of local services. As Batley comments it is extraordinary how much of the language and debate about public service reform is shared between European countries. The problem is large-scale bureaucracy and red-tape and many of the solutions are shared in terms of experiments with decentralised service delivery, user panels, opinion surveys, customer awareness training and competitive tendering. Various chapters in the book provide details of service delivery initiatives and experiments undertaken in the last decade or so.

At a broad level what is also clear is that the enabling role – of working with and through other organisations to achieve service delivery – is the norm for local councils in Europe. The chapters on the experience of France, Italy, Germany and Sweden in particular make this point. Lorrain describes the special role of private and semi-public companies in service production in the French system. The Italian system, as Dente confirms, is premised on local authorities working through voluntary organisations, workers' cooperatives and other service delivery organisations.

In the Swedish case, as Gustafsson makes clear, arms-length organisations have a crucial role and there is considerable interest in extending further the flexibility in production provided by the use of voluntary organisations or even private contractors (see also Riberdahl, 1989).

Moreover, as Batley points out, the practice of working through other organisations has enabled many European local authorities to retain responsibility for (if not control over the production of) a wider range of services. This point is confirmed in Chapter 2 in a discussion of the core functions of local authorities in Europe. As Batley comments, services which in Britain are managed at a regional level by unelected governmental or even private sector organisations are in a number of European countries the responsibility of elected regional or local government. Responsibility may be shared with other governmental tiers but it is not uncommon for local government to have a stake in water supply, sewage disposal, health services and energy supply.

Finally, in terms of broad strategies of service reform, a distinction can be drawn between those countries where the emphasis is on retaining but reforming the established systems of public service delivery and those that lay a greater stress on the introduction of market mechanisms, business-like organisation and private sector competition. Britain, in the last decade, has had a clear preference at central governmental level for market-orientated reforms and this is clearly a strong theme in Italy and the Netherlands. Germany, perhaps, provides a half-way house. Sweden and Norway are the most strongly committed to the strategy of public service reform. These generalisations, however, should not be pushed too far because in most countries a mixture of strategies and a rather pragmatic, experimental, mode of working tends to hold sway.

Local political control and democracy

Of the three themes which guide discussion in this book it is the issue of local political control and democracy which receives the least attention from the various contributors. In part this reflects the fact that it is an issue of greater concern in Britain than elsewhere in Europe. In Britain there appears to be a lack of faith in local political control and democracy. Central government has queried local authorities' electoral mandate, removed elements of the elected local government structure and handed key decision-making responsibilities to new and unelected bodies such as Urban Development Corporations and Training and Enterprise Councils. From below local authorities have found themselves criticised for their remoteness from the public and have had their legitimacy questioned by the tradition of relatively low electoral turnout. Elsewhere in Europe there appears a sense of satisfaction with the operation of local political control and the value of local democracy. However, Gustafsson expresses some doubts about whether public interest and support for the Swedish system will be retained. There are some fears in Italy that local administration is over-politicised. Blair notes various attempts to improve the working conditions of local elected representatives and extend opportunities for citizen participation. But overwhelmingly the impression is of a degree of relative satisfaction with the operation of local political control and democracy.

Why is it that Britain appears to have lost more faith in its local democratic representatives than other European countries? Batley suggests it may reflect the size of the councils which means the density of councillors per population is considerably less in Britain than elsewhere. He also argues that the majority voting system as opposed to the various versions of proportional representation that operate throughout the rest of Europe may be a factor. Blair refers to Britain's neglect of the local *governmental* role within our system and the lack of a clear and visible political executive as factors which weaken respect for local democracy.

A further factor may be tendency for politics to develop along functional rather than territorial lines in Britain. As Batley notes, central-local relations in Britain are characterised by the extent of the separation between the two tiers of government at both a political and administrative level. National parties' organisations and MPs are divorced to a greater degree from local party structures and representatives than is common elsewhere in Europe. The British civil service has a very distinctive and separate career pattern and recruitment base from that of British local government officers. Communication and inter-governmental working in the British case take place to a substantial degree through functional-based, service-specific, professionally-influenced policy networks. Territorial networks, although strong in the case of Scotland and Wales, are on the whole subservient to those functionally-based networks (Rhodes, 1988). In short, the governmental system in the UK pushes participants into functionally-based arenas and patterns and this in turn under-mines the support at both central and local levels of government for broad, community-based, local, democratic decision-making.

It is interesting to note that talk of extending democracy in the British case has in most cases involved setting up mechanisms for local decision-making by particular service users – parents, tenants – rather than the public at large. Whether this spread of functional democracy is a valuable development remains to be seen. What can be argued is that it stands in contrast to the preference elsewhere in Europe for sustaining a system of area-based local representative democracy.

Britain out of step

The sub-plot for this book – which has already raised its head to some degree – involves exploring a little further a theme sugges-ted by a number of commentators on developments in European local government (Goldsmith and Newton, 1988; Crouch and Marquand, 1989). The suggestion is that Britain is running counter to the trend. It is developing a more centralised political system with a diminished role for elected local authorities while elsewhere in Europe the agenda of change is favouring greater decentralisation and local autonomy.

This book does not support a simple picture of Britain heading in one direction and the rest of Europe heading in another. However, the evidence presented by much of the book does support the broad proposition that central-local relations in Britain have been uniquely conflictual and that the standing and status of elected local authorities has been subject to a more aggressive attack from the centre. It has to be conceded that the sense of crisis, uncertainty and loss of legitimacy is greater in British local government than is the case elsewhere in Europe. On the other hand the British debate about how to break down public bureaucracy into more responsive and accountable units strikes chords elsewhere in Europe. And in developing an enabling role – working through and with other public, voluntary and private sector organisations – British local authorities are moving much closer to the dominant tradition and norm of European local government.

Fiscal and spending constraints have been experienced in all of Europe's local government systems. As have the broad economic and social changes identified at the beginning of this chapter. What is unique about Britain is the sustained and active intervention by central government aimed at aggressively restructuring local government. In particular since 1979 the Thatcher administrations have maintained a major legislative onslaught.

In the first two terms of Mrs Thatcher's government the attention was largely focused on a series of measures aimed at restraining local government spending but after the third election victory in 1987 a greater emphasis was given to a broad concern with the role, organisation and management of local government finance, the extension of competitive tendering and the restructuring of local government's core functions in education, housing and community. Chapter 4 provides a detailed analysis of a number of the measures.

The driving principle behind the post-1987 reforms, from the perspective of the Thatcher administration, can be given the label 'marketisation'. The aim is to fragment public sector institutions and stimulate private and voluntary sector alternatives in order to create a marketplace of service providers. The production and allocation of state-supported provision will be increasingly conditioned by market or quasi-market systems as opposed to the established political, bureaucratic and professional forms of mediation. Who produces what and who gets what will become less a matter of political, professional or bureaucratic judgment and will depend more on the operation of quasi-market mechanisms. The language of the reform emphasises the virtues of the market mechanisms of competition, choice and opportunity cost. Competition between public sector agencies, and with the private sector, is seen as ensuring efficiency and responsiveness to the customer. Choice is to be made available to the customer in its market form of an exit option to another provider. A greater awareness of the opportunity costs involved in public spending decisions is to be stimulated by ensuring that both service providers and receivers have a sharper understanding of the costs of their choices. Accountability in that sense is thereby enhanced.

The reform package retains its concerns with financial constraint, but expands to cover broader issues relating to organisation, management and orientation of local government. Marketisation is promoted on the back of a claim that in the long run it will help to introduce the necessary discipline into public service provision to ensure 'value for money' and undermine the tendency for public spending to grow.

This 'official' explanation of the motivation and impact of the post-1987 reform package is challenged by many commentators on the British scene (for a review see Stoker, 1990). For those with a constitutional perspective these measures are part of a consistent and pernicious policy of centralisation pursued by the Conservatives since their election in 1979. The saddling of local authorities with a highly unpopular and difficult to collect tax – the community charge – combined with the establishment of a whole array of non-elected local agencies – Urban Development Corporations, grant maintained schools, Training and Enterprise Councils – outside the ambit of local authority control has contributed to a further undermining of the autonomy and power of local authorities. Still others argue that the programme is motivated by concerns of party interest and advantage. Thus reforms of housing are seen as undermining Labour's ability to maintain its electoral base on council housing estates by forcing Labour councils to eliminate subsidies and push up rents. The extension of competitive tendering is seen as a direct attempt to break the stranglehold of public sector trade unions in some local authorities. While the reforms in education, community care and an adjusted and adapted community charge are seen as providing rewards and benefits to Conservative party supporters.

Britain is out of step with the rest of Europe because it has had a national government uniquely and strongly committed to restructuring local government. The Thatcher administrations have seen themselves as promoting a more efficient, effective and responsible local government. Critics suggest they have manipulated local government to seek party advantage and have produced a grossly over-centralised political system. Most observers would agree that local government in Britain has been destabilised and is uncertain about its future role.

Paradoxically, as this book makes clear, the search for a new role may be bringing British local government more in line with that elsewhere in Europe. In particular the idea of the enabling authority – working through and with other organisations – is a concept of local government which is the norm in Europe. To a considerable degree the enabling concept expresses a new consensus in Britain about the future of local government. The vision of a more pluralistic system of production and provision is supported by Conservative ministers (Ridley, 1988), and the Labour Party's Policy Review (Labour Party, 1989). It is a vision that has been endorsed by a number of leading local government figures (Clarke and Stewart, 1988; Brooke, 1989).

The development of the enabling role in British local government may take a number of different directions. Some authorities see their future role as retaining the responsibility for production but contracting out the task of production. According to Mather (1989, p 233): 'This contract model separates the political process of determination of objectives and specification of services from their delivery, removing conflict of interest which occurs when those specifying a service are also its deliverers.' Local authorities will become more 'business-like' – selecting service producers from a competing range of private companies, in-house workforces and other agencies – and therefore become more efficient and responsive to customers.

Examples of the arms-length or contract mode of service provision are to be found elsewhere in Europe (see in particular the chapters on France, Italy and the Netherlands). Yet an overwhelming message from this book is that for most of European local government the enabling concept is not solely about more pluralistic service provision. It involves local authorities seeing themselves as political institutions giving expression to a wide range of local concerns. The contract model may find some resonance in Europe but it is a model of local authorities as community government that emerges as the dominant theme.

A point made by several contributors and one of the strongest points made in our discussions with our European colleagues is that the debate about and conception of local government is too narrowly focused on issues of service delivery. In particular for British commentators and practitioners at both central and local level, local government is seen almost exclusively as an instrument for the organisation and delivery of services. However, as many of our European colleagues argued, this view underplays the proper meaning of the term government. (Indeed they took a certain delight in suggesting we did not understand our own language!) The debate elsewhere in Europe, while taking on board issues of non-bureaucratic, customer, responsive service delivery, remains concerned with the idea of local government as a part of the political system aimed at identifying public concerns and fears, reconciling conflicting issues and identifying priorities in resource allocation and policy. Local government has a status and position as the first level of government of the community.

The prerequisites and implications of British local authorities developing a role in community government have been explored elsewhere (Stewart and Stoker, 1988; Stewart, 1989). The enabling authority acting as community government would take as its focus the needs and problems faced by its locality. It would develop sophisticated mechanisms for learning from its community. Working through local people and organisations – drawing resources from public, private and voluntary sources – it would seek to develop policies and programmes to meet the concerns of the community.

In so far as this wider conception of the enabling role is emerging in British debate and practice, then Britain is becoming more, rather than less, in touch with developments elsewhere in Europe. The challenge of meeting the demands of an effective community government role is shared by the local government systems of Western Europe, as the evidence and analysis of this book will show.

The structure of the book

As already noted, Chapter 2 provides essential background on the structure and organisation of Western European local government. Chapter 3 follows with some broad comparisons about the changing nature of these local government systems. There follows a number of single country studies.

Chapter 4 summarises developments in England and Wales. Peter John examines some of the factors influencing the process of change and examines the core reforms in detail. A concluding section suggests that, although some of the reforms may contribute to improved efficiency and responsiveness in service delivery, overall the package appears to undermine the scope for local choice and government.

In Chapter 5, Dieter Grunow focuses on developments in West Germany's local service delivery. The chapter opens with a brief account of the basic structure of local government in the Federal Republic. Grunow notes that local politics is increasingly driven by a concern to improve efficiency in service delivery and by the demands of a public who expect high quality services and are prepared to pay for them. The bulk of the chapter examines various reforms in service delivery. Some reforms involve the public on a collective basis by providing opportunities for participation, public opinion surveys and self-help groups. A particular radical innovation is the establishment of 'planning cells' – composed of members of the public supported by appropriate technical staff – which have the task of finding a solution to a particular social or economic problem. A second range of reforms aims at improving service delivery through better staff training and better coordinated provision. A third category involves the use of private contractors but Grunow notes that the contracting-out approach is only used in the case of a few services such as refuse collection.

In Chapter 6, Dominique Lorrain describes the major role in service production undertaken by private and semi-public companies in the French local government system. He shows how these companies have expanded their activities and diversified into a range of service functions including water, transport and refuse collection. Lorrain discusses some of the advantages and disadvantages of the system. In particular he notes that the operation of multi-functional, large-scale companies have facilitated the achievement of technical efficiency and economies of scale while allowing a highly fragmented, localised system of communes to continue to flourish. The basic units of local government have retained their closeness to the public and yet through the companies have been able to ensure effective service delivery. The chapter closes with a discussion of the different forms of control exercised by the communes over the companies. The virtues of a broad global regulation are contrasted with the strengths of a more detailed, contract-based system of control.

In Chapter 7, Bruno Dente stresses the distinctiveness of the Italian local government system in different parts of the country. The 1970s was a period of expansion, politicisation and welfarism which was checked in the 1980s by a growing fiscal crisis. Pressures to deal with this crisis encouraged two significant developments: an increased use of fees and charges for services and experiments in hiring staff via workers' cooperatives. These initiatives are seen as pragmatic, reactive and piecemeal. Dente, however, sees a growing demand for a public service revolution and an increasing interest in the possibilities of privatisation and contracting-out.

Hans Bekke's account of developments in Dutch local government in Chapter 8, describes a situation which will seem quite familiar to a British audience. Local government in the Netherlands is seen as having been over-ambitious, and over-loaded with responsibilities and tasks. The solution as seen by many is for local councils to step back from some responsibilities and develop a more business-like way of working. The bulk of the chapter discusses various approaches to contracting-out services and introducing modern management techniques into local government.

In Chapter 9, Armando Pereira, looking at local government in Portugal, describes a system in the making. Local councils are seen as central elements in the developing democratic structures of the society. Local government has considerable constitutional status but it is limited by lack of finances and appropriate technical skills. Pereira describes various programmes of reform aimed at improving the effectiveness and responsiveness of service delivery.

In Chapter 10 Juan Ferrer Mateo concentrates on developments in the system of administration in Spain. He notes the difficulties posed by the complexity and bureaucratic red tape of the system and examines how 'single window' reforms may open up access to the system for the citizen and challenge the controlling nature of public administration.

Tom Barrington in Chapter 11 provides an account of the trials and tribulations of local government in Ireland. He describes a system in which local government is dominated by the centre. Despite much talk of reform to increase local government's discretion and financial independence, he notes that it is in fact exposed to a continuous process of quiet decline in respect of its status, its role in service delivery, and local political control.

Agne Gustafsson describes the Swedish system of local self-government in Chapter 12 and presents a picture of strong and powerful local councils with substantial functions and revenue-raising powers. There is a clear commitment to decentralisation in the governmental system given even further emphasis by the development of the 'free commune experiment'. Gustafsson goes on to describe the system of local democratic control and various attempts to improve its effectiveness. The whole system, he notes, is underwritten by a strong local party influence.

Ore Nissen's description of local government in Denmark in Chapter 13 paints a picture of a strong system responsible for nearly 70 per cent of public spending. The fiscal crisis of the late 1970s created tensions. Nissen describes the 'control by agreement' exercised by central and local government over spending. He also outlines the arguments surrounding an ultimately un-successful attempt to abolish the upper tier of local government in the system.

In Chapter 14 Petter Lodden presents a detailed account of the 'Free Local Government' experiment in Norway which is prob-ably the most substantial and advanced of all such initiatives in the Scandinavian countries (for further background see Stewart and Stoker, 1989). The chapter describes the objectives and structure of the experiment. It describes the evolution of the scheme and evaluates the lessons that emerge.

In conclusion, in Chapter 15 Richard Batley discusses some of the key lessons that can be drawn from a comparison of the developments in the systems of local government in Western Europe.

References

Brooke, R. (1989) *Managing the Enabling Authority*, Longman, Harlow.

Clarke, M. and Stewart, J. (1988) *The Enabling Council*, Local Government Training Board.

Clarke, M. and Stewart, J. (1989) *The Future for Local Government: Issues for Discussion*, Local Government Training Board.

Crouch, C. and Marquand, D. (1980) (eds) *The New Centralism: Britain Out of Step in Europe?*, Basil Blackwell, Oxford.

Department of the Environment (1990) *Local Government Reform in Poland*, Report of visit of British Local Government Experts to Poland, HMSO, London.

Goldsmith, M. and Newton, K. (1988) (eds) 'Centralisation and Decentralisation: Changing Patterns of Inter-governmental Relations in Advanced Western Societies', *European Journal of Political Research*, vol. 16, no. 4.

Higgins, J. (1981) *States of Welfare: Comparative Analysis in Social Policy*, Martin Robertson, Oxford.

Labour Party (1989) *Quality Street: A Discussion Paper*, London.

Mather, G. (1989) 'Thatcherism and Local Government: An Evaluation' in J. Stewart and G. Stoker (eds) *The Future of Local Government*, Macmillan, London.

Norton, A. L. (1991) *The International Handbook of Local and Regional Government: Status, Structure and Resources in Advanced Democracies*, Edward Elgar Publishing Ltd, Cheltenham.

Riberdahl, C. (1989) 'Changes in Municipal Service Delivery and Management: The Trends in Sweden', Paper to ICL/INLOGOV Conference on Local Government in Europe.

Ridley, N. (1988) *The Local Right: Enabling Not Providing*, Centre for Policy Studies, London.

Rhodes, R. (1988) *Beyond Westminster and Whitehall: The Sub-Central Government of Britain*, Unwin Hyman, London.

Stewart, J (1986), The New Management of Local Government, Unwin Hyman

Stewart, J. (1989) 'A Future for Local Authorities as Community Government' in J. Stewart and G. Stoker (eds) *The Future of Local Government*, Macmillan, London.

Stewart, J. and Stoker, G. (1988) *From Local Administration to Community Government*, Research Series 351, Fabian Society, London.

Stewart, J. and Stoker, G. (1989) 'The Free Local Government Experiments and the Programme of Public Service Reform in Scandinavia' in C. Crouch and D. Marquand (eds) *The New Centralism: Britain Out of Step in Europe?*, Basil Blackwell, Oxford.

Stoker, G. (1988) *The Politics of Local Government*, Macmillan, London.

Stoker, G. (1989) 'Creating a Local Government for a Post-Fordist Society: The Thatcherite Project?', in J. Stewart and G. Stoker (eds), *The Future of Local Government*, Macmillan, London.

Stoker, G. (1990) 'Government Beyond Whitehall' in P. Dunleavy *et al.*, *Developments in British Politics 3*, Macmillan, London.

Stoker, G. (1991) 'Regulation theory, local government and the transition from Fordism', in D. King and J. Pierre (eds) *Challenges to Local Government*, Sage/ECPR, London.

2 Western European Local Government in Comparative Perspective

Alan Norton

This chapter aims to show the similarities and differences between the main systems of local self-government in the Western democracies and to provide a background to the developments in particular countries that are described in the following chapters, particularly having regard to local government status, structures and activities. It sketches, very briefly, some of the history necessary for an understanding of what is held in common and how principal differences are to be explained amongst the member states of the Council of Europe. It relates closely to the conclusions of Chapters 3 and 15 below.

Although Western European local government systems are often classified into Northern and Southern democracies (see for instance Page and Goldsmith, 1987), a wider analysis shows that this can be misleading, since the characteristics of the systems of the United Kingdom and Ireland are closer to those of the United States and the 'white' dominions of the British Commonwealth than they are to those of, say, Sweden and Italy, or to those countries that are really neither North nor South – France, the Federal Republic of Germany, Austria and Switzerland.

In a study published in 1983 I found sharp differences between advanced local government systems in North America and those in the non-English-speaking countries of Western Europe (Norton, 1983). The key characteristics of these latter countries were identified as:

- provisions regarding local authorities in national constitutions which to some extent guarantee their authority and entrench their position as organs of the state
- the concept of basic authorities as communities which place the responsibility for their own public affairs on accountable local assemblies or councils
- their unwillingness to allow their councils to lose an intimate relationship with local communities by amalgamations covering too wide an area
- general competence to undertake activities for the benefit of their inhabitants
- a wide spread of functions, reflecting the concept of general purpose local authorities exercising comprehensive care for their communities
- close integration of local authorities into the national governmental and administrative structure, with interdependency and mutual awareness between levels of government. Local authorities tend to be seen as implementors of national policies formulated in close consultation with all the interests concerned
- stronger political power exercised by local authorities upwards through their associations and more integrated political parties, local support being high in the minds of national representatives, a high proportion of whom have very close contact with their own local authorities and often significant experience in local government and administration.

While North American local democracy shares some of these characteristics, it lacks others. The analysis in Table 2.1 makes a further distinction between North European and South European countries: in particular between Sweden and Denmark on the one hand and France and Italy on the other, and it contrasts Britain with both groups. If the Irish system were covered also it would provide an example of a case derived from the British model but in which local authorities are more highly dependent on the centre than in any other case. Spain and other countries in Southern Europe based on the Napoleonic law model are obviously close to France and Italy. While there is more variety in the smaller Northern states, they tend to have characteristics in common with Sweden and Denmark. The systems of the Federal Republic of Germany, Austria and Switzerland are also omitted

TABLE 2.1 Characteristics of world systems of local government

	Britain	USA and Canada	France and Italy	Sweden and Denmark
Constitutional status	creature of Parliament	state constitutional	national constitutional	national constitutional
National structure			3-tier	2-tier
Powers	mixed limited by statute	mixed limited by statute	general competence and statute	general competence and statute
Control of legality by	courts	courts	regions and courts	state and courts
Control of local policy	local	local	interlocked	interlocked
Control of local policy historically	low	low	high	high
Decentralisation of functions 1949–89	reduced	various	increased	increased
Local authority expenditure as percentage of GDP 1985*	12 (UK)	11, 9	9, 15	28, 30
Public expenditure as percentage of GDP 1985*	44	35	49, 50	57, 60
Local executive authority	council	mixed	mayor or president	mixed
Representational system	majoritarian	majoritarian	proportional representation	proportional representation
Party system	strong two-party	weak two-party	strong multi-party	strong multi-party
Participation at elections	low	low	high	high

*Source: Mouritzen and Nielsen, 1988.

in order to simplify the table. They stand apart as federal systems, but relate in different ways to the southern and northern European groups, and even in different but relatively minor ways (ignoring the federal dimension) to the British and American systems.

The classifications are made on judgements; not, with exceptions, on quantifiable data. They are not strictly comparing like with like, and are to some extent open to debate. Moreover, if the classification is applied to groups there are a few clear exceptions under particular heads. One major problem in such comparisons is that the position of each individual service is often different from that of others. Nevertheless the classifications reflect general expert opinion.

On 10 of these 13 characteristics the North American systems most closely resemble the British, but there is a clear difference in matters of internal characteristics: not least the difference in the politicisation of the British system (where Britain is much closer to Europe) and the form of the executive. On politicisation, Europe contrasts sharply with North America, where levels of participation and party political activity are much lower. Britain has low voting participation, especially in local government elections, but nevertheless an active party system. Traditionally voting has tended to polarise between two parties, aided by the majoritarian electoral system, as is the case even more so in the United States. The two European groups stand together but differ from the British in about half their characteristics. Britain is arguably Atlantis: a separate continent with some institutions analogous to North American and some to European ones.

Historical heritage

The deep difference between European systems can be appreciated only through an understanding of their histories. Here there is space to make no more than two or three related observations.

The tradition of the free or chartered cities and boroughs, based on an acceptance by the state of the contribution they made to shared wealth as free centres of wealth and commerce, is a common root in virtually all European systems. They developed from institutions of self-government in towns, boroughs and

cities, controlling their own fiscal systems and levying direct
taxes on individuals according to means and on individual
consumption, also related to personal means.

We find here basic values: a high valuation of freedom amongst
their bourgeoisies and craftsmen, encapsulated in the German
proverb '*Stadtluft macht frei*' ('town air makes man free'); and
public provision of services in, for example, their development of
the regulation of commerce and industry, welfare services, road
systems, water supply, drainage and sewerage, rudimentary public
health systems, schools and facilities for the care of the poor and
elderly. They opened up new and distant markets for city trade,
activities generally appreciated by state governments as contributions to shared wealth (Pirenne, 1939). These systems at their best
were maintained by elected mayors and other officials who were
also magistrates applying law and under regulation by their
popular assemblies.

They were embedded in provinces governed either directly by
representatives of the central state or by local land-owning
oligarchs. The modern system of county and regional government was developed by the state by means of the reform of local
assemblies, the widening of the electoral franchise and the
extension of their responsibilities. In continental Europe traditional systems were transformed from the aftermath of the
French Revolution of 1789 onwards to provide a more rational
and efficient system of direct control of a local government
system based on communal institutions. The nineteenth-century
democratisation of the systems developed step by step in both
Britain and the continent, including France where elected assemblies were created for the '*départements*', whose executive nevertheless remained in the hands of nationally appointed prefects.
The prefects, assisted by sub-prefects, supervised the business of
the local communes closely. The model was widely copied and
democratised step by step from 1833 onwards. In Britain
responsibilities at this level were generally placed in the hands
of special ad hoc authorities. Towards the end of the century the
functions of these bodies were consolidated under new county
and district councils. The structure and procedures of these
councils were modelled on the political and administrative
patterns of the reformed boroughs. Chartered county boroughs
stood outside this system as all-purpose authorities, acquiring a

full-range of powers and frequently adding to them by obtaining approval of private acts in the national parliament. Under British rule Ireland followed step by step until the establishment of the Irish Republic.

The developing systems of local democratic government in much of Southern and Central Europe, increasingly based on the party system, were undermined by the fascist regimes of the inter-war period, beginning with that of Italy which since 1861 had developed a system of communal government with a uniform Napoleonic prefectoral system based on that which had operated in Piedmont. With the fall of the fascist regimes, the countries affected turned to the principles, traditions and structures laboriously developed in earlier years. Italy was a leader in the new wave of constitution-making. Like France and West Germany, it was determined to prevent the rise of a new authoritarianism by means of checks on the executive power. Decentralisation was seen as central to this objective. Portugal and Spain followed after the fall of the Salazar and Franco regimes. Not only were Germany's and Austria's federal systems restored, but provision was made in Latin countries for a new level of regional authority, led by Italy in its constitution of 1948. By the 1980s similar regions were exercising decentralised power in Italy, Spain, Belgium and the Portuguese islands, while France developed its own form of elected regional government within the framework of a previously existing constitution.

In twentieth-century Western Europe the most outstanding political developments have been the universalisation of electoral democracy linked with the maturation of the party system, both at national and at local levels. These have been guaranteed on the European mainland by the re-establishment where necessary and the development of the constitutional system as the principal under-prop to the maintenance of individual rights and the associated rights of local communal autonomy.

Local and regional government status

The word 'status' is used here to mean standing in law within the constitutional system. Local authorities have a position and a guarantee in the national constitutions or basic law of all the larger states of continental Western Europe, and in nearly all cases in the smaller ones. Their rights are defined, for example, as looking after the affairs of their communities (Denmark) or governing and regulating their own affairs (Germany). The main exception is Switzerland where local government is entirely a matter for the cantons and half-cantons, as described below. The communes of which they are constituted are nevertheless fundamental to the system.

Interpretations of the United Kingdom's 'unwritten constitution' used to give local authorities a special place within the structure, but local government has no special protection in law and it has become clear under Mrs Thatcher's government that local authorities are unprotected by tradition or consensus. Any sense of independence that the cities and boroughs may have enjoyed as creations of the Crown has virtually disappeared. The Irish Constitution, in the British tradition, also gives no special status to local authorities.

The doctrine of general competence – the principle that local authorities have a general power of jurisdiction over the affairs of their areas and inhabitants subject to the law – is the norm in continental Europe. In Germany this includes the 'power of issuing general regulations which represent substantive law', and such a quasi-legislative function determines decision-making procedures elsewhere. The doctrine of subsidiarity provides a justification for the special position of local government. This lays down that the responsibility for carrying out tasks should be held at the lowest level of government competent to undertake them, and that where necessary higher authorities should give support to enable them to fulfil the responsibilities that are appropriately theirs under this doctrine.

In English-speaking countries on the other hand local authorities have no general competence in law, with effects which Blair comments on in the next chapter. He also remarks on the extent to which British local government is regarded 'almost exclusively as an institution for the delivery of services – or at least for the making of arrangements for the delivery of services'. This is in the utilitarian tradition, the proponents of which in the nineteenth century by-passed the use of local government by setting up systems of ad hoc authorities. This tendency was to some extent reversed at the end of the nineteenth-century, but adopted again in a different form in the mid-twentieth century.

Federal states and regional governments

The status and influence of local authorities inevitably relate to the nature of the higher level authorities on which they are dependent. Thus in the countries in Western Europe which possess fully federal constitutions – the Federal Republic of Germany, Austria and Switzerland – they are subject in varying extents to the provisions of the *Länder* and cantons which share state power with the federal institutions. In Germany the ten *Länder* and West Berlin, which vary in population from 660000 (the city state of Bremen) to nearly 17 million (North Rhine-Westphalia), share sovereignty with the 'Bund'. Each has its own system of law and defines the responsibilities and powers of its local authorities in its Land constitution and in legislation. Austria has a centralised legal system and its nine *Länder*, which range in population from 265000 (Burgenland) to 1580000 (Vienna), have more restricted powers. Residual and 'implied' powers lie at the federal level. The centre has the right to determine the powers of local authorities throughout the country. In Switzerland the central state was created by the autonomous cantons to fulfil joint needs. There are 33 cantons, three being divided into 'half-cantons' with half the voting power of the others in the national assembly. Population sizes range from about 12000 (Schwyz) to 1123000 (Zurich). All but one canton entered the 'confederation' between 1291 and 1814. The relationships were formalised under the federal constitution of 1848 (revised 1874), and have subsequently been modified under national referenda which in general have strengthened the centre. The cantons and half-cantons however vote their own laws, levy their own taxes and determine their own local government systems.

In these three cases the member-states participate in national decision-making through representatives in central assemblies. This is not so in the 'regionalised' systems of territorial government of Belgium, Spain and Italy, but it has been the intention in Belgium to establish a form for such participation in the 1990s. In all these countries the regional authorities legislate for the local government systems within their boundaries and exercise supervisory roles of different kinds over their local authorities.

In Belgium regional institutions were set up in 1980 and the provisions revised in 1988. The three regions are Flanders (pop. 5676000), Wallonia (pop. 3206000) and Brussels (pop. 976000). Spain's regionalisation under the 1978 Constitution is the most radical – at least until Belgium's structure is completed. The regional authorities are the 17 'autonomous communities', ranging in population from La Rioja (260000) to Andalucia (6573000) and averaging 3331000. Italy embodied a regional level in its post-war constitution as one of the main measures towards democratisation and decentralisation of power. Most regions however were not set up until the 1970s, and it is only since 1977 that they have acquired wide competences from the central state. There are twenty regions, ranging in population from Valle d'Aosta (about 111500) to Lombardy (8500000). Their populations average 2865000.

The French regions acquired the same constitutional status as local authorities on the election of regional assemblies in 1986. There are 22 mainland regions (including Corsica for which there are special provisions), and four for territories overseas. Corsica apart, the mainland regions have populations ranging from 1084000 to 10073000. They enjoy the same constitutional status as other levels of sub-national elected government.

The Portuguese Constitution of 1976 provided for the setting up of regional governments which, amongst other responsibilities, were to prepare and implement regional plans and to coordinate and support the work of local authorities and the management of public services. Two 'autonomous regions' exercise powers in the Azores and Madeira, but mainland regions had not been established by 1989. There are however five Regional Co-ordinating Commissions to pave the way to regionalisation and exercise certain interim functions, with populations from 324000 (Algarve) to 3410000 (North).

Arguably the size of local authorities determines their conditions and abilities more than any other factor. It determines to a large extent the weight of the individual elector's vote in the choice of representatives, the extent to which he or she can understand and influence what is being decided in the council, the level of dependence of representatives on their paid employees, their knowledge of the whole of the local authority's business, the scale and specialisation of the officer organisation, its accessibility to the population – and in some ways to interference by the central state – and other matters. Population scale is in the majority of cases more significant than area, since even in a built-up area a major enlargement of scale increases remoteness and problems of understanding.

Despite the fact that in virtually all countries there is a wide range in the size of local authorities, the average population in each country may be taken as an indicator of scale, bearing in mind that a very big majority are below the mean. Countries form groups in this respect. Table 2.2 shows that in general the more southerly countries have shown most resistance to pressures for increases in scale. The line demarcating the regions most attached to smallness roughly follows a line around the Mediterranean and Atlantic coasts and the French side of the Channel as far as Belgium, and then continues south including Luxembourg, the south German Länder, Switzerland and Austria. We rank countries according to average size of basic main authority. The figures speak for themselves. In the following chapter Blair develops the theme of the effects of the bigness of British local government districts.

Where, as is the case in most countries, all basic authorities carry the same or nearly the same responsibilities and competences and there are great discrepancies in their ability to carry them out, ranging as they do from small villages to great cities, this is a matter that is often central to the problems of decentralisation of powers. It has of course been the main justification for extensive amalgamations of local authorities, particularly in Northern Europe. Where a general enlargement of scale has been rejected, governments have in most cases taken the initiative in promoting inter-authority collaboration, joint bodies, delegation of functions upwards, contracting and other means by which the limitations of smallness can be overcome. But the result can be that while the local powers are maintained in principle, effective local control is reduced. The successes and failures in this approach are too complex a story to summarise here.

TABLE 2.2   Size and populations of basic local authorities

Country	Average population of basic authority (approx.)	Number of basic authorities
The South		
France	1500	36000 (approx.)
Greece	1600	6036
Luxembourg	2905	126
Austria	3000	2417
Spain	4700	8049
Italy	6800	8000 (approx.)
Fed. Rep. of Germany	7240	8400 (approx.)
Portugal	34180[1]	275[1]
The North		
Norway	9145	454
Finland	10646	461
Belgium	16740	589
Netherlands	17860	800 (approx.)
Denmark	18500	276
Sweden	30000	282
The Islands		
Iceland	1100	222
Ireland	41910	92
Northern Ireland	60480	26
Wales	75870	37
Scotland	91620	56
England	127000	365

[1] Portugal has in addition to its municipalities 3848 parish authorities with an average population of about 2500 which carry out a range of statutory functions on delegation in addition to discretionary powers. They have much wider scope than the English parish and Welsh community authorities whose functions are entirely discretionary and not comparable with the other authorities above.

Provinces, counties and other intermediate authorities

The origins of the authorities that are intermediate between the basic local authorities and the central government – the provinces, counties, and '*départements*' – have been described briefly above. The development over the last two centuries of elected assemblies at this level, with the general transfer of state responsibilities to these counties or their executives has resulted in a variety of patterns, which may be seen as situated at stages in a progressive transfer of service provision to local democratic control. Thus we find the following arrangements:

1. A state-appointed governor or other high-level official responsible for state functions over a large area without an elected council of its own but including a large number of sub-areas with autonomous local assemblies, as can be found in Austria, Finland and the larger German Länder. In Luxembourg there is a state-appointed commissioner for each of the three administrative districts, whose purpose is to liaise with the communes, the single form of local government in the country.
2. A state-appointed governor for each province who acts as executive for and presides over an elected provincial council, as in Portugal pending the setting up of a new system of regional government. In Belgium there is a state-appointed governor for each province who heads a provincial executive board, but the provincial assemblies elect their own chairmen.
3. A governor or prefect who is responsible for central government functions in the same county or province in parallel with an autonomous assembly which provides major services and elects its own chairman and executive. In a number of cases he presides over a board of representatives chosen by the local assembly, so that there is close involvement of local councillors in decisions made and advice given on central government actions affecting the area. This is now a widespread arrangement found in Denmark and Sweden in the north of Europe and in Italy, Spain and Greece in the south.

In France the classic prefectoral system, in which the state-appointed prefect was the executive and chairman for the departmental council, was superseded under legislation in 1983 by one in which the council appoints its own executive and chairman, while the prefect has acquired the title of state commissioner (Commissioner of the Republic) acting for the state but not exercising detailed supervision.

All these systems, in different ways, provide for a close and often interlocked relationship between state-appointed officials and local government executives. They provide a means for close collaboration and joint action locally between central government and local authorities at both basic and intermediate levels. This close interweaving of state and county is achieved also in Ireland, where counties and towns appoint managers from candidates recommended by a national board. These officers are in practice very close to the government civil service. Such an arrangement however appears close to a direct subjugation of local government, although in what may be seen as a similar arrangement in the Netherlands where civic executives (the burgemeester) are appointed on the recommendation of the Crown commissioner in the province after consultation with the council, this does not seem to undermine the sense of local autonomy.

Britain stands apart in that although there are intermediate authorities for all areas excepting London and the other major conurbations – counties in England and Wales and regions in Scotland – there is no intimate relationship with a senior government official who carries specific general responsibilities for liaison and other matters in the interest of the national government. In fact there is no single senior government official whose task is to supervise and coordinate relationships with local authorities in an area.

Most countries have at least some authorities which cover all or most purposes, carrying out functions elsewhere split between levels. Examples are found in cities and large towns in France (Paris, Marseilles and Lyons), West Germany, Austria, Sweden and Denmark. The usual status is close to that of the former British county boroughs that were abolished in 1974. London Boroughs and Metropolitan Districts would be similar if it were not that important functions are carried out by mandatory joint bodies. The three Scottish island authorities are also general purpose.

The classical European system was one in which governors, prefects or other government officials supervised local authorities to ensure that their actions were in accordance with the law and government regulations, and had powers to annul or refer upwards decisions which they considered contrary to government provisions (see Chapter 3 below). In most countries some supervisory powers remain at such a level, but they are now in some cases the responsibility of a regional commission. The relationship is not in general an oppressive one: it is more one of advice and liaison, maintaining the mutual interests of state and local authorities by joint agreements. While, unsurprisingly, larger authorities may protest strongly where they believe their scope of action is being limited for political purposes with which they do not agree, respect for the law and the shared interests that arise between parties, and arguably the effects of proportional representation or two-round election systems, tend to create a different culture from that of the adversarial conflict which is typical of some British local authorities and central government.

The legal competences of local authorities

A recent survey of the powers of local authorities in Council of Europe countries has given a much clearer and more up-to-date picture of the distribution of competences than was previously available (Council of Europe, 1988). Blair describes its limitations below, but on analysis the data prove very helpful in giving an impression of the width of local government responsibilities between countries. The survey found that there was 'a certain homogeneity' between functions performed at the basic level of local government, whether or not local authorities worked under a general mandate of powers or a list of specific responsibilities. The sharpest contrast exists at the level of intermediate authorities. Second-level authorities such as counties and provinces tend to provide large-scale modern social services, and in particular health, social security and secondary education, which are seen as beyond the resources and ability of the basic authorities and which otherwise might be undertaken directly by state government.

In Sweden, Norway and Denmark, the counties are chiefly responsible for hospitals and other health services. In Finland, which has no second-level authorities, basic authorities are statutorily required to be members of joint authorities in 'general hospital regions', so that they are directly involved in an institutional network which brings together all aspects of health care. Responsibility for hospitals and in some cases the employment and payment of teachers and lecturers determine above all else the much higher relative expenditure by local government in Scandinavia. Provincial levels in Italy, Spain and Belgium were under threat until recent years because of the doubts about their essential role within systems of regional government, but in the Mediterranean countries at least it now seems to be accepted that they can fulfil intermediate functions better than other politically feasible arrangements.

In Germany the *Kreise* have been relatively secure in view of their longstanding rationale as a means for inter-municipal co-operation. They differ from other county systems in that they provide services such as public utilities, cultural and other relatively less expensive services that elsewhere are provided predominantly by the basic level. Their acceptability can be explained by their close relationships with the smaller municipalities and what is intended to be a rational distribution of responsibilities on the ground of the scale or areas of activity most fitted to provide a particular service. Authorities with populations considered large enough to provide a wider or complete range of services have an independent status. This is in a context of a system in which there exist many 'organic associations' of municipalities which carry out functions requiring larger scale management, particularly outside North Rhine – Westphalia whose basic authorities are exceptionally large.

Table 2.3 shows functions which are carried out by the basic authorities in 14 Council of Europe states on the mainland of Europe, including all the larger members. They are mostly within their general legal competence, but may in some cases be delegated to or performed under delegation from another level of government. In many cases provision in some areas of service is shared or divided with another level, either in accordance with legislative provisions or by joint arrangements. In the British-derived systems in Cyprus and Ireland (the latter was not included in the Council of Europe survey) functions are very much fewer. It is not possible in this type of table to distinguish between responsibility for implementation of part of a subfunction and comprehensive responsibility in a functional area. Where, as in most of these cases, the principle of general competence applies, it is not theoretically possible to set a limit on what an authority may legally undertake where there is no

TABLE 2.3   Powers of basic local authorities in fourteen council of Europe Member States

In all 14: water supply (11), tourism promotion (0), primary schools – construction and upkeep (14), library services (33), theatres (0), sport development and facilities (0), sewage disposal (12), refuse collection (14), homes for the elderly (4), social assistance (7), roads (14), local planning (14), building and demolition permits (14)

In 13: pre-primary schools – construction and upkeep (12), museum services (0), cultural and artistic heritage conservation (4), cemeteries (9), subsidised housing (3), fire service (12), organisation and management of land transport (6), nature and site protection/waste disposal (10), nature parks, recreation and open spaces (0)

In 12: abattoirs (0), baths and showers (0), financial participation in public/ private enterprises (0), development or conservation of employment (2: Netherlands and Portugal), land control (purchase, reserves etc.) (1), protection of the environment (7)

In 11: gas supply (4), electricity supply (5), financial or fiscal aid to public and private undertakings (0), fairs and markets (2: Netherlands and Spain), hospitals (5), response to disasters (11), planning control and building regulation (8)

In 9: pre-primary school administrative, teaching or technical staff (8), epidemic control (8), river or sea transport (1)

In 8: primary school administrative, teaching or technical staff (9), aid for religious worship and upkeep of related premises (4), housing assistance (4)

In 7: secondary school construction and upkeep (3), regional or national planning involvement (6), consumer protection (3)

In 6: cinemas (0)

In 4: secondary school administrative, teaching or technical staff (4), air transport (0)

In 1: higher education premises – construction and upkeep (0)

Note.   the figures in brackets give the number of states in which a particular function is legally mandatory

Source: Derived mainly from Council of Europe, 1988.

provision in law which prevents it. Moreover some functions on which individual countries might place high importance were not specified in the questionnaire, and some of these are known to have been omitted (for example non-university adult education). There are wide variations between systems in the extent to which functions are carried out and the means employed. It may be noted that British authorities are no longer responsible in areas of operation that are part of the competences of basic levels of service in all or nearly all the continental systems: in particular water, gas and electricity supply, hospital and other aspects of personal health care and social assistance involving income support (although they have wide responsibilities for social care for less advantaged groups in the population).

The wave of structural reform

The great wave of structural reform which swept through most of Europe between the 1950s and the 1970s arose from the belief of governments that a large proportion of the smaller local author-ities, characteristic of virtually all systems after the war, were inadequate to provide the services which an advanced society requires if it is to reach the high levels of economic, physical and social development which, with rising wealth, had come within the public reach. Britain nationalised energy, health, water and other services for this reason. Other states rejected this option and sought to meet the problem in other ways. Agency or contracting arrangements and the promotion of joint special or multi-purpose joint local authorities were the means adopted in France, Germany and elsewhere. In some cases major services were built up at the level of provincial and other second level governments. As we have seen above, in the Latin countries there was little rationalisation of boundaries and the small authorities survived. In West Germany and Scandinavia there were extensive reorganisations, raising the general minimum population size to 8, 10, 12 or 20 thousand: nowhere else to the norm of 60 or 80 thousand minimum adopted in Britain (see also Chapter 3).

After the reforms there was a counter wave of questioning and disillusion. The pay-offs were not automatic and were frequently questioned. Many politicians had feared that the reforms would

distance administration from the public and result in losses of
democratic responsiveness, accountability, sense of civic pride
and responsibility, and a distancing of the public from the locus
of community decision-making following the drastic reduction in
the number of elected representatives. Their fears were subsequently felt to have been justified.

Concepts and values underlying local authority status

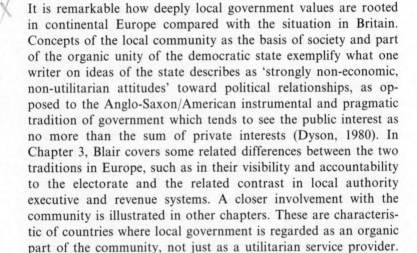

It is remarkable how deeply local government values are rooted
in continental Europe compared with the situation in Britain.
Concepts of the local community as the basis of society and part
of the organic unity of the democratic state exemplify what one
writer on ideas of the state describes as 'strongly non-economic,
non-utilitarian attitudes' toward political relationships, as opposed to the Anglo-Saxon/American instrumental and pragmatic
tradition of government which tends to see the public interest as
no more than the sum of private interests (Dyson, 1980). In
Chapter 3, Blair covers some related differences between the two
traditions in Europe, such as in their visibility and accountability
to the electorate and the related contrast in local authority
executive and revenue systems. A closer involvement with the
community is illustrated in other chapters. These are characteristic of countries where local government is regarded as an organic
part of the community, not just as a utilitarian service provider.
In spite of this, British local authorities have over the last few
years made much progress in building a two-way relationship
with the community, despite the problems of relating to large and
dispersed populations.

Conclusion

There is a tradition in British government of seeking simple
answers to what appear to be complex problems, which dates,
some might say, from the medieval principle of Occam's razor:
'No more things should be presumed to exist than are absolutely
necessary.' This has resulted (no doubt against Occam's meaning,
let alone his intentions) in attempts to simplify and condemn as

unnecessary the kind of organic complexities described in some of the papers that follow in this book. Simplification may be seen to require fewer local authorities, fewer elected members, fewer relationships with the community and with external bodies. European experience points us to some models which display complexity but which have been resilient and successful, perhaps because their complexity matches that of the society they serve.

We have surveyed here only a few of the aspects in which the British system differs from systems elsewhere in Europe. Others of importance are electoral procedures, party systems, status of the elected member, sources of revenue and the extent to which local government is involved in national decision-making. These features contrast and challenge aspects of modern British thinking about local government. Apparent complexities are in fact overcome in practice, so far as they are overcome, by a pragmatic approach aiming to reach a level of agreement that will mobilise sufficient support, resulting in a degree of solidarity between segments in the local community. For centuries Britain was outstanding both for its centralisation of power and also for the autonomy of its local authorities, but in recent years local autonomy has in various ways been undermined. Perhaps in Britain there should be less fear of complicating the process of decision-making by wider involvement with the community and bargaining. Levels of government should be active in seeking closer relationships and a wider basis of support outside themselves if they are to emulate some of the best characteristics of developments on the West European mainland.

References

Council of Europe (1988) *Allocation of powers to the local and regional levels of governments in the member states of the Council of Europe*, Council of Local and Regional Authorities of Europe, Strasbourg.

Council of Europe (1986) *Explanatory Report on the European Charter of Local Self-Government*, Council of Europe, Strasbourg.

Dyson, Kenneth H. F. (1980), *The State Tradition in Western Europe*, Martin Robertson, Oxford.

Mouritzer P.E. and Nielsen K. H. (1988) *Handbook of Comparative Urban Fiscal Data*, DDA, Odense.

Norton A. L. (1983) *The Government and Administration of Metropolitan Areas in Western Democracies*, INLOGOV, Birmingham.

Page, Edward C. and Goldsmith, Michael J. (1987) 'Centre and locality: explaining cross-national variations' in *Central and Local Relations: A Comparative Analysis of West European Unitary States*, Sage, London.

Pirenne, Henri (1939) *History of Europe*, George Allen and Unwin, London.

3 Trends in Local Autonomy and Democracy: Reflections from a European Perspective

Philip Blair

Introduction

The purpose of this chapter is to identify some current trends in local government in various European countries. To complete the picture, reference is also made to certain background conditions which exert a continuing influence on the functioning and status of local government. In so short a chapter, the treatment is bound to be selective in terms of both the aspects raised and their illustration by reference to experience in various European countries. Inevitably also, the discussion of each topic is superficial. But the aim is to raise a number of issues which may be of interest from a comparative perspective.

Most of the information which has been drawn upon derives from work done within the Council of Europe in the local government field. However, the opinions expressed do not necessarily reflect the views of the Council of Europe and are solely the responsibility of the author.

Autonomy, decentralisation and government control

When comparing trends in different countries with regard to local autonomy, it is important to bear in mind the quite different

41

starting-points from which each system is evolving. Decentralising
tendencies which may be observed in some traditionally highly
centralised systems may still leave them more centralised than
some other countries in which local autonomy is being eroded.
The problem, however, is that the actual degree of local
autonomy in different countries is not easy to compare, depending as it does on the interplay of a large number of factors which
are often difficult to measure.

The range of responsibilities of local authorities is perhaps the
most obvious of these factors. A recent survey carried out within
the Council of Europe sets out a detailed list of possible
functions, as a basis for comparing the actual allocation of
powers in each country. The resulting tables suggest that the
basic level of local government in most European countries has a
wide range of functions, which are broadly comparable. However,
appearances may be deceptive: even with a relatively detailed
classification of functions the actual role of the local authorities
often remains unclear. In the circumstances of modern government many functions are not assigned exclusively to the local
level but are shared with a higher level of government; in this case
the problem is to identify where the major competence lies or
whether one of the levels is responsible only for relatively minor
aspects. Moreover, a function may be performed by a local
authority in its own right or on behalf of another (central or
regional) authority, in which case the discretion it enjoys may be
very limited. More generally, any of a local authority's functions
may take the form of tasks which it is obliged to carry out or of
activities which it is permitted to engage in if it wishes. But the
fact that it is *authorised* to carry out a particular function is in
itself no indication as to how far it actually does so; especially in
the case of small municipalities in some countries, lack of
financial resources or of qualified staff may result in discretionary powers remaining purely theoretical.

A general idea of the size of the local government sector as a
whole can be obtained from the statistics on total local authority
expenditure as a proportion of total public expenditure as shown
in Table 3.1. But the impression gained from these figures is only
a very vague one, so long as no account is taken of the extent to
which local authorities can determine their expenditure freely.
The strikingly high proportion of public expenditure accounted

TABLE 3.1 Local authority expenditure as a proportion of public expenditure

Country	1980 (%)	1984 (%)
Austria	39.0	37.1
Belgium	19.2	14.1
Denmark	76.3	65.4
France	27.8	27.1
Federal Republic of Germany	27.5	25.5
Greece	4.9	6.2
Ireland	16.8	15.8
Luxembourg	35.0	33.8
Netherlands	28.9	–
Norway	45.5	42.7
Portugal	9.8	7.5 (1983)
Spain	8.2 (1981)	27.9
Sweden	32.3	31.6
Switzerland	34.9	35.3
Turkey	6.4	7.2 (1983)
United Kingdom	29.2	27.5

for by local authorities in Denmark, for example, has to be seen in the light of their agency role for social security payments, old age pensions, etc. More generally, local decision-makers may or may not be subject to detailed, binding norms with regard to the services they are to provide. Thus in the Scandinavian countries, the local authorities' larger than usual share of public expenditure seems traditionally to have been counterbalanced by close government regulation leaving relatively little discretion. It is against this background that serious efforts have been made in these countries in recent years to reverse the tendency of legislation to go into unnecessary detail about the manner of service provision and to reduce regulation by state bodies. For example, in Sweden the previous detailed legislation in the field of social services and health and medical care has been replaced by general enactments laying down the goals but leaving it to the relevant local authorities to decide how these goals are to be attained and what their internal organisation should be.

The clearest indication of governmental willingness to extend the scope of local autonomy in Scandinavia is the so-called 'free local government' experiments which are in progress in Sweden, Norway and Denmark. The aims are to test new approaches to local government activity, to increase the possibilities of adapting policies to local conditions, to enable members of the public to exert greater influence and to improve the use of resources. To this end, certain selected municipalities and county councils may, on their own initiative, obtain exemption from state regulations which they see as standing in the way of more efficient or democratic organisation. Among the main areas of action are the simplification of rules, less compartmentalisation of committee and administrative structures, greater flexibility in the provision of services to the citizen and the transfer of more powers of decision from state bodies to local authorities. Undoubtedly the end-result will be a general reduction of state regulation and control. Although some of the innovations of the free local government experiments in Scandinavia appear to relate to constraints to which local authorities in countries like Britain have traditionally been less subject, there is no mistaking the strength of the trend towards greater local autonomy.

Elsewhere in Europe analogous developments towards reinforcing local autonomy may be observed. In France, the 1980s have been dominated, in the field of local and regional government, by the major decentralisation reforms. Apart from giving *départements* at last an independent executive elected by the *conseil général*, these reforms have transferred various important functions to the sub-national authorities: town planning and primary education to the communes, social assistance and the intermediate school sector to the *départements*, grammar schools and vocational training to the regions. At the same time the traditional system of *a priori* supervision by the prefect was abolished and the *a posteriori* control was limited to the possibility of appeal by the prefect (or members of the public) to the administrative courts in cases of alleged illegality. Even if the reality of central control has changed less, especially for the small communes, than the texts might lead one to suppose, it is clear that a substantial transformation of the traditionally centralised French system has been effected.

Other countries, such as Italy, Spain and Portugal, had preceded France in moderating the traditional system of supervision and reducing it in essence (as in West Germany) to a control of legality. More recently, the new Local Government Act in Luxembourg provides for the abolition of virtually all *a priori* supervision by central government and a major reduction of *a posteriori* control, with a right for municipalities to appeal to the Council of State when their measures are annulled or approval is refused. In Belgium, too, where responsibility for supervising local authorities is being transferred to the regions, the scope of such supervision is being considerably reduced.

Developments in the finances of local authorities are complex and not easy to summarise. However, a parallel to the reinforcement of local autonomy described above may be seen in the policy pursued in certain countries (most notably Norway, France and the Netherlands) of shifting the relative weight of specific and general grants in favour of the latter. It is of course clear that recourse to specific grants restricts a local authority's freedom to exercise its discretion with regard to expenditure priorities. But it is also reasoned, for example in the Netherlands, that even for functions which local authorities are obliged to perform, financing by general grants leads to greater efficiency in the use of resources; otherwise detailed definition of the task in relation to the resources will be necessary, of a kind which the national level is too remote to carry out effectively. Of course the fact that it is easier to reduce a general grant than to cut individual specific grants may not be entirely foreign to some governments' reflections: during the crisis years of the early 1980s a number of governments resorted to reductions in the size of the grant pool as a means of restraining the rate of growth of local spending.

The British government appears to be more concerned with controlling local government expenditure than other European governments. There are no doubt several reasons for this. In the first place, if the share of the GDP represented by local authority fiscal and grant receipts is under 5 per cent (Greece, Portugal, Italy, Luxembourg), the government can take a more relaxed view of the economic impact of local spending than in Denmark (27.6 per cent), Sweden (20.9 per cent), Norway (19 per cent), the Netherlands (11.8 per cent) or Britain (9.6 per cent) (figures for 1987). Secondly, if local authorities are so heavily dependent on government grants or on a system of shared taxes that they have only modest access to local taxes of which they can determine the

rate (the Netherlands and Norway), the government will have less
need to control the expenditure side, especially if it can also
restrict local government borrowing. Finally, of course, some
governments are less ideologically committed to cutting public
expenditure (and also more committed to local autonomy).
Taking all these factors into account, it is no coincidence that
the country which has come closest to the United Kingdom with
controversial efforts to cut local government spending seems to
be Denmark.

The pursuit of accountability

The concept of accountability, which has so dominated British
debate about local finances, appears to have played little or no
part in other European countries. Indeed, the term itself seems to
be regarded as rather mystifying. Everyone is of course familiar
with the idea that local elected representatives, like all democra-
tically elected authorities, are responsible to their electorates in
the sense that they must present themselves periodically for
election. In this way they must 'render account of their steward-
ship'. In the financial field, systems of audit are no doubt seen as
the principal means of ensuring that local government funds are
spent economically and effectively in terms of value for money.
Some governments, for example in Italy and Sweden, have been
active in seeking effective means of measuring the efficiency of
local service provision, as have many local authorities themselves
or bodies jointly established by them. The results of such
initiatives may, at least theoretically, assist local electorates in
judging the performance of local authorities. However, the
conception does not seem to be widespread that there is a
fundamental distinction in this respect between, on the one
hand, local financial resources derived from taxes levied on local
electors and, on the other hand, those obtained from taxpayers
who have no vote in local elections or, for that matter, from
government grants. For all these there is presumably the same
responsibility on the local authorities to spend the money wisely
and to answer to their electorates in this respect.

What is absent, therefore, is the narrow conception of accountability which consists in the attempt to establish a direct and

automatic link between councils voting for higher levels of services and the level of contribution by local electors. If calls are made (or in some instances – for example in Belgium in 1982 – measures are taken) to increase access to local taxes of which the local authorities are free to determine the rate, it is in the name of local autonomy, not accountability. As for the argument that every local resident who can afford to should contribute to the financing of local government, those countries (Scandinavia, Belgium, Switzerland) which have some form of local income tax would no doubt agree, but they would probably add: 'in proportion to his means'. The community charge is generally regarded as rather exotic, and has certainly found no imitators.

The reason for this difference may well lie in the tendency, which seems to be stronger in Britain than in most other countries, to view local government almost exclusively as an instrument for the delivery of services – or at least for the making of arrangements for the delivery of services. It thus becomes natural to see in local taxation nothing other than a system of payment for services. The situation alters significantly if local government is regarded as what the (English) name implies: the first level of government of the community. In that case it becomes as anomalous in relation to local authorities as it would be with reference to central government to question whether they should be allowed to levy taxes as they see fit on categories of taxpayers who do not have the right to vote.

Of course in any local government context it may seem appropriate to establish a clear link between enjoyment of certain kinds of service and payment for their provision. But in that case the usual solution is direct user charges. However, the local authorities are generally left substantially free to decide whether to have recourse to this method of financing and, if so, to what extent it should cover the cost. That they have increasingly done so in many European countries during the 1980s has had more to do with a search for other sources of revenue in a period of fiscal austerity than with a commitment or obligation to increase accountability in the British government's sense of the term.

Probably the closest approximation on the Continent to the British concern with accountability is the pursuit of 'transparency' in government. Thus it is interesting to note the recent reform of the property tax in the Netherlands: previously collected by the national revenue service on the basis of information supplied by the municipalities, this local government tax was not perceived as such by the taxpayers; in future, therefore, it is to be administered by the local authorities themselves. Nevertheless, the impression persists that transparency is only one value among several to which the organisation of local government aspires, and that there is less confidence in the extent to which it can be achieved in the complex circumstances of modern government.

Local democracy and participation

The search for greater responsibility and transparency in local government is part of a general concern with the quality of local democracy, which has been manifested in political debate and in various initiatives in many European countries. Often this concern may be related, as in Britain, to a conviction that the 'product' of local government does not correspond as well as it should to what its consumers want. But the current British answer to this problem – which is to give more power to the individual *qua* consumer, and to take functions out of the hands of local authorities and disperse them among a variety of public, private and voluntary agencies – is no more than one trend, and hardly the most important, in thinking on these matters on the Continent. Certainly some governments of a conservative tendency (for example in the Netherlands) have been determined to make the public sector retreat from what they see as its exaggerated aspirations to regulate society and care for its needs. And even governments of a different political complexion (such as Sweden) have been interested in schemes to promote organised influence by the users of local government services at the level where these are produced, although this may not amount to the introduction of market mechanisms. But the emphasis is not so much on restricting the scope of local government as on improving the functioning of local democracy.

Once again, this difference of approach seems to be based on the fundamental conception of the role of local government. If it is essentially about providing services, then the idea of user power is certainly plausible – even if it begs eminently political questions such as the appropriate compromise between efficiency and equity or between economic use of resources on the one hand and attaining certain basic standards or ensuring a degree of general coverage on the other. The situation is quite different, however, if local government is conceived as involving making strategic policy decisions, deciding priorities as between different public services or different investment projects, setting orientations for the development of the local community and trying to protect the community as a whole or individual citizens against hardship or disaster. It is in the weighting of these objectives and their achievement that the democratic process at the local level makes its contribution to the effectiveness of local government.

But that presupposes that the democratic process is itself effective. This issue is of course not a new one. During the 1970s measures were introduced in many European countries to improve the status and working conditions of local elected representatives, the provision of information to local residents or the opportunities for citizen participation between elections. But these concerns are again coming to the fore in several countries, as may be seen from a number of current initiatives. In Austria and Luxembourg, new obligations have been imposed on local authorities to provide information, while in Austria there is now legal provision for citizens' initiatives in relation to planning questions, for example in the field of environment protection. The recent Local Government Act in Luxembourg makes provision for the holding of referendums on the initiative either of the local council or of the inhabitants of the municipality. The French government also intends to improve participation by local residents in planning decisions, as well as to facilitate access for all social and professional groups to elective office and to strengthen the rights of minorities within local councils. In Norway and Sweden reforms are in preparation, one of the main aims of which is to improve the working conditions of local councillors and strengthen their position especially vis-à-vis the local administration. And five member states of the Council of Europe – Sweden, Denmark, Norway, the Netherlands and Ireland – have granted resident non-nationals the right to vote in local authority elections, while Luxembourg has made compulsory the establishment of consultative committees to represent the interests of foreign residents in municipalities where they constitute more than 20 per cent of the population.

These developments naturally reflect the existing situations in the individual countries, which vary considerably. For example, citizen participation in planning procedures is much stronger in some countries than in others. Again, the wish to reinforce the position of local elected representatives is naturally stronger in Northern European countries which have developed highly professional bureaucracies at local level; in other countries, such as Italy, some argue rather that the influence of the local politicians is too strong. Nevertheless, there are clear signs of concern with reinforcing the (direct or indirect) democratic mechanisms for the collective government of the community.

It is not, of course, suggested that there are no parallels in the United Kingdom to these trends: the follow-up Bill to the Widdicombe Report contains some relevant provisions, for example in relation to the position of minorities on local councils. But the impression remains that the general aim is rather that of curbing perceived abuses than the positive one of strengthening democratic participation.

Contrasts in status and structure

Under this heading three disparate points will be touched on briefly, which have in common that they exert an influence on the general status of local government in society and the atmosphere within which it functions. In contrast to most of the aspects dealt with hitherto, it is not so much a matter of identifying trends as of recalling background features of local government.

The first of these features is the general competence which the municipalities possess in most European countries. This right to intervene and take initiatives with respect to any matter relating to the local community in so far as the law does not explicitly provide otherwise is in direct contrast to the British doctrine of *ultra vires*, whereby local authorities may only carry out such responsibilities as are specifically assigned to them by Parliament (although the 1972 Local Government Act did introduce a limited exception to this principle). Historically, it was important in that the municipalities were often the first to recognise newly arising problems and attempted to deal with them long before the government turned its attention to them. With a general competence they were – and are – able more easily to react to new situations and take on new tasks.

However, it is questionable whether the existence of the principle of general competence *per se* necessarily entails a higher degree of autonomy. It is not just that governments nowadays usually take up problems more rapidly, so that the potential scope of the principle is more limited. In addition, the existence of the general competence seems in some countries to be accompanied by a lack of precision in the allocation of specific responsibilities: where tasks are not assigned exclusively but shared with higher levels of government, the exact demarcation of responsibilities may in practice be left to the latter. Moreover, the freedom to carry out functions which are not explicitly provided for by legislation may be purely hypothetical if, as in certain Southern European countries in particular, the financial and staff resources of the municipalities are not sufficient even to carry out effectively all those tasks which are specifically imposed on them by law. In this respect, it is arguable that British local authorities, with their still relatively broad range of well-defined functions and often substantial degree of discretion, are quite well off even without a general competence.

The importance of the general competence lies perhaps rather in the symbolic and psychological sphere. It bolsters the conception of the municipality as a general political authority which acts in its own right to foster the welfare of its inhabitants and confront whatever problems may arise in the local community. It encourages the citizen to see in the local authority not one agency among many for carrying out administrative tasks, but the corporate manifestation of the local community (*collectivité locale*) which is the first resort in case of difficulty.

This symbolic effect should not be exaggerated in itself, but gains more significance in combination with the second factor to be mentioned in this section, namely the absence in the United Kingdom of a separate political executive. This is a characteristic which is shared to some extent with the Nordic countries as well as with Ireland and the former British Occupation Zone in Germany. Most of these countries have modified or mitigated the effects of the system whereby executive as well as policy-setting functions are vested in the council itself. Denmark divides up executive responsibilities between the relevant council committees and the mayor; in Norway an executive committee, elected by the council, supervises the municipal administration and the implementation of council decisions; in Northern Germany the political appointment of the chief executive *(Stadtdirektor)* constituted a step away from the British-imposed system and back towards the German tradition of strong executive leadership, even though he remains dependent on the council and without real political initiative of his own; finally Ireland has developed the system of the (non-political) autonomous manager who, in his executive sphere, is largely outside the direct control of the council. Nevertheless, a basic similarity remains by comparison with the continental tradition of the strong political executive.

Whether the political executive is constituted by the mayor alone or whether, as for instance in the Benelux countries or Italy, he heads a collegial body, his authority is considerable. It not only derives from his simultaneous function as the representative of the State in the municipality, but is also due to the fact that he prepares and implements the decisions of the municipal council, controls the administrative apparatus, manages the municipal finances and is responsible for public order in the municipality. In most countries he is elected by the municipal council; the direct election of the political head of the municipality in southern Germany, as well as in Portugal and in some Swiss cities, gives him the added advantage of relative independence.

The existence of a strong political executive has a number of consequences. In Germany, for example, where the contrasting systems of local authority organisation can be observed within a single country, it has been plausibly argued that it is far more conducive to responsible financial management. The mayor's strong central position and co-ordinating role in the council makes it easier to control spending initiatives, while his control of the staff and influence over their careers tends to screen them from too close a relationship with the relevant committee. This contrasts with the position in Northern Germany (or Britain), where strong spending committees usually cooperate closely with the relevant department, a practice which certainly furthers participation by individual councillors in the practical administration of local affairs but which also, by creating sectoral alliances interested primarily in increasing their slice of the cake, tends to impede the overall weighing of political priorities and firm financial discipline.

More important in the present context of the status of local government, however, is the effect of a strong political executive on the popular perception of the municipality. In continental countries, the municipality tends to be personified in the mayor or in the college of mayor and 'aldermen', in much the same way as with a national government. On the other hand, few British local politicians are as well-known among their electorate, or indeed beyond, as a French mayor, and none enjoys as much prestige. This undoubtedly has some impact on the turn-out in local government elections.

It also substantially affects the attractiveness of local political office to the ambitious and its place in the national *cursus honorum*. In France, this attractiveness is reinforced by the system of *cumul des mandats* (despite the restrictions introduced in 1985) and the importance of a local power base for a national political career. One by-product of such overlapping of local and national politics in what remains a markedly centralised country is a degree of understanding at the centre for the interests and needs of local government which is much less apparent in a country like Britain. But even in those countries where combining political office at more than one level is less widespread or partially prohibited, the influence and prestige of the mayor of a major city is certainly greater than that of a simple member of parliament and his position may be just as good a spring-board for ministerial office.

The third feature affecting the general perception of local authorities is the size of the local authorities and in particular of the basic level. For reasons of space this major topic can only be touched on here, but as a background condition for the functioning of local government its importance cannot be overlooked. Britain was of course far from being the only country to implement far-reaching local government reforms in recent decades to take account of the perceived requirements of efficient service provision, technical complexity and economies of scale. In proportional terms, the number of local authorities was reduced almost as much in West Germany and even more drastically in Sweden, Denmark and Belgium. It was, in fact, only in the countries of Southern Europe (including Switzerland and France) that the amalgamation of local authorities made little or no progress. That the process has not necessarily come to an end in Northern Europe is indicated by the current review of the municipal and county structure in Norway, prompted by the fact that (at least by Scandinavian standards) Norway still has a large number of municipalities with a relatively small population.

What is unique in the British case, therefore, is not the fact of the reform but its results in terms of the average size of the lower-tier authorities. In this respect, Great Britain diverges dramatically from the European norm. The average district in the shire counties is over 13 times as large in population terms (96 000) as the average of all the German or Italian municipalities (somewhat over 7 000), which are themselves five times the size of the average French commune (1 475). Of course in the latter case the parish might seem the more appropriate unit of comparison; but then the discrepancy would reappear in terms of the negligible functions of the English parish.

It is common for independent observers in France to conclude that the 80 per cent of French communes with less than 1 000 inhabitants can hardly be capable of carrying out autonomously the tasks of modern management and service provision calling for professional staff. The solution is often found in single- or multi-purpose consortia of municipalities, but in many respects dependence on the assistance of the state authorities or a *de facto* exercise of the function by a higher administrative level is inevitable.

In Britain, on the other hand, the single-minded pursuit of criteria relating to service delivery capacity has produced solutions which a comparison with other European countries suggests must be excessive. Planning and organisational considerations were undoubtedly implemented at the expense of the sense of the identity of the local community as a framework which local citizens can comprehend and within which they can contribute to determining their own living environment. In other Northern European countries too the major programme of amalgamation produced complaints of remoteness and loss of identity, and it is interesting to note that in Sweden there has for some time now been a reaction aiming to decentralise the structures of participation within the municipality. But nowhere were the local authorities removed so far from the citizen as in Britain, a fact which, especially in conjunction with the lack of a 'visible' political executive, is bound to affect the perception of local government within society. Moreover, with the replacement of the self-sufficient authority by the enabling council, the justification for such large units may appear even less evident.

If the lower level of British local government is exceptionally large, it is interesting to note that, by comparison with other European countries of equivalent size, the highest level of sub-national government is unusually small. In other words, there is no regional level of government. Regionalisation, which must be accounted one of the major trends in Europe since 1945, has in fact passed Britain by. Yet Germany (like Switzerland and Austria) has a genuine federal system, while in Italy and Spain (as in Belgium) there are autonomous regional authorities protected by constitutional guarantees and endowed with legislative powers over a broad field. Only France among the European states of comparable size to Britain has been at best half-hearted in going down this road, for it has created regional authorities with no legislative powers, which have the same legal status as the local authorities and, despite their recent reinforcement, are still weak in terms of their range of responsibilities.

Whatever the reasons for its creation, it seems clear that a fully-fledged federal or regionalised system offers a real alternative to the national level for the exercise of many functions of the modern state. The inevitable complication of political structures is counterbalanced by a reduction of the load on the centre, by the bringing of basic policy-making in important fields closer to the problems on the ground, often by a harnessing of regional loyalties and, indeed, by the stimulation of inter-regional competition in seeking the best solutions. British reticence is understandable, of course, considering that genuine regionalisation involves a willingness to rethink the state and to countenance a vertical division of powers which must at least put a dent in the system of parliamentary sovereignty. But in considering local government in other European countries, it is important to bear their regional structure in mind, as it is not without influence on the local authorities, whether positive (in terms of a general philosophy of decentralisation or subsidiarity) or negative (by squeezing the autonomy of the upper-tier local authorities).

Concluding remarks: Britain out of step?

It is not easy to draw conclusions from the sometimes rather impressionistic and certainly incomplete sketch which has been attempted in this chapter. Nevertheless, as far as the chapter goes, it does suggest that local government in continental Europe and in Britain is moving in quite different directions. Where in the one case there are numerous instances of decentralisation of powers and transfer of functions from state administrations to the local authorities, in the other there is a reduction of local responsibility through privatisation or transfer to appointed bodies. A gradual increase in local financial autonomy in several countries (more own taxes, more general, as opposed to specific, grants) contrasts with less discretion as regards revenue (business rates, more specific grants) and increasing control of expenditure in Britain. On the one hand there is a decline in government control and an increase in freedom as regards the means of carrying out statutory obligations; on the other hand an increasing tendency to prescribe management methods (competitive tendering) and internal organisation. Here attempts may be observed to improve possibilities of participation in the collective decision-making process; there the emphasis is on widening the individual's choice of services provided from whatever source. Finally, a number of basic characteristics of British local authorities – their size, the *ultra vires* doctrine and the lack of a political executive – help to explain their undeservedly low status in society.

It is no doubt against this background that the failure of the British government to sign the European Charter of Local Self-Government must be viewed. This Council of Europe Convention, which has so far been signed by 17 member states and ratified by ten, attempts to set out the basic principles which should be respected by any democratic system of local government. Indeed, it is providing inspiration for current reforms of local government in several countries of Eastern Europe. In order to take account of the sensitivities of national governments and the wide variations in structures across Europe, the charter's terms are not excessively detailed and flexibility is permitted with respect to the undertakings of the contracting parties. The fact that the United Kingdom has nevertheless not found it possible to accede to the Charter has caused some sadness and perplexity in Strasbourg and raises the question whether the prevailing British conception of local government now diverges too far from the European norm.

4 The Restructuring of Local Government in England and Wales

Peter John

Introduction

This chapter looks at the ways in which the relationship between central and local government has altered in England and Wales since the late 1970s. It examines the growth in the power of central government and the reduction of local government's policy-making role. The theme of the paper is that more recent changes have seen a more concerted move by central government to restructure local government, changing the way local authorities exercise their functions so that local government reduces the services it directly provides. With the aim of enhancing consumer choice, central government has tried to increase the numbers of service providers. Local government is to be moved to an 'enabling' role, organising other institutions to supply services. Central government wishes to increase accountability of local government to the electorate and the consumer through the community charge and the new roles for schools and housing authorities. If the aims were realised, the changes would significantly alter the role of local government.

The recent changes pose several questions. What is the role of central government in the new reforms and to what extent do the new measures reduce the role of local government as a political body? How successful are the reforms and what are their effects on local government? How far does the new 'enabling role' and new version of accountability retain an element of local choice and discretion? This chapter attempts to provide some answers.

1976–86: The central control of local government

Before the 1970s central government traditionally had a wide range of powers and exerted control over local government, but the character of central control tended to be concerned with setting the broad outlines of policy, its implementation being left in local hands. Central departments sought to influence and use their authority over local government, through primary legislation, circulars and the selective approval of projects and schemes. Local authorities were given permissive powers to carry out their functions through legislation that was enabling in character. It allowed local authorities to set for their area the preferred standard of service providing that basic duties were fulfilled. The model was that local authorities were multifunctional organisations subject to political control. They were agencies that implemented central government policy and received funds for that purpose, but they had a broad discretion about how to carry it out.

It is important not to overemphasise how far the system was decentralised. The legal framework contained elements of central control, as did the financial framework, particularly for the approval of capital projects. Britain does not have a constitutional protection for the functions and role of local government which have been continually changed by central government. The position of local government may be summarised as having a tradition of the local administration of services, but central government has often altered the services which local authorities provided.

Since the late 1970s, and since 1979 in particular, it has often been alleged that there has been a change in the relationship, with a shift in power and influence to central government and a restriction of the role of local government in setting local policy (e.g. Loughlin, 1985; Jones, 1988; Stallworthy, 1989; Travers, 1989). The finance of local government and concern by central government about local government expenditure have been the main factors leading to central concern with, and then in the

1980s, control over local government. The control over the level of central grant started with the introduction of cash-based limits in 1976. The momentum increased after the election of a Conservative government in 1979 which acquired new types of powers over local authorities, such as to alter the amount of grant going to groups of authorities and reduce central grant as a penalty for overspending. Later changes were crucial in adjusting the central-local relationship when the Rates Act 1984 allowed central government to reduce the rates of groups of local authorities.

One of the problems was that there was a failure to control the total level of spending of local government, even though central grant was reduced and capital spending in certain areas fell. It was the relative failure of the national government's objectives on spending levels that led to a succession of central controls (Travers, 1986). Some local authorities increased rates to maintain spending; they used the mechanisms of creative accountancy to avoid spending controls; they disregarded the consequences of penalty or sought procedural devices to avoid it.

The central government was also committed to introducing policies to reform and reduce the role of the welfare state and increase the rights of the individual. Hence, council tenants were given the right to buy their own homes and parents given greater choice in schools. A shift in the central-local relationship was signified by the power to transfer local authority planning functions in certain areas from local authorities to agencies designated by central government, the urban development corporations. These allow central government to promote local economic development without the participation of local authorities.

In other areas central government acquired wide discretionary powers over local government. The Local Government Act 1985, which abolished the Greater London Council and the other metropolitan county councils, gives central government considerable power of control (Hebbert and Travers, 1988). In 1987 the government ended the consultative arrangement for deciding teachers' salaries and took a direct power itself. There has also been an expansion of central grants for specific programmes which has reflected the wish of central government to ensure that certain policies are followed or activities supported. This removed some of the freedom of local authorities to decide how they spend their grant, since as specific grants rose so the main central grant fell.

Local authorities lost some of their discretion to set policy. The Local Government Finance Act 1982 extended the powers of the district auditor. It set up the Audit Commission which had a remit to ensure that local authorities secure economy, efficiency and effectiveness. The London Regional Transport Act 1984 removed local government's control of public transport in London. The Local Government Act 1985 reduced the activities controlled by local authorities in all metropolitan areas by abolishing the upper tier of local government and not transferring all of its functions to the lower tier but instead giving them to appointed bodies, such as the fire and civil defence authorities. The Transport Act 1985 abolished the bus licensing system controlled by local authorities and allowed private operators to provide passenger transport. Local authorities have been restricted in the degree to which they may subsidise transport services and do not now have a direct providing role. The Education Act 1986 gave further powers to parent governors, forbade 'political indoctrination' in schools and created a duty to consider political issues in a balanced way.

Summarising, the change in central-local relations involved central government acquiring and using broad discretionary powers over local government, particularly over its financial decisions, and increasing specific grants to local authorities. The discretionary powers of local government have been restricted. Local authorities are obliged to observe market disciplines in some of their activities. There has been a reduction in the real level of central government finance for local government. Although, at first, the increase in rates made up for the shortfall, since the mid-1980s financial austerity added to the constraints on local government and reduced its ability to carry out new policies. The reduction in the level of capital finance affected local government's traditional role as a provider, for example of housing. There has also been an increased role both for other government organisations, such as the urban development corporations and the Manpower Services Commission (now the Training Agency), for voluntary agencies, private companies and the wide range of agencies which now supervise services within metropolitan areas. In addition to the abolition of the upper tier of metropolitan government, local authorities have also lost strategic functions in planning and transport. The style of relations between central and local government has altered. Policy for local government has tended to be introduced without its consent. Central-local government relations have tended to become legalised (Loughlin, 1986), with more precise legal controls over local government and an expansion of the number of regulations. There has been rapid change in the law affecting local government, and both central and local government have increasingly resorted to the courts to resolve disputes.

Some of the changes may be summarised by the term 'centralisation' and this may be appropriate if the term refers to the extent of change attempted by central government at the local level. But central government did not always succeed in achieving its aims for local government. The controls over current expenditure did not prevent local authorities from using their powers to experiment with many new policies in the fields, for example, of local economic development and local educational management.

The reasons for change were partly to do with political conflict and partly due to background tensions in central-local relations. Many controls were imposed to limit the increase in the general level of local government spending, and to control the spending of certain councils in particular. Central government sought to reform the services administered by local government and, since services such as education and housing are controlled by local government, a degree of control over elected authorities was needed if the new policies were to be implemented. Central government also tried to prevent local authorities from exercising their existing powers in novel ways. The politicisation of some Labour controlled local authorities in the early 1980s and the new policies they formulated antagonised the Conservative controlled central government. Many controls were added as a reaction to earlier failures to control local government: the lack of success in controlling finance in particular led to firmer restrictions in a spiral of ever more stringent legislation. Conflict has emerged because the reforms appeared to challenge the traditional role of local government as a welfare and strategic agency.

Underlying the changes were long-term social and political causes. First, the financial crisis of central government in the late 1970s and the expansion of the demand for local government services led to a higher than average expansion of local government services at a time of fiscal austerity. There was thus a need, or a perceived need, to control local government spending. Second, there have been pressures to adapt the welfare state and to recast the institutions and professions which administer it. Since the 1970s there has been a change in the intellectual climate. Professionally administered bureaucracies have been criticised as inefficient and unresponsive to the consumer, and consumers themselves have become more demanding of the services provided by the state (Gyford *et al.*, 1989). In the private sector the structure of organisations has been changing toward smaller central bureaucracies and decentralised or contracted-out bodies carrying out specialist activities. Such changes challenge the traditional structure and functions of local government (Stoker, 1989); they meant that policies to increase the formal rights of consumers and introduce pluralism in the provision of services had a level of popular support.

Finally, the decline of political consensus, both on the right and on the left, led to the emergence of the neo-liberal policies of the Conservative government at the central level and the collectivist policies of Labour councils at the local level. This change has particularly affected central-local relations because of the longevity of Conservative central administrations and the increase in the number of Labour controlled councils. Ideological and party political conflict has thus reinforced the traditional conflict of interest and culture between levels of government, based on the Treasury's concern to control and account for government spending, and local government's role as the representative of the needs and demands of public services and their clients. It is the highly political dimension to central-local disputes that has prompted the centre to make wide-ranging changes to local government, and that has been the cause of the opposition of some local authorities.

Local government since 1987

The reforms of the Conservative government from 1987 differ from those that went before. In the preceding period there were many influences affecting central policy towards local government. These derived from longstanding commitments (for example, council house sales), the pressure on public spending, political factors and a reaction to the lack of success in controlling local government. The legislation after 1987 appears to have more direction; it is more coordinated and comprehensive.

There is some evidence that central government rethought the role of local government in a consistent way across the whole range of local functions (Ridley, 1988). This again derived, first, from the overriding concern with finance and a perception that the whole system was too complex and ineffective. The new community charge, which replaced the property tax or rating system, led to a new approach to central grants and capital spending. Capital controls led central government to reconsider housing finance, and finance was also at the heart of education reforms. Second, the reform of public services derived from a slowly emerging philosophy of consumer choice and pluralism which fitted both into the pre-existing Conservative beliefs in cutting back the state and promoting private institutions and into the newer models of individual choice promoted by bodies such as the Adam Smith Institute. This philosophy was developed across a range of public bodies, and influenced the reforms introduced for the civil service and the National Health Service.

Finance

The main change in finance, the community charge or poll tax, continues the trend towards increasing central control and declining local discretion, though on first inspection the new tax appears not to alter the powers of local authorities which remain able to set their own tax level. However, the legislation removes local authorities' power to set the non-domestic rate and replaces it with a uniform business rate set nationally. Local authorities do not retain the income from the rates but are entitled to a standard amount for each adult. The new system thus reduces, by about half, the level of local revenue which may be decided locally.

The aim of the new system is to promote the financial accountability of local authorities. This will be achieved, in the government's view, by the community chargepayer bearing the cost of a local council's decisions to increase expenditure and perceiving the link between spending and the level of local tax. This follows from the parallel reform of the central grant system which, by removing the compensation for the differences in rateable income, tries to ensure that the level of community charge directly reflects the level of spending in each authority. Moreover the 'gearing effect' (the ratio between an increase in local expenditure and local taxes) is increased since the business rate is fixed and the local authority can therefore only increase its income by raising the community charge.

Because low income groups bear a higher proportion (in terms of their income) of the community charge, there may be pressures to reduce spending if councils, particularly Labour councils, are sensitive to the burden of the community charge on their voters. These pressures may increase if local authorities' costs exceed the Retail Price Index since they will have to find the increased costs from the community charge payer. The regressive aspect of the new tax system, the automatic nature of the gearing effect, and the reduced proportion of their income local authorities control may reduce local discretion rather than increase choice and accountability. Spending outcomes depend more on the mechanics of the new system than an electoral choice. Moreover the Secretary of State may limit the local power of decision by reducing community charges.

Capital controls over local government have also been reformed. The Local Government and Housing Act 1989 introduces a new system, the basis of which is to shift control from spending to borrowing. There are limits, called credit approvals, on the level of commitments which individual local authorities may enter into in any year and finance by borrowing; these are calculated according to the government's assessment of the needs of the authority. Although local authorities are now free to use revenue contributions to finance additional capital expenditure, the new system is more restrictive because local authorities were previously able to raise revenue through the sale of assets.

Services

The Education Reform Act 1988 has changed the relationship between the Department of Education and Science and the local education authorities. It vests more legal powers in the Secretary of State and reduces local authorities' discretion to set policy through the provisions for a national curriculum and for the delegation of budgets to schools. Local authorities are required to obtain central government's approval for a financial management scheme for the delegation of budgets. The authority determines the total resources available to schools but can have little influence on how they are allocated. Three-quarters of the delegated budget is allocated on the basis of the number of pupils; the remaining quarter is allocated for special purposes, but the authority cannot earmark the resources for specific uses. It is the schools which have the discretion about how their budgets are spent and how staff may be deployed.

Local authorities also lose control over education in a number of other respects. Schools may 'opt out' from the local education system and become central government 'grant maintained' schools, after a ballot of the parents and with the government's approval. However, they are still required to rationalise educational provision and remove surplus school places, a task which becomes harder to fulfil when threatened schools can opt out. Special inner city schools, City Technology Colleges, responsible to central government, can also be set up to compete with the local education system. Finally, local government loses powers over polytechnics, colleges of higher education and teacher training colleges.

The education reforms are part of the general attempt to introduce 'pluralism' into the services which local government administers. The local education authority has lost its directive role: grant maintained schools, schools with delegated budgets, city technology colleges, polytechnics and higher education colleges now make their own decisions about the provision of education. In theory, the role of the consumer is enhanced by parental participation on governing bodies and by the quasi-market which is generated by the funding formula which rewards schools according to parental choice. Local authorities have to adapt to a more strategic role, providing a service to the schools and persuading them to adopt policies, but their power of influence is strictly limited by financial and legal controls.

The 1988 Housing Act is designed to reduce the direct providing role of local authorities by providing for the transfer of the tenancies of council houses to other bodies. Initially it appeared that 'housing action trusts' would be an important part of the policy. These are organisations with powers to act as the landlord over local authority housing stock with the powers and finance to refurbish it in areas seen by central government to have particular public housing problems. However, since none have been created so far, they are unlikely, in the near future, to be an important way of transferring housing stock.

The second and potentially more far-reaching aspect of the Act, is the measure which allows groups of tenants of a local authority to change their landlord to a tenants' group, to a housing association or to a private landlord, decided in a ballot of the residents. If there is a substantial transfer to alternative landlords, the housing role of local authorities will diminish and they will come to cater mainly for the homeless, for the special housing needs of deprived groups and for the management of low quality public housing. At the present time no transfers have occurred; only one tenants' group and about five housing associations have obtained approved landlord status, the first step to transfer. Local authorities may also transfer their property voluntarily to housing associations or private landlords, with the consent of the Secretary of State. This has met with some response from local councils with a few transferring the whole of their stock to housing associations. Another influence on transfers, and one which will become more marked over time, is the reform of local authority housing finance in the Housing and Local Government Act 1989. By prohibiting subsidy of council rents by the local authority it tries to ensure that the rent that tenants pay is commensurate with the cost of providing council housing. The higher rents which result may cause tenants to favour the transfer provisions in the Housing Act.

The reforms in housing continue the developments of the preceding years. Central government has increased its powers over local government: to create housing action trusts, to approve transfers and to control housing subsidy. Local authority discretionary powers are restricted: they lose the power to subsidise council rents, are required, under certain circumstances, to transfer their stock and may be subjected to more stringent capital controls. Their providing function is also reduced as they become one among other suppliers, with housing associations and other bodies subject to the supervision of the national Housing Corporation.

The most recent reform is in the field of social services. A government-sponsored review of community care policies for elderly and mentally ill people concluded that local government, should be the coordinator of these services, becoming 'arrangers and purchasers of care services rather than monopolistic providers' (Griffiths, 1988, p.17). The government decided, if reluctantly, to implement the Griffiths Report. In one sense this was a reversal of the trend to take away functions and responsibilities from local government. But the reforms also fit into the government's version of the 'enabling' approach, separating provision from regulation and promoting the use of the private sector in providing public services. Local social services departments are to be the assessors of an individual's needs and are to enable private bodies to provide the care. Community care plans have to be produced to show the steps being taken to increase the use of non-statutory provision, and there are financial incentives for local authorities to arrange for care in the private sector. Central government has the power to inspect local plans, to issue directives and to give guidelines.

The control of procedures

The Local Government Act 1988 requires local authorities to contract out or to offer to tender to private companies the provision of services such as refuse collection, cleaning of buildings, school catering, ground and vehicle maintenance; the management of sports and leisure facilities have since been added. More than any other reform this pushes local government in the direction of enablement.

The legislation restricts local authorities' discretionary powers and sets out in detail the procedures to be followed. The process for putting work out to tender is defined precisely so as to prevent the restriction of competition. When deciding about supply and works contracts, councils may not take into account non-commercial matters such as the terms and conditions of employment by contractors and the country of origin of the company. They are prevented from laying down any contract

compliance requirements and are prohibited from unfairly awarding a contract to their own direct labour organisation; indeed the
Act even allows central government to close one down.

Contracting out may increase the efficiency of local government services and reduce the size of their workforce; it will also
tend to change their role from provision to supervision and
monitoring. Even their supervisory discretion is, however, limited: they can re-allocate contracts if they are dissatisfied with the
performance of the contractor but cannot pursue social or welfare
objectives when awarding or monitoring contracts. In the short
term they may keep a certain influence with contractors since, so
far, it is mostly ex-employees' organisations which have won
contracts.

Other important reforms are the controls over the discretionary
and incidental powers of local authorities and the way the
internal procedures of local authorities are regulated. These
reforms originate from the government's concern about the
politicisation of local government and the new practices which
have been developing in local government in recent years, such as
the commissioning of political appointees and 'political' advertis-
ing. For example, the Local Government Act 1988 introduced
controls on the publicity issued by local authorities, especially
material designed to support a political party. The Local Government and Housing Act 1989 limits the political activity of senior
officers, alters the power of local authorities to provide finance
for activities which are not covered by statute and restricts the
interests a local authority may have in companies. This legislation
has tightened the legal framework governing local government's
discretionary powers and its freedom to order its internal
procedures and staff. It is likely to lessen the political nature of
local government, vesting more powers in the hands of officers
and restricting the range of decision-making through the introduction of checks and balances in councils.

Conclusion

The reforms since 1987 have affected most aspects of the
functions and procedures of local government. Many of the
trends observed since the late 1970s have continued: there has

been an increase in the powers of central government to intervene at the local level and restrictions on the discretion of local authorities. The legislation of the relationship between central and local government has continued. Central government may be more successful in achieving its objectives than before 1987, through its design of precise controls on local government activities, such as in housing finance and general capital controls.

A key change has been the financing of local authority services. Decisions about the allocation of funds to services are increasingly based on the cost of providing that service on a per capita basis, as in the case of the delegated budgets to schools or the allocation of central grant generally. The redistributive function that local authorities performed may be restricted in future, and this is likely to be reinforced by the effects of the community charge.

A new non-political model of local government is emerging. Accountability is defined more by the responsiveness of local authorities to groups of consumers of local government services and measured by its performance according to market and efficiency principles rather than through the political process. Procedures to increase efficiency, to control local authority procedures and increase consumer choice over institutions such as schools promote this role. The reforms effectively challenge the traditional model of local government, reducing local discretion in the development of policy.

The reforms have become less piecemeal and there appears to be a new role being created for local government, as it loses responsibility for certain decisions to new institutions at the local level. These include schools with delegated budgets, urban development corporations, housing action trusts and new housing bodies, while private companies will have an increasing role in undertaking contracted out services. The local authority may still have an enabling role to play, becoming the leading party in coordinating other local institutions and private organisations; the recent government decision to make local government the lead authority in community care encourages this view.

Recent writings from different perspectives (Ridley, 1988; Local Government Training Board, 1988) claim that the enabling concept is consistent with local democracy and that the reforms have fostered a new management culture within local government which will favour further development in this direction. The problem is that it is still not really clear what 'enabling' means: the concept seems to cover a wide variety of different policies and institutional arrangements. It has different implications for different services and may only be applicable to some. In social services the idea seems to be clear: the local authority is the lead authority and other institutions, such as voluntary agencies, are encouraged to provide services. With contracting out, the service is provided by other agencies, leaving little discretion to local authorities. In housing the role seems limited to the fulfilling of statutory functions, such as to house homeless people. In education the concept does not clearly apply since schools already exist to provide education and it is not clear how the education authority will fulfil its remaining role in the servicing and rationalisation of educational provision.

There are several obstacles to the emergence of the enabling authority in the broad sense of the term. Firstly, the community charge may mean that, in future, local government may not have access to a buoyant source of local finance; funding new and innovatory projects may become more difficult. Secondly, central government retains broad discretionary powers to direct and control how local authorities exercise their enabling role. Thirdly, the decentralised institutions of service delivery and contracted out services are formally separated from local authorities, and there are therefore limits on local authorities' power to control them. Fourthly, local government's powers have been constrained: it is less able to promote policies with a redistributive or welfare aspect.

The 1990s may require local government to respond to new needs, such as those of the elderly or the environment, but central controls and the reduction of local authority powers appear to constrain the response. The contradiction underlying the recent reforms is that whereas the central control of local government and the changes in the way local authorities exercise their functions may be ways of improving performance, efficiency and responsiveness to the consumer, the cost is the reduction of local choice which undermines the realisation of the enabling authority.

References

Brooke, R. (1989) *Managing the Enabling Authority*, Longman, London.
Grant, M. (1989) *Local Government Finance Act 1988, Annotations*, Sweet and Maxwell, London.
Griffiths, R. (1988) *Community Care: Agenda for Action*, HMSO, London.
Gyford, G., Leach, S. and Game, C. (1989) *The Changing Politics of Local Government*, Unwin Hyman, London.
Hebbert, M. and Travers, T. (1988) *London Government Handbook*, Cassell, London.
Jones, G. (1988) 'The crisis in British central-local government relationships', *Governance*, vol. 1, no. 2, 162–83.
Local Government Training Board (1988) *The Enabling Council*, LGTB.
Loughlin, M. (1985) 'The restructuring of central-local government legal relations', *Local Government Studies*, vol. 11, no. 6, 59–74.
Ridley, N. (1988) *The Local Right*, Centre for Policy Studies, London.
Stallworthy, M., 'Central government and local government: the uses and abuses of a constitutional hegemony', *Political Quarterly*, vol. 60, no. 1, 22–37.
Stoker, G. (1989) 'Creating a local government for the post-Fordist society: the Thatcherite project', in J. Stewart and G. Stoker (eds), *The Future of Local Government*, Macmillan, London.
Travers, T. (1989) 'The threat to autonomy of elected local government' in C. Crouch and D. Marquand (eds), *The New Centralism*, Basil Blackwell, Oxford.

5 Customer-Orientated Service Delivery in German Local Administration

Dieter Grunow

Developments in the West German administrative system

This chapter is concerned with the changes in the goals and strategies of consumer-orientated, responsive service delivery at the local level of the West German political administrative system. In this introduction a few background details are given concerning the formal position and role of local government in West Germany.

The political administration system in Germany is formally organised on three levels of political representation and public administration: national level (*Bund*), state level (*Länder*) and local level (*Kreise* and *Gemeinden*). This federal structure, which is defined by the German Constitution, implies an incomplete and in part contradictory division of labour. In this, local government is given a 'guarantee of local self-government', that it is to shape all local affairs according to specific local circumstances and demands – *within the boundaries of existing law*. In spite of the strong commitment to decentralised structures in West Germany since the Second World War, there has been an increasing shift of legislative and executive powers to the national level. Although communes have to fulfil ever more tasks, the strength of the local level is now and then 'rediscovered'. This is a matter not only of efficient service delivery but also of the function of political legitimation, especially in times of scarcity of public resources.

In practice these structures lead to many forms of cooperation between the levels as well as to conflicts about the allocation of competence and resources. With reference to the three models which were described in the introduction to this book, the recent situation in Germany comes closest to the interaction model. The following examples describe some major changes in the formal position and functions of local government (during the last twenty-five years) which have influenced the means of service delivery in many respects. They refer to reforms in the size of local government units, changes in tax sharing, the relationship between political representation and administration, and new forms of co-operation and coordination.

During the 1960s and 1970s the number of local government units was changed: by 1978 the counties (*Kreise*) were reduced from 425 to 236; the communes which were part of the counties (*kreisangehörige Gemeinden*) were reduced from 24371 to 8506; the independent municipalities (*kreisfreie Städte*, not part of a county) were reduced from 141 to 88. The basic idea was to strengthen local administration by making use of the economies of scale within larger bodies of administration. This goal implied the necessity to change the division of labour between region, county and communes. However, the functional reform that was supposed to follow the territorial reform was only partially implemented. The attempt to abolish regional administrative offices of the states failed. Thus, a delegation of tasks to lower levels of government did not take place to a sufficient degree. The same deficiency could be observed with regard to county-commune relationships. Although local institutions grew larger the delegation of tasks from the county did not take place accordingly. Altogether, the results of this reform are at least ambivalent.

One major consequence of the reform is the increasing spatial and communicative distance between administration and citizens. Also the possibilities of participation seem to be practically reduced. Thus, many local governments had to implement decentralised or at least deconcentrated substructures of administration in their municipalities, in order to cope with these deficiencies (Holtmann and Killisch, 1989).

Since 1969 a new system of tax sharing has been established. It has made the local government more independent of trade tax which formerly was collected by and only for the local level. This had led to a situation in which the settlement of business firms overruled all other ideas of community development. Now the trade tax as other taxes (including income tax) is divided up between all administrative levels. Thus, there is more independence with regard to business firms (concerning tax-income), but more dependence on the political and administrative factors which decide upon the respective tax-shares. An important aspect of the fiscal situation at the local level is now the proportion of citizens who are entitled to welfare payments and social services. There is not yet an accepted mode of compensation between the various states and local governments concerning the different welfare pay loads (Rosenschon, 1980).

The debate about the relative importance of local councils and local administration relates to the general modelling of the federal system. If the 'agency model' of local government holds true, the dominance of administration is quite evident. If there are many autonomous functions of local political bodies, the representation of citizens' interests is more important. A more specific debate has recently started with regard to the role of mayor (*Burgermeister*) and of the head of the local administration. There are different models in Germany so that a comparison is possible. Basically either the two functions (mayor and head of administration) are divided up between two persons or fused into one position. Another difference is the direct election (by the voters) or the indirect election (by council members) of the mayor. Although there seems to be a preference for the strong mayor model it is still difficult to measure precisely the effects of the different models (Schimanke (ed.), 1989).

The development of new functions at the local level and the definition of new goals and means of local development is not just the consequence of formally defined rights; it is as much a matter of initiative and of the ability to decide. Non decision-making may lead to the foregoing of new opportunities at local level; or other administrative levels may be included in the decision process, with the consequent danger of transferring the decision to those other levels. Sometimes local authorities may try to avoid difficult local choices by presenting alternative projects to the state level for selection.

During the last few years in North Rhine-Westphalia the state government has tried to reverse the process of increasing local government dependency. With the crisis of coal and steel production many cities in the Ruhrgebiet face severe problems and many programmes for restructuring working and living conditions in this area have been installed. In this context an attempt was made to increase the participation of local actors: regional and local developments were identified as a matter for local initiative, participation and coordination. The traditional tools of regional planning (in the sense of moving through a hierarchy of responsible institutions) were not applied. The state government asked for joint projects developed with the participation of all relevant local groups, and/or for priority lists. Intercommunal arrangements were also encouraged so as to strengthen the scope for local initiatives for development. Although there is no solid proof of the efficiency of this procedure, state and local authorities seem to welcome the new strategy. The losers seem to be other intermediate levels of administration – the regional offices of the state and other regional institutions.

Relevance of service delivery at the local level

Among German people there is a frequent complaint about 'space-ship Bonn'. In contrast to the national level of policy-making and implementation, local government is seen as much more 'down to earth'. It is the field where the practical work of policy implementation has to be done (for example all welfare and health services). It is the field where unsolved problems of policy-making still have to be dealt with (for example the refugees from East Germany or foreigners applying for asylum). It is the field where new problems and public demands are first observed. It has become quite clear that most of the legitimation for the political administrative system has to be secured by local politics and administration. The quality and efficiency of local service are of great importance to the acceptability of the system as a whole, a fact which can be seen especially well by comparison with East Germany. This basic point, that local institutions are the place where government executives and citizens meet and where therefore the responsiveness of the system is assessed, has not always been given enough attention.

During the mid-1970s the disappointing results of national planning led to the realisation that good policies and programmes were not enough for efficient government; the importance of implementation was acknowledged (Wollmann (ed.), 1979). At this time the idea of responsive local administration was developed, and models of good practice were installed and evaluated. By now, the responsiveness of the administration is accepted as a measure of quality as are efficiency, effectiveness and legality. Some of the implications and practical applications will be discussed in the following paragraphs.

Responsiveness as a standard of service delivery

The early ideas and initiatives concerned with responsiveness in public administration were rather simple and sometimes almost superficial. Friendliness of staff or better furniture in waiting rooms seemed at first to be a sufficient answer. But it became increasingly evident that responsiveness was a complex and difficult measure of performance in service production and delivery (Grunow, 1988; OECD, 1987). Practical experience and empirical research shows that the adequacy of urban services vis-à-vis citizens' needs and demands is a key issue and problem for all types of service delivery organisation whether private, public or other. None of them is *per se* responsive to consumers' demands and the extensive legislation on behalf of consumer protection in the context of capitalist economies is proof of this fact.

The following considerations centre around the questions, how to measure and how to improve the responsiveness of urban services. If these two issues are seen in close connection, it will be seen that the investigation of consumer needs is not sufficient. The concept of need is ambiguous and controversial. It has to be supplemented by other indicators and an adequate matching of clients and services. Even if needs are well known, this is not a sufficient prerequisite for responsive action by service organisations. There are different ways of analysing the degree of failure and success of urban services in meeting consumers' needs: comparing needs and need fulfilment on the consumers' side; comparing the output and impact of urban services; comparing the relationship between needs and output or impact whether through formal statistical relationships or qualitative assessments; and evaluating the responsiveness of service organisations as an indicator of an adequate relationship between needs and services.

Responsiveness can be considered from a consumer's or a service agency's perceptive. For the consumer's view one would have to consider levels of knowledge, participation or co-production, proportion of clientele contacted by the service, the continuity of utilisation, levels of acceptance and satisfaction, impact and costs. In terms of a service-focused view one would have to consider the degree to which the organisation takes into consideration needs and demands, the communication capabilities of consumers, the participation or co-production abilities of different citizen groups, and the ability of service personnel to comprehend the delivery system. For all of these indicators there is no maximum criterion of performance. At best, a relative optimum within a mixture of criteria can be looked for and eventually reached. The aim of establishing such standards for performance in service delivery faces many obstacles. Firstly, it is very difficult to monitor and tune the performance of public services in detail; instead of preparing a well-composed menu, local authorities ask for 'fast food', the instant solution to the responsiveness problem. They do not look for solutions but for (more or less plausible) instruments. Thus, some officials support the idea of training, others want to reorganise, others are supporters of privatisation. Most often the effects of these strategies are not examined. Thus, at least for Germany it is much easier to find examples of practice, than of *good* practice.

Secondly, responsiveness as a quality standard for service delivery is seen as being in competition with legality, economy and efficiency which have often been used to repel initiatives for better services. Although there might be fields of incompatibility between the different goals, there are also service modalities which allow a simultaneous adaptation of those goals or quality standards. In addition, it is typical for policy cycles to give special emphasis only for a short period to one particular goal. During the late 1970s responsiveness was such an emphasised goal in Germany. Many boards were established and initiatives were started on behalf of responsive administration and better service quality. A better approach would have been to include responsiveness as a normal feature of administration with lower expectations and enthusiasm.

Lastly, it is always possible for a widely supported concept to be misused. Cutback policies, reduction of services, decay of public institutions may be sold as debureaucratisation and privatisation.

The experience of the last 10–15 years has demonstrated many ideas and practical ways of improving services at the local level. It is not possible to describe the entire field of activities, so what follows is a subjective selection. Three main types of initiative will be mentioned: 1) to strengthen the position of the client, user or consumer; 2) to improve the public system of service delivery; 3) to support solutions outside the public sector. As a general evaluation, it can be said that the second option is the one which is by far the most often chosen in Germany, but examples will be given from all three types.

1. *Strengthening the position of the client or consumer*

There has not been a consumer movement in Germany as there has in the USA, but consumer protection has always been a part of national legislation. During the 1970s, the interest in this policy field increased and it was an important part of the discussion of state interventions in economic processes. Thus, pieces of legislation were constantly added but they were all quite moderate in their effect and, in the case of strongly conflicting interests (housing, drug production, credit selling), the consumers were the losers. The general importance of consumer protection and rights was rediscovered in the context of environmental problems where the debates about safe levels of contamination have shown the increasingly difficult role of the consumer.

Most of the examples of the position of the consumer are taken from the private economy and are related to goods. It is difficult to apply these ideas to (personal) services and public institutions. Although there are consumer information centres everywhere in German communities, they are not concerned with the quality of public services. The role of the consumer is increasingly embedded in local citizens' initiatives and protest groups, which share specific experiences and problems in regard to public services. Instances were: the opening of the housing market, which led to rising prices and deficits in social housing projects; the use of atomic energy for local energy supply (some groups tried to withhold payment of part of their bills); the formation of interest groups amongst those who were suffering from poor services or unfair treatment; groups that depend on monopolistic public services (such as schools and local transport).

It is evident that the idea of a competent consumer acting in a polypolistic market is rather idealistic in general, and especially with regard to public services. The idea of choice has not played a major role so far. For many services the creation of alternatives and competition seems to be too expensive (for example in public transport or energy supply) so we have either a public or a private monopoly. In other cases (like health and social services) there is a long tradition of voluntary organisations (and also of private providers) besides provision by public institutions (Fink, 1988). The idea of choice is a different one here: as the voluntary institutions are bound to the churches, alternative service delivery (according to religious affiliation) was demanded for and by the users. This again might lead to small scale religious and regional monopolies, so the effect of alternative provision on quality of service is at least ambivalent. Moreover, since the services are not directly or fully paid by the users, this type of choice strategy does not necessarily lead to improvements in quality; costs often seem to increase because of an oversupply which has to look for the necessary clients. This is the reason why local sickness funds now hesitate to accept further private nursing institutions.

In a corporate society, consumers also are forced to act in an organised form. In recent years the formation of self-help groups and organisations has been strongly supported within the German political and administration system (Vilmar and Runge, 1986). In many cities bureaux have been established to assist self-help initiatives with organisational and technical support paid for from public funds. However, the early expectations of politicians with reference to the self-help initiatives failed. They are not the expected cheap substitute for public services, but they are important additions to public services, and they may also promote quality.

As empirical studies show, self-help groups also lobby to influence local policy-making (Trojan, 1986). In this sense, they are part of a strategy for the improvement of services through participation. In general, national legislation has extended participation within city planning procedures, but has only loosely connected it to service institutions. An important instrument is the consultation of concerned citizens; very often, however, this excludes the 'silent majority'. Therefore, representative surveys help to detect needs and demands as well as difficulties or complaints about utilisation. This is often done for plans concerned with service provision for sub-groups of the local population such as the elderly, the handicapped, youth and the unemployed. Another project started a few years ago in some cities of the Ruhrgebiet has been repeated comparative surveys (twice a year) of the inhabitants. These surveys cover a broad spectrum of living conditions and their development.

A more radical innovation in representation has been the creation of the 'planning cell' as an instrument for many small scale planning tasks in a community. A sample of the inhabitants is drawn and exempted from normal work for the necessary planning period (6–24 months or so), during which they have full access to the local administration (staff, technical support, data). Experience has shown a convincing and often surprising quality in the results, for example in the designing of the central square around Cologne Cathedral.

The strengthening of the role of the consumer vis-à-vis public services does not enjoy high priority in West Germany. It is moderate in its aims and well adapted to 'economic necessities' and the social welfare system.

2. *Improvements in the system of public service delivery*

As already mentioned, attempts to improve the public system have been and still are dominant in Germany. They are closely connected to the concept of responsiveness and, during the conservative government in Bonn, increasingly fused with ideas about debureaucratisation. The concern with responsiveness and its practical implementation is not so much a product of insight among public officials, but rather the effect of a demanding clientele. In two respects citizens nowadays meet public institutions on quite different terms than in earlier decades: they insist on their rights and entitlements; and they expect competence and orientation to service rather than bureaucratic and presumptuous attitudes from public officials. As described above, in some instances citizens have organised themselves into interest groups or self-help groups, so as to address their demands and complaints not only to local politicians but also to local administrators (Grunow, 1988).

A dominant response on the part of administration has been to focus on training for better interaction or communication skills. This focus makes it possible to blame the lowest level staff for the observed deficiencies, and thereby to avoid difficult changes in the local administration.

Typical improvement strategies have been about improving the quality of interaction and its environment in or close to the public office. This has involved, for example, sending staff members on training courses about interaction styles and behaviour, formulating manuals of rules, improving offices and waiting areas, improving signposting, making sure there is a first contact person in a building, organising transport for people with restricted mobility and increasing the number of telephone numbers to reduce waiting time.

There have also been initiatives to meet citizens or clients elsewhere: in their homes, at their workplace, in other public places and during leisure activities to create a less official environment.

All these activities, aimed at an improvement of the style of service delivery on the basis of existing structures and procedures, were quite widely applied in local administrations. Less often, there has been an extension of services: the police installed new information centres for the improvement of property protection and introduced new subway controls during the evening and night, and new patrols in dwelling areas. Public transport widened its network of information and ticket selling, using shops which are highly frequented by citizens.

It is much more difficult to find examples of a more profound change in local agencies. One important and widespread change-strategy was to give more weight to staff members and organisational units having intensive contacts with citizens, clients, or consumers. Those 'boundary positions' most often were the worst paid and had high rates of turnover. They have now been raised with regard to status and payment, making them more attractive and even the subject of competition among staff members. In this context, the ability to develop service and consumer orientations became an important feature in the personal records of staff members, and a criterion for selection.

The boundary units became more important in other ways too. Superiors were also obliged to participate in training courses so that trained staff members were not hindered by ignorant superiors when they tried to change their style of client-interaction. In addition, the experience and insight of boundary units have been given more weight in planning organisational structures and procedures. Staff members are expected to act as advocates of client and consumer groups and to use the files, complaint statistics and special surveys to detect systematic deficiencies in service production and delivery. In very few instances a whole local office was reorganised according to ideas of responsive administration. One prominent example is the citizens' office in Unna (Burgeramt), which includes in one building all public departments with frequent contact with citizens. It applies a 'single-window' procedure for access and makes intensive use of information technology. As models or points of orientation the service strategies of travel agents, banks or insurance companies are used.

Typically the new emphasis on responsiveness is being introduced as part of a modernisation strategy. This implies the use of information and communication technology, the reduction of rules and regulations, an increase in efficiency and a reduction in response time. The participation of staff members is guaranteed by law; with reference to clients or consumers participation is still weak or non-existent. An exception was a recent experiment in social welfare offices where the introduction of a computerised procedure for welfare payments was discussed with client groups in an attempt to preserve case-oriented discretion.

Most of the initiatives and actions taken to improve public services at the local level have taken place within public agencies. However, many deficiencies in service production and delivery are a result of lack of cooperation and coordination between organisations. The lack of coordination can be observed especially well at the local level, where services take concrete shape as buses, schools, hospitals, welfare offices and police stations.

Citizens are sent from one office to another and infrastructure stands unused.

Local service institutions and services are becoming ever more multifold and difficult to use for citizens, providers and producers of the services. Available services are more and more differentiated with regard to specific user groups: for example for age groups or with reference to a specific problem or demand (unemployment; single parent families; car drivers, etc.). It becomes increasingly important to use modern information technology to keep up with the available service arrangements and alternatives, and to coordinate the quantity and quality of supply. Even where only public institutions or offices are concerned different policies and styles of service delivery lead to conflicts and deficiencies at the cost of consumers. Often these conflicts develop out of the different structural position of the local offices: some are part of local government, some are local units of state administration (like tax offices), others are local units of national administration (like unemployment offices). Thus, in the context of local (horizontal) coordination many vertical ties have to be considered. Some coordination problems (for example between the social welfare office and the unemployment office) have been resolved by the installation of coordination groups composed of members of the relevant offices. This 'solution' may increase the complexity, especially where direct ties have been developed across different levels of administration, different policies and different political affiliations.

The complete picture of coordination and cooperation has to include all non-governmental service producers as well. In many areas (like local transport, education, refuse collection, energy provision) a public monopoly exists at the local level. But there are also areas where different types of institution can deliver specific services. This is especially true for personal services (in social welfare and health) where there is a long tradition of German voluntary associations which are engaged in service delivery: from kindergarten and home-help services to nursing homes and hospitals. The availability of services is still guaranteed by local authorities, but production and delivery is realised by voluntary associations and, recently, increasingly by private enterprises. Nevertheless, the costs are mainly covered by public institutions and are part of the budget of the local government.

Only in a few cases does this transfer of tasks to non-governmental organisations lead to a market situation. Although there are many suppliers of the same service, choice is limited because: (a) due to financial rules and legally defined standards, services are very similar in quality; (b) there is no direct relationship between fees and service quality assessable by the users; and (c) often a corporatist arrangement prevents competition (for example by dividing up the city into service regions, which are almost exclusively served by one specific institution).

Nevertheless, where a market is opened for new and more suppliers, competition for consumers can develop. It is not easy to show, though, that this improves the quality. Choice in the context of personal services is probably quite different from choice among products. In service delivery, very specific if not idiosyncratic expectations and judgments play an important role. As personal services are not easily conservable or transportable, there is a high probability of the development of local or neighbourhood monopolies, whether they are run by the administration, voluntary associations or private enterprise. Some recent examples (ambulatory and institutional services for the elderly, for example) still show that the quality of service has to be ensured and sometimes even practically demonstrated by local administration. One major exception is the services for the very rich, which are based on high fee payments. The increasing competition between sickness funds during recent years has had the effect primarily of increasing their public relation budgets and furthered the notion that the poor should pay more, because in the lower social stratum there are more health risks and higher costs per insured person.

The examples above indicate that the idea of competition plays a rather minor role in the context of service delivery. However, there is competition between communes or cities either of the same region or county or between similar types of city depending on their size, infrastructure, industry, employment or budget. The KGSt (the Local Authorities Joint Institution for Organisational Studies) and the Deutscher Städtetag (the Association of German Cities) are providing comparative data which allows more precise self-assessment and mutual imitation.

In the German context, debureaucratisation is mainly addressed to public interventions (guidelines, controls, etc.) in economic affairs; it tries to reduce regulations and 'red tape' vis-à-vis private enterprises. Privatisation has at least two meanings: one being the retreat of the state from running business firms like Lufthansa, Volkswagenwerk and Veba at the national level and energy production or the public utilities at the local level. The other meaning is a 're-privatisation' of tasks of local government and administration. It is a strategy of getting rid of public tasks, either by abolishing a task or service altogether or by giving it explicitly to groups or non-government organisations. A review of these activities shows that a broad range of tasks has been privatised in this latter sense. Some tasks were just defined as private affairs of private persons or households; some have been contracted out to private firms; some have been placed in differently organised but publicly controlled institutions; some have been delegated to voluntary associations or even to self-help initiatives, which rely on public funds and are controlled by the administration.

In spite of the broad scope of types of privatisation only a few cases have been realised with any frequency: privatisation of cleaning services in public buildings (contracting out), slaughter houses and refuse collection are examples (KGSt, 1976). Some more interesting recent examples are the semi-public organisation of the local promotion of the economy and privatised local broadcasting.

Altogether, the discussions and the practical experiments have not led to a remarkable shift of former public tasks to other (local) institutions and organisations. It must be acknowledged, though, that the provision, production and delivery of services at the local level are already and increasingly a joint product of a complex and heterogeneous set of organisations. Public institutions play an important, sometimes also a dominating role, but they also depend on the other local actors with partly different approaches to service delivery. We are increasingly observing a mixture of principles and qualities of service delivery at the local level of the German political administrative system.

The role of political culture

Political culture can be defined as the values and expectations that are held by the population with regard to the political system. It connects political or administrative institutions with the orientations and actions of their clients or customers and can therefore explain some aspects of the status quo in service production and delivery. Summarising the results of recent empirical studies of the political culture in Germany (Böhret 1988), the following observations can be made. There is still a strong state-centred orientation in the German population: the state is seen as somewhat separate and probably superior to society; thus, following the rules of the state seems to be the most relevant duty of the citizen. The population's judgment of administration is more favourable than that of political institutions; political participation (besides voting) is not highly valued and political conflict and competition are less favoured than cooperation and harmony. The evaluation of the system is highly efficiency-oriented, concerned with problem-solving, especially in economic terms. The expectations of public administration are that it should be primarily concerned with delivering services of high quality. Most people prefer higher taxes and more public services in contrast to lower taxes and less public provision. There are also signs of a change in orientations especially among youth: social movements, self-help initiatives and the development of the Green Party are seen as indicators of a more participatory orientation and of the general (Western) trend toward post-materialistic values.

These indications of the dominant political culture help to explain the dominant role of public institutions as providers and producers and the demand for an improvement of public services rather than the installation of new service markets.

References

Böhret, C., *et al.* (1988) *Innenpolitik und politische Theorie*, Westdeutscher V, Opladen.

Fink, U., *et al.* (ed) (1989) *Der neue Generationenvertrag*, Piper, Munchen.

Grunow, D. (1988) *Burgernahe Verwaltung*, Campus, Frankfurt. a.M.

Holtmann, E. and Killisch, W. (1989) 'Gemeindegebietsreform und Politische Partizipation', *Politik und Zeitgeschichte* no. 31 27–39.

KGSt (1976) *Privatisierungsmassnahmen*, Köln.

OECD (1987) *Administration as Service – the Public as Client*, Paris.

Rosenschon, J.E. (1980) *Gemeindefinanzsystem und Selbstverwaltungsgarantie*, Kohlhammer, Köln.

Rudzio, W. (1987) *Das Politische System der Bundesrepublik Deutschland*, Leske, Opladen.

Schimanke, D. (ed.) (1989) *Stadtdirektor oder Burgermeister*, Birkhäuser V., Basel.

Trojan, A. (ed.) (1986) *Wissen ist Macht*, Fischer, Frankfurt. a.M.

Vilmar, F. and Runge, B. (1986) *Auf dem Weg zur Selbsthilfegesellschaft?*, Klartet V, Essen.

Wollmann, H. (ed.) (1979) *Politik im Dickicht der Burokratie*, Westdeutscher V, Opladen.

6 Public Goods and Private Operators in France

Dominique Lorrain

This chapter is concerned with the organisation of urban utilities in France: water distribution and production, sewage and waste water treatment, refuse collection and treatment, collective heating systems, urban transportation, large-scale housing and collective provision for culture, sports and social affairs. Even though these sectors are technically different they have a unity: the same organisational set, the same internal principles and a common political culture. These three factors define the French model of urban services (Lorrain, 1991).

What strikes foreigners is the role played by large private companies in France. They were founded a century ago initially for water distribution but now operate in all the other sub-sectors of urban services. Operation of these sectors, by municipalities and private companies, is long-established and does not reflect the current privatisation trend in many industrial countries but dates back to the end of the nineteenth-century. The privatisation of urban services is not something new but a tradition. This is a paradox in a country with a tradition of state control and generally because these are sectors which are considered in economic theory to be public goods and which are frequently run by public authorities in other countries. This solution doubtless corresponds to a specifically French approach to the urban phenomenon, based on a certain view of local public affairs and a specific political culture. The following discussion will focus on the private dimension of the French approach: the history of the enterprises, the reasons for their growth, the organisation of the urban utilities sector and the question of control.

The growth of private corporations

The majority of companies currently operating were formed a century ago. The Compagnie Générale des Eaux was incorporated in 1853 and the Société Lyonnaise des Eaux in 1880. The dates for the leading transport companies are relatively close: CGFTE in 1875, and Transexel-GTI around 1905. The newest water distribution companies were formed after the First World War (SAUR, SOBEA). These companies were originally engaged only in water distribution and none at that time had reached its present size. Nevertheless many elements which characterise the present system already existed.

Firstly, the companies aimed for vertical integration in a single market. Taking the water market as an example, this involves intervention in distribution, treatment, maintenance and pipe manufacturing activities. The Compagnie Générale des Eaux was to achieve the best results in this field by the creation of a number of subsidiaries. Secondly, these enterprises were all interested in foreign investment and had subsidiaries in other countries: Northern Italy, Spain, North Africa, Central Africa and Indochina. Due to war or to movements for decolonisation not all these connections have been maintained, but their orientation to foreign investment is a permanent feature.

The third common characteristic of these companies is the territorial basis of their markets. The municipalities, which hold a monopoly for the organisation of public services, are placed between the consumers and the private operator. This means that, for the companies, progress can be achieved mainly by increasing the number of contracts with municipalities or by taking over another company with contracts of its own. Winning a market share means winning territories. Since their origins the logic of growth of these enterprises has been a mix of market competition and of a process of encirclement and 'conquest' of new municipalities. The major cities have a special place in such expansionist strategies. They serve as a reference, making it possible to develop the most complex solutions which are subsequently applied to the whole of France. Paris – at the time of the world exhibition – Lyons and other cities have thus served as shop-windows for private sector know-how.

Since the beginning of the twentieth-century the companies have implemented policies of diversification into other urban services. For example, by the Second World War the Société Lyonnaise des Eaux et de l'Eclairage had begun to achieve greater sales in the electricity sector than in its original activity of water distribution. Nationalisation of the gas and electricity sectors deprived the company of a substantial part of its activities (Sedillot, 1980, p.82).

From the 1950s onwards the companies experienced rapid expansion for obvious reasons of urban growth. The companies expanded in their original market and also diversified into other directly complementary markets. Starting with water distribution they turned to water treatment, district central heating and cleaning. In some cases this diversification has been quite recent. For example, the development of Compagnie Générale des Eaux in to cleaning and electricity equipment began in 1972 with an alliance with a Swiss company: la Continentale. These diverse activities are organised through leading companies which play a central role in each sector. In the Lyonnaise des Eaux group we find: Dégremont for water treatment, Sita for cleaning and refuse, Cofreth for heating. The urban transport sector went through a major crisis period from 1964 to 1968, followed by a revival from 1975. The transport networks were modernised, new funding sources were created and municipalities accepted a greater level of involvement. The resultant new conditions of financial return enabled groups still in existence, but sluggish in 1964, to develop by taking over the operation of new transport networks.

This period was also marked by the emergence of a new institutional pole of attraction, in the form of the semi-public company: *l'économie mixte*. This formula had been used by the State during the 1920s for the implementation of economic activities but was subsequently abandoned in favour of nationa-lisation. It gained a new lease of life in 1958, when, in order to accelerate development and make up leeway in the housing construction sector, the state called on the CDC (Caisse des Dépots et Consignations) to mobilise its financial and human resources. A number of new companies were formed in the space of a few years to intervene in the management of land for industrial zones, housing or commercial facilities, the construction of motorways, the development of harbour facilities, the modernisation of wholesale markets, and the provision of leisure and urban transport facilities. The organisational structure combined national companies at the top, specialising in particular markets and backed by engineering enterprises, with Sociétés d'Economie Mixte (SEM) functioning at the local level, responsible for operations and linked directly to mayors or deputy mayors. As a result of these various elements it can be said that an industrial quasi-sector was created in France towards the middle of the 1970s. It had macro-economic importance, an industrial scale and a limited number of leading companies.

A new general context emerged from 1975, marked by the economic crisis and a sharp deceleration of urban growth. The companies operating in the sector could have experienced adverse effects, but, in fact, this did not happen. The companies continued to grow throughout the crisis years, as evidenced by the expansion of the turnover of the two leading companies (see Table 6.1). These results were achieved by the implementation of different policies.

TABLE 6.1   Group turnover Générale des Eaux and Lyonnaise des Eaux 1975–87 (bn Francs)

1975	1977	1978	1979	1980	1981	1982	1983	1984	1985	1986	1987
Générale des Eaux												
5.4	7.45	8.3	10.0	13.1	23.5	26.8	29.7	39.9	44.2	48.0	53.0
Lyonnaise des Eaux												
4.9	7.2	8.4	9.7	12.4	14.4	10.0	12.9	13.5	14.8	15.7	16.7

The private companies continued to expand their markets, either by winning new territories to the detriment of public enterprises or by buying up other autonomous private enterprises. Starting from a situation where the private sector share was already substantial, the private sector now dominates many urban markets. For example, 60 per cent of drinking water distribution

was under private control in 1983. With the privatisation programmes which have taken place since then – Paris 1985, Lyons
1986, Toulouse 1990 – this share has further increased so that the
private sector now holds three-quarters of the total market. It
should be noted that the ratio of public and private market shares
was exactly the opposite of that in Great Britain, before the
privatisation of Water Authorities; the British water boards had
75 per cent of the market and the 29 private companies –
statutory water companies – the remaining 25 per cent. In the
case of provincial urban transport, representing about 150 networks, 85 per cent of operators are private, 24 per cent being
SEMs and 61 per cent fully private companies. The Transexel-
GTI group alone is concerned with more than 30 networks. The
share of the private sector is also strong for collective heating
facilities and for refuse treatment plants.

The companies also diversified into sectors where they were not
previously present, and which have in common the production or
management of urban facilities: building and public works, public
lighting, car park management, local cable networks, cellular
telephones, funeral activities, public health, collective catering,
leisure activities. This strategy is implemented to a greater extent
by the Compagnie Générale des Eaux than by the Société
Lyonnaise des Eaux which explains the spectacular upsurge in
the turnover achieved by the former. CGE public works and
building subsidiaries today form the second national group after
Bouygues. In certain respects, Bouygues has adopted a similar
strategy. Starting in the public works and building industry, the
Bouygues group has diversified into a number of urban services
sectors over the last few years, including water distribution –
SAUR – and public lighting. By these policies of cross-diversifi-
cation, the two largest private groups in the sector are accelera-
ting the process of inter-penetration between the building
industry and urban services; this represents a new phenomenon.
More than ever, the physical production of urban utilities
constitutes a vast market, unified by the strategy of a few large
private multi-sectoral companies.

The other major feature of the period was the implementation
of policies for penetrating foreign markets. This strategy was
adopted principally by Société Lyonnaise des Eaux. While CGE
opted for national development and diversification into a large

array of activities, Société Lyonnaise followed a substantially different policy. The company has concentrated its activities in a limited number of service sectors, in which it reckons to possess genuine know-how, namely: water distribution and treatment, energy and cleaning. This has led Lyonnaise to shed the other activities in which it was engaged – public works, safety, lighting – in order to develop its basic trading skills more efficiently in foreign markets. The company has set up in the USA, Canada and Asia, as well as other European countries (Spain, Belgium). The share of total group turnover achieved outside France exceeded 30 per cent in 1986, compared to a figure of 12 per cent for CGE. With the prospect of the European market, water privatisation in UK, and the possibilities in other developing countries, the other companies have now adopted the same orientation (Drouet, 1989). They are increasing their involvement in Italy and Spain, and have an interest in the German market. All of them have significant shares in the UK water companies.

The semi-public sector, corresponding to the group created around CDC, also experienced a number of changes during this period, not surprisingly when we consider its origins. The group was created for the purpose of making up leeway in the provision of urban facilities and establishing an intermediate channel between the traditional public sector and the private sector. At this time, the semi-public sector was therefore the central point for a strategy aimed at the modernisation of French society. For many years, the member companies of the group were carried along by this driving force. This was the most expansive period for the mixed economy societies (the SEMs), with major projects to be executed, active support from the state, and readily available funds. The group was therefore doubly affected by the changes of the period, both in its markets and in its role. The initial urban markets became less fruitful, and there was a decline in the level of demand for housing, a slowing down of the motorway construction programmes, and the end of large housing programmes, the so called *grands ensembles*. All these are well-known phenomena and each produced its financial consequences.

In addition, the concept of the semi-public sector, which had stimulated and facilitated company strategy, became less precise. On the public side, the municipalities were transformed, with regard to the mayors and to elected and appointed officers. Younger and more fully qualified personnel appeared on the scene towards the middle of the 1970s; working methods also changed. The newly elected officials claimed a more important role in the management of the local SEMs. In some cases severe criticisms were made of group practices. On the private side, the companies also changed. In many cases they adopted types of contract which introduced some cooperation with municipalities. The division between public and private consequently became less strong and visible than in the past, and the case for the SEMs less obvious. In a word, the semi-public sector was set up to fill a gap between the municipalities and the private groups, and the gap was a large one. By the end of the 1970s, however, the gap had been bridged as the participants on each side evolved. They had changed their mode of action and gained a share of the market. The SEMs were then confronted by a double challenge; they had to find new markets and to define a clearer image of themselves.

After taking some time to respond to the changes in its environment, the CDC group embarked in 1983 on a set of reorganisation policies. The links between the specialised subsidiaries and the funding institution (CDC) which is a state bank, were clarified. A new holding company designated C3D (Caisse des Dépots Développement) was funded in order to run and to coordinate the subsidiaries. In each sector the group set out to re-establish its profitability situation: policies of diversification and development were to be undertaken on re-established financial bases. Although this group is currently smaller in size than the private companies it nevertheless holds a number of strong positions. It is the second group in the urban transport sector after Transexel, and is the leading car park operator ahead of a CGE subsidiary. The group is the leading French producer of residential buildings. It also holds strong positions in engineering, consultancy and forecasting. It has the major role in raising finance for utility development which was its original activity.

The urban utilities sector from two points of view

At the present time the features of the urban utilities sector can be interpreted from two points of view, depending on whether we examine the industrial organisation and membership of groups, or consider the municipalities with their organisational network and territorial organisation. These two visions are complementary and illuminate one of the lines of tension present in the sector, between group strategies and municipal policies. The two perspectives are described below.

From the industrial point of view, the organisation is based on a number of large groups which are among the leading French companies and among the most highly valued on the stock exchange, a unique situation among developed countries. This is the result of continuous policies of diversification which have led them from water distribution into the other urban utilities. Another original feature is the fact that these companies combine several functions besides their original activity, the operation and management of water services; they now also undertake engineering, construction, and manufacturing activities. Some differences can be seen among the companies. The Compagnie Générale des Eaux, the leader in water management, is at the same time the second French construction company after Bouygues; some of its subsidiaries are leading pipe manufacturers, as well as manufacturers of machinery for refuse collection. The activities of the Société Lyonnaise des Eaux are more concentrated on the operation of services and engineering. However, the combination of various functions in one company is what distinguishes the French utilities from those of other developed countries. Elsewhere, owing to the political philosophy of public-private relationships and to different industrial histories, private enterprises are less often involved as operators of public services but do contribute to the engineering, construction and manufacturing functions.

So, if we are interested in the dynamics of urban utilities or in the effects of the single market of 1992, we have to consider what may happen to the four different functions: operation, engineering, construction, manufacturing. If it is true to say that the private French utility companies are larger than those elsewhere it should also be remembered that this is partly because of their role in the operation and management function. But when we consider all four functions large groups are active also in other countries. Large engineering companies do exist both in the UK and the USA; large manufacturers in Japan and Germany – but their activities in operation and management are very limited. One effect of the separation of activities in the UK is that especially in the case of water, the political debate about privatisation policy has concentrated only on the most emotive aspect – the character, public or private, of the management – without any discussion of the other functions. However, hardware production and patent ownership are equally important matters for both the national trade balance and industry.

Consider the scale of the main French utility groups:

Compagnie Générale des Eaux has a consolidated turnover of 53 billion Francs, the result of a consistent diversification policy implemented since the 1970s, 80 000 employees and no fewer than 620 subsidiary companies provide a deeply rooted territorial base. Its subsidiaries are active in each French *département* which creates a permanent relationship with the local officials and state civil servants. CGE is present in practically all sectors which concern urban life.

Société Lyonnaise des Eaux, since its formation, has held the second position in the water distribution sector, with a global turnover of 16.7 billion Francs and 36 700 employees. In certain other sectors however, the company is in the first place; these include water treatment (Dégremont), cleaning and undertaking services. The group is smaller, but more concentrated on services, more internationalised, and its profit margins are higher.

SAUR (*Société d'Aménagement Urbain et Rural*) was formed in 1933, and holds third position in the drinking water distribution market, well behind the two leaders. Diversification is substantially less developed, and the only other activities in which the company is engaged is sewerage and household refuse collection. In 1983, SAUR served four million inhabitants, employed 2 500 people, and achieved consolidated net sales of two billion Francs. In 1984 the company was taken over by the Bouygues group.

The C3D group (*Caisse des Dépots Développement*) achieved direct net sales worth seven billion Francs in 1986, and employs 11 000 persons. A further 12 000 persons are employed by the semi-public companies (SEMs) of the C3D network. The group generates approximately 18 billion Francs of new investment each year: seven billion Francs for housing, six billion for public facilities and five billion for motorways. These figures represent a minimum which does not take account of the direct activities of the local SEMs; as the group only has minority interests in these SEMs their activities do not appear in the consolidated turnover.

Mention must also be made of the urban transport groups, which occupy a special position in this context. Transexel is the leader in this field, and now associated with the largest French inter-urban transport company, GTI. SCET-Transport, which holds second position, only entered this activity in 1974, and is a branch of the C3D group. CGFTE is the third operator; this company was for a long time a subsidiary of a private commercial bank, the Rivaud group. Early in 1987, CGFTE was bought by a transport subsidiary of Compagnie Générale des Eaux, which previously had an extremely modest share in this sector. At the beginning of 1990 CGFTE and Transexel also began to work more closely together. The effects of this type of regrouping within the sector will be felt in due course.

From a municipal point of view the urban utilities sector appears quite different. It is not so much concentrated in the hands of a limited number of groups, as organised by a large number of municipalities. It is the municipality which delegates its monopoly, issues contracts and provides a certain amount of funding. Various organisations participate in the public service operations, but they all centre on the traditional municipality with its municipal budget and personnel. Distinctions can be made between various types of satellite organisations in the three main areas of local community intervention: urban utilities, housing and socio-cultural provision.

The urban utilities or, to use the terminology of public law, the industrial and commercial public services (SPIC), cover the technical fields of water supply, sewerage, district heating, collection of household refuse, transport and parking. The communes can intervene directly via public corporations, but frequently employ the services of subsidiary companies of the large multi-sector groups already described. Local operators are classified according to their legal status, into three categories: public corporations where the municipality operates the service itself (*régie municipale*), semi-public companies (SEMs), a solution extensively employed by the C3D group, and conventional joint stock companies in other cases.

In the housing sector, the communes operate via communal or departmental HLM (low-cost rented housing) agencies, HLM joint stock companies, semi-public building companies and property renewal associations. This action is frequently complemented by a development company. A number of different legal forms, ranging from the public to the private, cohabit in this sector: HLM agencies, semi-public companies, entirely private joint stock companies, and non-profit making associations operating in the renewal sector as a part of redevelopment programmes with a welfare character. Many medium sized communes have created their own urban development agencies.

Thirdly, the communes frequently use non-profit associations for intervention in the welfare, educational, sports and cultural fields. Some of these local associations form part of national federations, for example, in both the leisure and the educational fields. Others, however, only exist as a result of support from the municipality. These are local organisations, operating on a precisely defined basis, and in some cases the period of their existence is linked to the implementation of a specific programme. This vast associative sector is currently much more heterogeneous and fragile than the multi-sector groups. Nevertheless, several signs of change are starting to appear. The personnel employed in these sectors have changed and national networks are being formed reducing the balkanisation of these non-profit associations. The multi-sector groups are also entering the scene, and this will doubtless upset a certain number of established practices. These groups are penetrating the communications, leisure and public health sectors.

To complete the picture, it must be remembered that in the majority of major urban agglomerations, the central communes participate in higher tier structures, to which they have transferred certain of their responsibilities for various services: syndicates, districts, *communautés urbaines*. Once again, these organisations can either operate directly, or delegate to the private sector. This further increases the complexity of the institutional situation.

In the major cities, this results in organisational systems which can incorporate as many as 50 different organisations. As a consequence in order to analyse local policies it is necessary to shift from the concept of the 'municipal institution' to that of the 'communal public sector' (Lorrain, 1987, p.11). An analysis of local power through the management of urban utilities and their production leads to a reconsideration of theories of local regulation. The municipal game is not only articulated around the figures of the mayor and the chief town clerk; large operations are run by municipal 'satellites', and those who manage them have some power. The mayoral model (Dupuy and Thoenig, 1983) which characterised French local political life up to the 1970s loses some of its strength when the number of full time deputy mayors running municipal satellites is expanding. Local power is now more shared and the regulatory mechanisms are more open.

As an example, the Nancy city hall has a staff of 2000 civil servants, and symbolically represents the centre of local political power. However, this image, which reflected the reality of the situation forty years ago is now substantially out of line with changes in local systems. Alongside the city hall, full account must be taken of the weight of the suburban communes, which have extended the scope of their interventions and increased their staff numbers, now employing over 2000 persons. Since 1959, this metropolitan area has set up a district authority, employing 660 persons and an increasing volume of responsibilities. Its action in the urban services sector is extensively sub-contracted to private companies; this 'paramunicipal' network has a payroll of 800. Mention should also be made of various other paramunicipal organisations, such as the welfare bureau, with its 400 employees. Taking all these organisations together, the 'communal public sector' of Nancy employs more than 6000 persons, with the relative weight of the symbolic city hall segment representing no more than one-third of the total. Close to the mayor and to his town clerk, other people of position and of power become visible.

Why a private sector in France?

An international comparison is interesting: it shows that privatisation of service operation is not the most frequent solution in the developed countries. Municipal enterprises are the tradition in Germany, Italy and Japan, which means that the municipalities operate these utilities through local public corporations – the equivalent of the French *régie*. The management remains public, and consequently the private sector comes in mainly as manufacturer or as constructor. In the USA, many services are managed on a public basis; the private sector has never expanded into all the urban utilities throughout the national territory. In some cases the contractors are still local firms, specialising in narrow markets which require low capital investment and high levels of labour management, such as snow removal and refuse collection.

This raises the question why private corporations have been able to expand in France whereas elsewhere among the developed countries we find public management and private enterprises which generally remain small. There is no single answer. In order to understand this French peculiarity, we have to consider a variety of different factors, some technical, others historical and some which are rooted in the political culture (Lorrain, 1991). The general question can be broken down into three specific questions.

1. *Can the French situation be explained economically?*

The specialised socio-economic literature does not give clear evidence that delegation to the private sector is a more efficient way to run urban services. On each element the experts are divided, the same advantages or drawbacks can be attributed to either system: public management or private delegation. This seems to be a general phenomenon since the case of the British privatisation has led academics to the same conclusion (Wright, 1987, p.131). This difficulty in assessing the performance of the management of urban utilities shows that in a complex environment the classical tools of evaluation are inadequate.

The public sector is generally considered a better guarantor of the continuity of the service. This is certainly true when the private operator is small and can be bankrupted, but this classical argument can be reversed if we consider that in some French cities the water service has been operated on a private basis for fifty years or more. They have passed through economic crises, wars, constitutional crises, but nevertheless the continuity of the service has been maintained.

Private monopolies generate scale economies in research, capital investment and labour management, which might explain the growth of the French companies. This classical argument is only partly true. If it is the private sector which has the capacity to achieve scale economies in France it is only because the operations of the *régies* are strictly limited by the law to the boundaries of their commune. They cannot export their know-how. Other countries, such as Germany with its *Stadtwerke* which operate in several sectors, show that it is not a difference per se.

Is it possible to show that the private sector's scale economies induce lower prices? All the comparisons on this point (Gruson and Cohen, 1983; Cour des Comptes, 1976 and 1989) have established that private water is sold at higher prices than public sector water. A more controversial point is to question whether the methods of calculating costs are the same, and we have good reason to think that they differ. In the public sector there is a tendency not to allow for the depreciation of assets, and not to incorporate all the costs of long-term development, such as funding of research, or renovation of fixed capital assets like pipes. Many mayors believe that a low price is proof of good management. Public accountability does not set up a clear difference between the operating budget and the balance-sheet. The consequence is a tendency to evaluate the costs mainly in terms of annual budget expenditure. On the other hand private sector accounting incorporates all these costs in addition to the operating budget, and companies do this more especially as these charges are deducted from their profits before tax. So the tools of accountability, as well as their philosophy, differ between the public and the private sectors.

The debate is constrained both by the difficulty of establishing criteria to compare and evaluate the management of urban services and by the deficiency of the tools of management. All debates about privatisation are beset by these difficulties, showing that a precondition for a fair debate is the development of knowledge about public sector management.

2. *Why are the private operators profitable?*

This is the question our Anglo-Saxon colleagues ask observing that in their countries private companies have remained small and that the urban utilities sector has not (until now in the UK) been considered a market for high rates of profit. Several elements, ranging from the more general to the more specific provide an answer.

a) The French enterprises operate in monopoly situations with long-term contracts and low risks. Moreover, if deficits emerged they would be balanced by municipal grants; for example, if there were abrupt economic change, unexpected inflation, major losses or war. A whole juridical corpus has been compiled since the First World War to deal with such eventualities (Auby and Ducos-Ader, 1975).

b) Profitability is written into the framework of the pricing itself. Since the origin of the utility companies it has been asserted that the final price of a service should include all the costs of production plus the return to the operator (Goubert, 1986, p.18), whatever are the economic conditions of the sector. The system does not work on market principles, in which an enterprise can be bankrupted if the demand does not match the cost of the product. As a result, it is possible to have private, profitable and expanding enterprises in markets which are in a situation of permanent deficit. This is the case of urban transport, where 50 per cent of the turnover comes from public grants and specific taxes.

c) New types of contract set up for the management of facilities and for the financing of the more capital intensive investments combine public property and private management. If it is true to say that these contracts have given more power to the municipalities – the power of property – at the same time they have reduced the financial burden on private companies and contributed to maintaining their rate of profit.

d) Economies of scale in each group mean that once a contract has been signed in one town, the groups can optimise the management and reduce the costs, owing to their experience in other towns. This know-how includes not only a technical dimension but knowledge in commercial management which includes a capacity to handle the relationships both with the municipalities and with the users. This explains, for example, why the Lyonnaise has had the capacity to diversify into funeral services where it had no previous experience, and why Générale can move into cellular radio telephone systems.

e) The benefits of vertical integration make it possible to control profit-making along the chain of production: engineering of new facilities, their construction and equipment, operation and maintenance.

f) Marginal benefits are accepted by municipalities. For example, maintenance works are not always submitted to bidding as they should be. The private companies have a perfect knowledge of contracting and of the long term variations of the pricing formula. They know how to use a whole range of contracts and rates of return and to delay tax and other payments so as to make important short-term gains.

3. *Why is the private sector expanding?*

The private sector has demonstrated a remarkable capacity to pass through wars, nationalisation programmes and constitutional crises. How can this continuous growth be explained?

Structural factors are part of the explanation. In a competitive market – on the stock exchange – the enterprises which do not grow die (Lorrain, 1987). In order to attract funds, or to keep their shareholders, they must show prospects of growth. The history of the private groups shows that those which have existed since the beginning of the century are the ones which are still expanding. On the other hand the municipalities are not allowed to expand but only to operate within their own territory. The rules of the game are different for the public and private sectors. The public sector has, first of all, the responsibility to satisfy the needs of a population in a certain place, and as long as this goal is achieved there are no reasons to innovate. On the other hand the private enterprises operate in a market game which ignores boundaries. These structural differences explain long term dynamics.

Secondly, the municipalities are weak, often very small in size and with inadequate human resources. This has presented another opportunity for the private enterprises. When they compete with a municipal *régie* within its limited boundaries, they can use their critical mass – research capacity, human resource potential and diversity of experience.

Thirdly, the multi-sector groups have developed a capacity to adapt to situations, and to solve problems while maintaining a low profile. Their prominence in the media is quite recent; up till now they have been able to expand while remaining almost unknown. They are pragmatic, close to everyday problems, modest and discreet. This attitude makes them acceptable to politicians. It is quite different from the culture of the state officials who speak of the 'general interest', set up ambitious projects and look for rational solutions.

Lastly, the multi-sector companies have had the capacity to conduct their own strategy independent of variations in public budgets. This position was created by the pricing system which effectively guaranteed returns to the operators (see above). So the cashflows generated in water supply could be used to finance operations and investments.

Advantages, drawbacks and the question of control

Insofar as advantages are concerned, mention must first be made of the question of local autonomy. The municipalities have not been dispossessed of all this family of responsibilities, in favour of larger public (and now private) agencies such as the British water authorities, or the Dutch and Danish transport authorities. When municipalities work together in a higher tier structure, it is generally based on voluntary membership. The French model is based on strong political power. The fact that there is a hierarchy which puts elected representatives at the top explains the system's effectiveness. The mayors and other elected representatives have a position within the urban service system which allows them legitimately to express the needs of the population. Consequently, they have the authority to coordinate the services and to avoid professional and technical control. The French system is one of 'local government' and not of 'local agencies'. This difference highlights a very important hierarchy of powers: political legitimacy is above technical legitimacy; political control restrains professionalism.

Sectoral integration eliminates the paradox of institutional fragmentation. The municipalities are independent and small in size; no substantial reform of the institutional framework has been implemented, but the system works because the large multi-sector companies reintroduce scale economies. This is one of the differences with the American system, which is also based on municipalities but with smaller companies, a situation which has tended to accelerate the public infrastructure crisis in certain areas (Beyeler and Triantafillou, 1988). These companies do not have the financial strength to carry out the necessary policies or to cope with the random factors in public service management. If economies of scale are to be sought, they can be obtained either at the organising authority level (the British solution) or at the operator level (the French solution) of the system.

The French system also embodies a number of drawbacks. Firstly, there is the obvious risk of actors misusing their power. And the power is in the hands of the private groups as a result of their concentration. The numerous local communities, engaged in varied activities as a result of their multiple social purposes, do not have the resources to monitor the operations of delegated public services on a permanent basis. Consequently, a group on the lookout for opportunities inevitably finds many occasions to serve its own interests as a first priority. This is a genuine risk.

The second drawback in solving the paradox of the 36 500 communes, is that this results in complex – doubtless excessively so – organisational sets in the large urban areas. This complexity can be considered to have a dual cost. The first is political. When a local council takes a decision, the organisational systems employed to implement this decision are geared down to such an extent that part of the process is no longer under the control of the decision-makers. This results in the all-too-familiar gap between intentions and results. The second cost is economic, and one which cannot be measured, as the accounting systems cannot produce breakdowns on the basis of urban areas (*agglomérations urbaines*). In this case, the risk exists of producing public assets at excessive costs, and of being ignorant of the facts, owing to the absence of appropriate measuring tools (see above).

The cost of system complexity will have to be measured sooner or later. While differences in the cost of production and management of urban services exist between urban areas, the presence of barrier mechanisms cannot mask the reality of the situation for much longer. This will be reflected one day by a lack of competitiveness on the part of certain towns. We can therefore consider that one line of reform must involve action in order to set up management tools for urban areas. The tendency should be towards greater organisational simplification and the installation of management systems designed to achieve a global approach in the case of each urban area. One priority would be to obtain consolidated accounts for each urban area and for all the organisations involved in the sector of urban facilities.

With regard to the question of control, we are currently alternating between two solutions, neither of which will necessarily prove satisfactory in the longer term: 'global regulation' and 'detailed control'. In the global regulation system the communes delegate, and apply the logic of delegation, putting the matter entirely in the hands of the private company concerned. In fact, when a municipality delegates a service to the private sector it is precisely because it cannot operate on its own, or does not want the trouble of direct management. In that case the delegation concept effectively means transfer. How, then, can the elected representatives keep control of the private operator? They aim to achieve this through global and indirect control. So long as the service works and the users do not complain, the operator is assumed to be doing his job well. The control by the elected representatives is thus based on global and political criteria rather than technical ones. In a normal situation, without complaints, the question of the level of profits is of minor importance; the private enterprise has great flexibility to initiate policies on its own. This solution has a major advantage. Each party is competent in its sphere of action, responsibilities are clear, and there is no duplication of effort. However, all this is based on self-limitation of power by the private company.

In the case of detailed control, the communes seek real control of the companies. This situation is encountered in particular in the transport sector, and appears relatively close to the British contracting-out system. The communes delegate but retain or set up a department responsible for controlling the operation. This produces closer control of policies, but increases operating costs. If the commune wants to be genuinely capable of assessing private company policies, it needs suitably qualified personnel. This also results in situations of cross-responsibility, where it is no longer entirely clear who decides, or who is responsible for this or that. For example, responsibility for a transport service is shared between a deputy-mayor, behaving in the manner of a departmental head, one or more other senior town-hall employees, the manager of the private operation and headquarters staff experts of the group. If a new bus service generates deficits, each party involved can easily throw responsibility for the failure onto the others.

To sum up, the solutions adopted tend to oscillate between delegation and duplication. In the first case there is an absence of knowledge, and in the second, the knowledge is available but at a high price. In the light of this history and of the increasing internationalisation of this sector as a whole, the forms of control applied by the public authorities to the private sector might evolve in two directions. Control could be developed at all levels, as in the transport sector and adopting an Anglo-Saxon view of public-private relations, but this will certainly introduce a rigidity factor and additional costs. Alternatively, the principle of global regulation, applied extensively in the water supply sector, could be generalised; this certainly represents the simplest solution. However, the multi-sector groups must then clarify the ethics of the public service within which they operate.

References

Auby, Jean-Marie and Ducos-Ader, Robert (1975) *Grands services publics et entreprises nationales*, PUF, Paris, 2nd ed.

Beyeler, Claire and Triantafillou Catherine (1988) 'La crise des infra-structures urbaines aux Etats-Unis et en Grande-Bretagne', in *Réseaux territoriaux*, Paradigme, Caen.

Cour des Comptes, 'Rapport au Président de la République, années 1976, 1989' *Journal Officiel*, Paris.

Drouet, Dominique (1989) 'The French water industry in a changing European context', Séminaire OTAN, 22 juin, RDI, Paris.

Dupuy, François and Thoenig, Jean Claude (1983), *Sociologie de l'Administration Française*, Armand Colin, Paris.

Goubert, Jean Pierre (1986) *La Conquête de l'Eau, Robert Laffont*, Paris.

Gruson, Claude and Cohen, José (1983) *Tarification des services publics locaux*, La Documentation Française, Paris.

Lorrain, Dominique (1981) 'Le secteur public local: entre nationalisation et décentralisation', *Annales de la Recherche Urbaine*, no. 13, Paris.

Lorrain, Dominique (1985) 'Textes et contextes', *Annales de la Recherche Urbaine*, no. 28, Paris.

Lorrain, Dominique (1986) 'L'industrie des réseaux urbains en France, (des origines nationales à une dynamique mondiale)', *Revue d'Economie Régionale et Urbaine*, no. 1.

Lorrain, Dominique (1987) 'Le grand fossé? Le débat public privé et les services urbains', *Politiques et Management Public*, vol. 5–3, Paris.

Lorrain, Dominique (1991) 'The French model for urban services', *West European Politics*, Oxford.

Sedillot, René (1980) *La Lyonnaise des Eaux à Cent Ans*, SLE, Paris.

Wright, Vincent (1987) 'Actualité de la dualité public-privé dans la société britannique', *Politiques et Management Public*, vol. 5, mars, Paris.

7 Italian Local Services: The Difficult Road Towards Privatisation

Bruno Dente

Italian local services: a background

The basic unit of Italian local government – the *Comune* or municipality – is by far the most important public service producer at the local level, having a wide competence for social services, cultural facilities, local transportation, as well as all the usual urban services (like refuse collection and disposal, street cleaning, parks, sport facilities, etc.). Moreover the municipalities have an important role even in the two big services not entrusted to them, namely education and health care. In the case of education, municipalities build, maintain and equip schools, provide activities supplementary to the bare state curriculum and provide assistance to pupils and students. Furthermore there are many civic initiatives, notably in the field of vocational education and training. In the case of health care one has to recall that the board of directors of the local health district is appointed by the municipalities.

But the picture is far more complex than that: first of all the Italian *Comuni* are very numerous (more than 8000) and are very different in size, political orientation and level of service provision. One should at least differentiate between the North and Centre of the country, where the situation is comparable to that in most of Western Europe, and the South where the basic services are often non-existent or very scarce. But also in the

North the different political orientations combined with the different sizes of the units of production bring about some very sharp contrasts. Moreover there is a long tradition of intertwining between central and local competences, in such a way that the state, regional and local administrative powers are combined in almost every field. Finally, at least since the beginning of the 1970s, the municipalities have lost any sort of fiscal power and are totally dependent, as far as money is concerned, on the national grant, supplemented by the financial income from the fees and charges for the services themselves.

During the 1970s some very important developments took place. First and foremost was an enlargement of the supply of local services resulting from the growth of demands coming from social movements, as well as the growth of the electoral power of the left parties which are traditionally welfare oriented. In the second place there was a strong orientation towards an increase in the public provision of services, which has resulted in the nationalisation or municipalisation of nearly all the private or quasi-public bodies that provided an important part of these services. This preference for public provision was probably meant to achieve, and certainly resulted in, a strong politicisation of local services, in the sense that the managerial powers were entrusted to the elected officials, and/or to a new class of political appointees. The third trend is in the basic ideology that public services must be free, or at least provided at a 'political price' not reflecting the actual costs of production and distribution; this orientation, mostly, but not solely, shared by the progressive, welfare oriented, left-wing local elites, had probably its biggest success in the Communist-dominated city of Bologna, when during an experimental period urban transportation in rush hours was totally free. Even if the experiment was short-lived, the orientation against fees and charges, motivated by the belief that the biggest possible share of public expenditure should be financed through progressive income tax, was (and still is) hard to abandon. Fourthly and lastly, as a consequence of all the previous trends, the financial burden on the local authorities increased greatly. Local expenditure skyrocketed, well beyond the official figures, because at the same time some previous local financial burdens were shifted onto the shoulders of central administration and the national grant was increased significantly.

One indicator is the size of the municipal bureaucracy which between 1976 and 1981 increased by at least 15 per cent, and probably more, taking account of the fact that in the same period a number of local employees were transferred to the newly created National Health Service.

Local services in the 1980s: a shift of mood

If this was the legacy of the 1970s it is not surprising that the following decade shows a quite radical shift in the prevailing mood. The triggering element was of course the financial problem. The double digit inflation rate was at the same time the cause and the effect of the huge increase in public spending, because of the explosion of the interest rate on the already appalling public debt. Some way of containing public expenditure had to be devised and one of the obvious candidates was local expenditure, because of its total dependency on central financial transfers. The ways in which this goal was pursued, if not actually attained, lie beyond the scope of this chapter, and it need only be recalled here that cash limits were the main tool; one result was the creation of off-budget hidden deficits whose amount is still unknown. On the other hand the various attempts to reintroduce some form of local taxation have until now been unsuccessful and only in 1989 did it begin to look likely that a permanent local tax would be raised (on commercial and professional premises), but still for a marginal amount compared with total local expenditure.

As far as the objective of this chapter is concerned two important parts of the financial legislation are more relevant. The personnel policy is the first. Already in the mid-1970s this matter was dealt with by means of three potentially contradictory measures. The first was the provision that any increase in the total number of permanent public employees had to be linked to an overall reorganisation plan to be passed by a central committee staffed equally by state administration and local government associations. In fact this provision proved less than stringent, mainly because the style of the national commission was more consensual than confrontational, bringing about a co-management of the increases. More important was the second development, the legislation which made national collective agreements with the trade unions compulsory for every single municipality. The employers' delegation to the bargaining table was in fact dominated by the representatives of the state administration, and this meant that the local authorities were no longer able to have autonomous personnel policies, while they had to bear growing costs – all local services are work intensive – without any ability to increase the revenue. Local budgets became more and more rigid, salaries representing the biggest part of the expenditure. From this point of view the behaviour of the central administration was to say the least contradictory, because the collective agreements granted quite large additional pay increases, when at the same time there were attempts to reduce national grant. The third and more recent development which took place in the personnel field was the provision that local authorities could not fully replace permanent staff lost through retirement. Here the goal was more clearly a decrease in public spending, but it is easy to figure out the kind of problems this provision brought about.

The second aspect of financial policy we have to recall here is the legislation concerning fees and charges. At the beginning of the 1980s a legal requirement was introduced that some services (such as refuse collection) had to be entirely financed through user fees, while others (the so called 'individual demand services' such as school lunches, kindergartens, theatres, etc.) had to introduce charges covering at least one third of the total cost. There was still a lot of leeway, because a municipality could cover the full cost or even make a profit on some services, while at the same time providing others almost free of charge. But of course an important principle was established: other, more detailed, norms concerned important services like water provision and urban transportation. Finally, in 1988 an attempt was made to transform the provision so that at least 36 per cent of the total cost of every single service had to be covered through its own user fees, gradually increasing the ratio to 100 per cent in five or six years. This attempt was defeated by the opposition of local authorities, but it seems clear that the blueprint is already there and that it is only a matter of time before this plan will be put into practice. The general effect is already clear in the sense that fees and charges constitute by now an important part of municipal income, even if the differences between the various areas of the country are immense.

If the two above-mentioned shifts – the constraints in personnel policy and the compulsory introduction of fees and charges – are very important because they had a legal status, one should not forget that an equally important cultural change took place in the 1980s. In Italy, until now, the anti-welfare backlash has not been really introduced into political discourse, but neither has a neo-conservative mood gained weight. But what on the contrary has gained recognition is the growing dissatisfaction at the politicisation of public administration. The result of the reforms of the previous period, namely the strong presence of political appointees in the management of services, has been regarded, rightly or wrongly, as the single most important cause of inefficiency and ineffectiveness. Even if this has not brought about, until now, significant changes in the organisation of the services, an attentive observer should be able to detect a growing interest in managerial techniques, the training of public servants, and the need to give more responsibilities to the professional managers. This development is not without dangers, mostly because of misunderstandings with regard to the action take, as we will see later, but it is nevertheless there, and explains quite a lot of what is happening in the field.

Privatisation 'Italian-style'

The combined result of the shifts outlined above is the growing difficulty, and sometimes the clear impossibility, of managing local services as in the 1970s. Organisational and financial constraints are by now at work almost everywhere, and something must be done. Of course one finds all the usual rhetoric: left-wing and trade union forces officially declare that there is the need to build up a 'new relationship' with the private sector, at the same time protesting against any 'indiscriminate privatisation'. The conservative parties, on the other hand, emphasise the financial problems, at the same time declaring that they are not ready to follow the Reaganite or Thatcherite example (whatever they mean by that) and that the welfare state has to be preserved.

Everybody is against political interventions in management, and nobody does a lot about it. The result is, of course, that until now no privatisation in the field of public services (and very little in the field of nationalised industry) has taken place.

This does not mean that nothing is being done. On the contrary it is possible to define a likely future for the introduction of new organisational and managerial arrangements in the field of local public services, even if one has to recall that decisions are often incremental and that an overall strategy is apparently lacking.

The starting point is the ideal-type of service provision according to the standards of the 1970s: in this tradition the personnel should be permanent professionals fully integrated into the territorial agency, working in a planned way. A distinction can be drawn between the cultural and social services on one hand, to be dealt with within the municipality, and the so-called 'network services' (water, refuse collection and disposal, transportation, etc.) where the preferred structure is the semi-autonomous communal agency (the *asienda municipalizzata* created as early as 1902). In both cases, however, there is the need to define short-term and long-term programmes and to secure political control through directly or indirectly elected officials. The financing of the service should be secured in part from fees and charges (with a character we will examine later on), but mostly through taxation and notably through progressive personal income tax. There has been very little critique of this model which continues at the back of the minds of politicians and professionals alike even as change takes place.

The first step towards a new form of organisation is usually quite marginal, often unconscious and taken under constraint. The triggering events in this case were the above mentioned norms concerning staffing. When the municipality cannot hire new staff needed in order to cope with an increased workload, and/or replace retired permanent personnel, the first possibility which comes to mind is to hire temporary personnel with short-term (usually three to four month) contracts. This practice, originally meant to solve emergency problems (maternity leave, for instance), has been quite widespread in the recent past as a way to get around the stringencies of the legislation. The advantages are several: it provides a way of hiring the needed employee immediately without waiting for the cumbersome and slow recruitment process to take its course; at the same time in this way it is possible to test the temporary person on the job before entering a permanent contract; last but not least the practice easily allows clientelistic deals, and this is a permanent feature of the Italian political system. The effects on the organisation of public services are small, in fact the only different is that some employees are doing the same tasks, have worse conditions of service, no tenure and lower pay (because they are at the bottom of the salary scale). The latter aspect became more and more important as the financial constraints began to have their impact, giving new impetus to the practice. But still this first step can hardly be regarded as part of an overall strategy, and was taken more as an emergency measure.

The second step is, from this point of view, much more important. The idea that it was possible to make temporary hiring permanent arose when someone created the first so-called 'service cooperative'. In short, what happened was that some of the people hired on a short term basis created a co-operative firm selling work to the local authorities. The advantages for both partners in the deal are clear. The local bodies are able to avoid the legislation on personnel hiring, because they are buying services from a firm, not hiring staff, and at the same time have a much more flexible way to increase their own permanent staff. The workers have much better protection, because they are collectively able to work for many different local authorities at the same time. Furthermore, at least at the beginning of the experiment, the costs were quite low, even if by now the situation is somewhat different and the direct costs shouldered by the public agency for the contracts with the co-operatives are more or less comparable with those implied in the hiring of permanent personnel. This practice has become quite widespread (partly also because the cooperative movement has strong political linkages), and contract staff are today an important part of social services personnel. From the organisational point of view the existing arrangements alter very little: every single worker, regardless of his or her status is subject to the hierarchical power of the manager (always a permanent officer or a politician) and the fact that a part of the total staff is provided through contracts means only a greater short-term flexibility in defining the programmes.

The third step follows naturally. Once the practice of hiring contract workers is established, the possibility of buying the product comes quite easily to mind. If the school lunches, for instance, are produced in a municipal kitchen filled with outsiders, it becomes natural, sooner or later to buy the lunches from a catering firm directly, using the permanent personnel only for the distribution to users. And this is what actually happened. Important functions within the existing services are by now entrusted to outside producers: apart from school lunches, these include cleaning, laundry, summer camping for boys and girls, but also less obvious candidates like night care in residential homes for elderly people. There is no need to entrust this type of task to cooperative firms, but given the political links mentioned above, this is what happens most often. Here the consequences for the management of the services are far more serious: first of all there is no need to invest any more, as the production is done outside the municipality itself. Even more important is the fact that the organisation of work is no longer a problem of the public agency as it was in the two previous instances (interim staff and contract personnel); the agency usually buys the product of outside work having only to specify its characteristics and not to determine the production process. The flexibility is even greater than in the previous case, because often the payment is made according to the quantity of goods purchased (number of lunches, kilograms of linen laundered, etc.) and therefore the possibility of getting good value for money is greater. One must remember, however, that the overall strategy and organisation of the services within which this functional delegation takes place still remains in the hands of the public body.

This is no longer true in the fourth step, where the whole of a service is entrusted to an outside organisation. The latter may be a non-profit body, sometimes formed by the clients themselves, or a market oriented organisation, and the public agency's role is restricted to specifying the conditions of service (performance standards, for instance) and to financing all or part of the costs. The examples are numerous and too wide ranging to be dealt with in a few lines: from private sector health care to the use of outside contractors in street cleaning and refuse collection. This is by no means a totally new development. On the contrary it is in many respects a re-emergence of the old way of producing services. And therefore in a country like Italy one can see the paradox of the new strongly anti-mafia political coalition in Palermo, where the modern direct provision of some basic services never took place and the use of outside contractors was traditionally a clientelistic and mafia dominated affair, actually contemplating the use of the same organisational mechanism in sharply different terms, favouring deals with non-local big companies, with the after-thought that they will be able to resist illegal pressure better than the municipality itself. In any case to contract out the production and provision of services means that the public role changes totally and becomes one of regulation and financing. The use of outside contractors, however, in the most advanced part of the country, is still quite exceptional, partly because of the problems involved in recycling the existing personnel and partly because of the lack of some of the conditions for an effective use of this possibility.

These four steps exhaust the organisational imagination of the Italian policy-makers in the field; there are no significant instances of other, more daring and imaginative alternatives to the public production of local services. However, two further steps could be suggested.

The fifth would be financing not the production but the consumption of the services themselves, giving the clients the money for buying what they need in the market. The use of vouchers is but one obvious example, much debated in the field of education, but very little used in any specific field. The sixth and last step, of course, would be simply retreating from the policies, totally entrusting the whole of the matter to the private sector, or to charities. Privatisation in this extreme form has not taken place and it seems unlikely that it will in the short run, unless a very deep financial crisis forces radical measures.

Summing up, we must underline that privatisation Italian-style is not privatisation at all, and that the process we can detect, at least in those parts of the country where the welfare oriented philosophy was more effective in widening the range of public local services, is always based upon the public financing and often the public production of the collective goods. Moreover we must emphasise that even the measures drifting away from the welfarist ideal-type were not inserted in any sort of overall strategy but were more or less incremental changes devised to tackle contingent situations, mostly the legal constraints on personnel policy and the financial stringency of the late 1980s. The almost total lack of empirical research prevents any conclusion about the effectiveness of the resulting situation in preserving or improving the performance standards of the services, and about efficiency in saving money.

Indirect privatisation: fees and volunteer work

The picture of the new developments in service provision at the local level in Italy would not be complete without a mention of two aspects that, if not directly challenging the dominant form of organisation, are nonetheless important because they alter the context within which the basic decisions are made.

The first development, already referred to, is the introduction of fees and charges, required under the new legislation of the beginning of the 1980s. The aim of the provisions was of course to reduce the financial burden of many services, substituting the monies provided by the state with the income collected from the users. Less important was a second possible goal, namely to avoid the excessive and useless consumption of services. The norms were quite effective, at least in raising money, but had some unintended consequences. The first is a probable growth in inequality between areas of the country, because citizens of similar municipalities pay very different sums for the same services. The second is that, reproducing the logic used by the centre in introducing fees and charges, local governments tend to view them as a form of taxation, to be employed only if actually needed. In other words they are not regarded as a price for a given good, but as a form of contribution to the overall income of the community. A clear clue in this direction is the fact that, more often than not, the fees are fixed in relation to the income of the client, in a progressive way, as if they were a form of income tax. This poses another equality problem, because of the very different proportion of tax evaders among the different occupational groups. But even more important, regarding the fees as a form of taxation and not as a price, the communes tend to underestimate the effect on demand of a rise in the fees (so that it happens that a rise in the fee reduces the total income), and more generally to shift the burden for inefficient production onto clients. The general trend, however, is towards a still bigger stress on this source of income; it will be interesting to observe whether this will be accompanied by greater attention to the marketing of services, as it should. For the moment there is very little evidence in this direction.

The second development is the growing importance accorded to volunteer work in many social and cultural services. After a long period during which this phenomenon was regarded with suspicion because of the ideological and religious underpinnings of many charitable organisations, and because of a general diffidence towards the alleged amateurism of the volunteers, the mood has totally changed. Communist and Christian Democrat dominated local authorities alike are more than willing to promote and finance volunteer work in the field of public services. This is mostly done through some sort of official recognition of the organisations working in this field, and negotiating with them the conditions of cooperation between public administration and the charities. In general terms one can detect in these agreements some negative characteristics: the tendency to subordinate official recognition to bureaucratic criteria and the risk of policies more oriented towards the charitable organisations than towards the well-being of the clients. Moreover in many cases the constraints on personnel policy and financial stringency are again the most important reasons behind these agreements; local authorities often feel that they have no option. The importance of volunteer work, however, cannot be underestimated, at least because it prepares the field for a more free relationship between the organisation of public services and outside contributions. There are some examples in which the contribution of volunteer work is actually able to change the content and the organisation of the services: for instance home care or meals for elderly people are sometimes produced through agreements between neighbours, improving the quality and the quantity of the service provided at a cost which is only a fraction of what would be needed for public provision.

If such developments do not remain isolated they may effectively alter the philosophy of the 'big state' underlying most welfare trends in Italy.

The 'service revolution': conditions of success

As we have seen, there is still very little evidence of major changes in the way in which Italian local public services are produced and distributed. It is possible that careful empirical research would be able to show some instances of real innovation, but observation suggests that no such thing exists. The process is very slow, quite unconscious, motivated by outside factors. A cultural change would be needed for real change to occur and, despite some declarations of intent, this seems only at the beginning.

However, there is little doubt that this is the road along which Italian local authorities have to walk and therefore it seems necessary to figure out the conditions under which such a development might be fruitful. Of course willingness to start the innovative process is essential, and the cultural change already referred to is fundamental. In this concluding section I will briefly elaborate two other interrelated aspects sometimes forgotten by the advocates of reform.

The first concerns the characteristics of public bureaucracies involved in the provision of local service. In brief, if contracting out is to be developed, what are the consequences for the local bureaucracies? The first, and most obvious, is the need to find new jobs for the lower rank personnel previously involved in the production of services. This will pose a lot of problems, with the trade unions for instance, but they can be solved through a mixture of retraining, financial incentives, early retirement, and so on. More difficult to solve is the problem of the managers of the services contracted out: even if one could imagine an easy transfer to the private sector, this would not be without consequences for the public administration as a whole. First of all the managers of the public services were often the more modern part of the local bureaucracy, as opposed to the old style bureaucratic administrator: the loss of such people could have regressive consequences on the overall organisation. In the second place, and even more important, to contract out a service cannot mean that a local authority can wash its hands of what will happen afterwards. And neither the traditional legally minded bureaucracy, nor the production managers of the existing services, are trained, or probably skilled, for the new control and evaluation role required by the new situation. To start a policy of contracting out without thinking of this aspect can result in the diminished effectiveness of services and, in the long run, even in an increase of costs, because the municipalities could find themselves unable to counter the demands of the private contractor having lost the alternative of directly providing the service. Contracting out, in other words, needs a careful consideration of the managerial skills left in the public body and this seems a fundamental condition of success.

But there is a second condition even more easily forgotten: contracting out services can also result in a loss of information about the means of satisfying the needs and demands of the population. If, as seems likely, direct production will no longer be the dominant way of providing services, there is a need for management control systems able to monitor and evaluate policy outcomes and impacts. This implies the ability to build up adequate models, as well as to collect the relevant information. Those tools, as we know only too well, are scarce commodities in the intellectual market let alone the public administration field. The few existing management control systems have been usually designed to monitor economic efficiency in service production, much more than the social effectiveness of service provision. From this point of view the successful implementation of new radical forms for producing collective goods until now entrusted to the municipalities, depends not only on the above mentioned conditions, but also on the ability of experts to devise effective tools for the management of services. These tools must not be solely derived from the experience of the private sector, but must be really apt to cope with the much more complex reality of the public services.

8 Experiences and Experiments in Dutch Local Government

Hans A. G. M. Bekke

Introduction: a changing Dutch local government

The concept of the decentralised unitary state in the Netherlands, which can be found in the Constitution of the beginning of the eighteenth century, only gave a really autonomous position to local government for a very short time. In the last four decades in particular a growing central government has brought about a situation in which local authorities function to a great extent as offices for central government in the local community. Departments and ministries in the Hague take most of the main policy decisions, giving instructions and financial resources to their local outstations. Only a small part of real political policy-making is reserved to the city councils. The very pluriform system of Dutch municipalities with strong local characteristics, differences in size and differences in intensity of tasks can be cited as a major reason for central guardianship.

Nevertheless some important recent changes can be observed in the position of government, both central and local, within Dutch society. The most important changes that are now taking place can be identified as:

- government stepping back from many traditional tasks and redefining its position in society;
- government working in a more businesslike manner.

In local government especially, a growing self-awareness of its role can be seen, one which has been gained not only through a changing relationship to the central level, but also by looking for new local tasks in cooperation with other local and regional partners, both in the public and in the private sectors.

The changing position of government in society

Particularly since the end of the 1970s, the increasing complexity of society and the speed with which one development follows the other have placed totally different demands on (local) government. In the years following the Second World War, the Dutch government directed itself particularly to rebuilding society by increasing the amount of public services. In the prosperous 1960s and 1970s, the variety of tasks increased because the government tried to meet those needs which the private sector did not take care of, and took action by issuing regulations with respect to the side-effects of economic growth. At the time it was thought that developments in society should be guided and controlled by regulations as well as by government provision, and ample finance resulted in ever more demands for social benefits.

Public administrators came increasingly to realise that the problems of increasingly complex societies, with their conflicts of interests, were becoming more difficult to solve in spite of technical developments and burgeoning information banks. In the 1970s, organisational solutions were sought, such as the introduction of management planning and the restructuring of municipal organisations. It can be said, with only a little irony, that the making of decisions came to seem more important than the real effects they produced.

Society's belief in government has slowly diminished. The problems encountered by municipalities nowadays are also of a totally different nature, not so much the building of schools or new suburbs, but more the questions of waste disposal, city renewal, drug abuse, caring for the aged, football vandalism, criminal behaviour, etc. In the 1980s, it has become more and more clear that social problems could not be solved easily and alone by government, which came to be seen as only one of the players in the social game. This knowledge, together with the uncontrolled growth of the collective sector in society and the budget problems of government (and not least those of the municipalities), has led to a revaluation of the position government ought to take in Dutch society. The image has emerged of a super-caring and super-regulating government which has gone beyond its capability to manage itself as well as its ability to manage society. The solution for government in the 1980s is: on the one hand to step back, and on the other hand to carry out its remaining tasks in a more businesslike fashion.

The position of government as a whole is becoming that of a partner in governing society together with other (private) organisations while central and lower authorities are becoming aware of a growing interdependence of all the parts of the governmental system. Especially for the local authorities, development is in the direction of a network of agencies and of competition with other (private) organisations for the delivery of services. Effectiveness and efficiency have gained importance as criteria of performance together with the old ones such as democratic control and political responsibility.

Processes of redefining the position of (local) government

As a result of changing relations between government and society, two processes – deregulation and privatisation – have started in recent years to redefine the position and function of central and local government in Dutch society.

Particularly in the last decade the codifying function of regulation has changed to a modifying function directed towards the manipulation of future behaviour. Deregulation in the Netherlands started in the first instance at the central level and then extended down to the lower levels of government, provinces and municipalities. The attempts to deregulate law seem to have had little success up to now, owing to the fact that these attempts are directed only towards the restriction and the limitation of the number of rules. If deregulation is to become successful, the emphasis will have to lie more in answering the fundamental question whether regulation, in a given situation, is an effective instrument at all. It is surely possible that other steering instruments may be more suitable, such as subsidising and facilitating, or making regulations more global in nature so as to leave more self-regulation to the market or social organisations. Deregulation in this sense could put greater demands on the capacity for municipal or self-regulation.

A few examples of deregulation of local authorities can be given. One example is the attempt by central government to shift from specific to general grants to local government in order to give municipalities more room to make their own policy choices. The discussion has started, but so far little movement to specific grants has occurred. One difficulty is that it needs to be combined with a simplification of rules and laws in the specific policy-fields. Such a broad project needs the collaboration of the several departments at the central level, but all are frightened at the loss of power resulting from this process.

Another example of deregulation, which is important for local authorities, is the successful transformation of the control function of intermediary authorities (provinces). In the recent past they had very detailed supervision of the financial operations of the municipalities, but this supervision in most cases has now been changed from a preventative to a retrospective role.

'Privatisation' covers every change in the way of supplying 'government products' whereby the input of the private sector increases. The involvement of the private sector may be associated with decision-making, provision of funds and implementation of policy. Broadly speaking, the following types of privatisation can be identified:

- private firms are involved on a contract basis;
- the municipality remains responsible and continues to take care of financing while implementation is given to the private sector;
- the municipality is no longer responsible as far as management is concerned, but remains interested in management by others through the provision of funds and/or rules;
- the municipality altogether ends its involvement and leaves it to the private sector.

As regards the first two forms of privatisation, the municipality may contract with private companies (for example in the maintenance of parks and city cleaning or in the policy areas of research and town planning) or with private individuals and voluntary associations. Examples of the latter are the sports facilities managed by clubs, parks maintained by neighbourhood associations, council houses managed by tenant associations, ambulance services operated by companies, and the organisation of socio-cultural activities left to coffee-house proprietors. The second two forms of privatisation involve a transition to full opting-out by the public authority. Initially the government might retain some form of involvement in terms of regulating finances, which would diminish over time. One could think of entrusting swimming pools, libraries and socio-cultural services to companies or private institutions. Also municipal utility companies might be made progressively more independent with the municipality at first remaining the sole shareholder before it sells the shares on the stock market.

An inquiry amongst 200 of the more than 700 Dutch municipalities concerning the level of privatisation, showed that about 60 per cent of these municipalities had contracted companies to manage services. This contracting out particularly concerned the operations which were already undertaken more or less as businesses by the municipalities themselves: the provision of green space and city cleaning. Furthermore, the inquiry showed that it was not ideological reasons, such as reconsidering the function and place of municipalities in society or the strengthening of the private sector, which were the deciding factors in favour of contracting out. The dominant factor was the need to reduce expenditure.

There are few cases of privatisation in the more complete senses. The problem of the viability of privatised services plays a part in the attitude towards privatisation. Products and services need to have a commercial value to be of interest to the private sector. This means that a former municipal department or service would have to be sold on the market as a competitive and customer oriented operation. Factors such as personnel practices, work culture and methods and employment conditions are difficult obstacles to such full privatisation.

Working in a more businesslike manner

There is an increasing tendency to expect a no-nonsense business-like style in Dutch local and national government. Like private enterprise, government is expected to be run on profitable, effective and efficient lines. Effective management and rapid intervention require new instruments, new municipal organisation and a transformed bureaucracy. To clarify the way in which the municipal organisation is changing, we will first examine the shortcomings of the classical organisation before looking at new forms of municipal organisation.

The basis of the traditional municipal organisation lies in the municipal law of 1851. In those days no one foresaw the size and diversity of present municipal organisations and the extent of their tasks. Nor had anyone foreseen the social complexity present municipalities have to deal with. Municipal organisation, as it has developed, separates policy-making and policy implementation. The model was that the town clerk's office looked after the legal and administrative preparation of policy and the support given to the administration, while technical implementation was left to the appointed services and companies. With the increase in the number of tasks in the 1950s, the number of services and companies, and with that the size of town clerk's departments, have also increased.

The growth of public tasks has subsequently led to division into different portfolios through which several separated organisational sub-systems have been set up. New tasks, such as the environment and city renewal, demanded increasingly more technical contributions from the service departments, while the town clerk's office was also increasingly obliged to advise on policy. The borderline between policy-making and execution diminished, but support and advice to the politicians still came via the town clerk's office. The result was a separation of the management of services from political administration.

From the results of an investigation published in 1987 with respect to the reorganisation of 15 municipalities each with a population of 100000 to 200000, it seems that the main bottlenecks in the traditional organisations were as follows:

- the indistinctness of clearly defined tasks between the town clerk's office and service departments;
- insufficient coordination between sectors at clerical, managerial and policy levels;
- lack of clear political direction in the main issues of management and too much involvement of managers with details;

- poor communication between political and administrative organisations;
- poor management as a result of the culture of advancement by seniority and technical experience.

Next to this there is the 'disease' sometimes described as 'government-autism' from which both the Dutch government and also the Dutch municipalities are suffering. This is a situation where the government is exclusively self-centred, having a minimum amount of contacts with the outside world. Social problems seem inferior to its own governmental problems of coordination, division of tasks and management. This can perhaps be most strikingly illustrated with the example of a clerk who is busy writing a management memorandum and regards a telephone call from a citizen as an interruption. The government seems to forget that it is there to serve the citizen. Governmental organisations know their own reality; social developments are expressed through filtering of information as a simplified abstraction. The known gives peace and offers 'security', but at the same time forms a denial of the social reality which it becomes more and more essential to understand in order to manage effectively.

The first reorganisations in several large municipalities, at the start of the 1970s, were particularly directed towards the clarification of the division of tasks between the town clerk's office and the services. At this time the classical division between policy-making and implementation was still considered the leading principle.

In the mid-1970s there was a slow movement away from this principle until, particularly in the last few years, municipal reorganisation has placed the emphasis on the development of a product-oriented organisation. In this arrangement, policy-making and execution are integrated and the task of the town clerk's office is to support the political administration in its overall integrating function. In the ideal type of the new organisation, all functions of policy-making and policy-implementation are integrated in one organisation. Each policy domain, such as Education, Energy, Housing, Economic Affairs, Health and Social Welfare, has its own integrated sub-system in which administrative and technical disciplines work together in order to produce well-integrated end-products, such as policy proposals and concrete services for citizens. At the central level only maintenance functions for financing, personnel, organisation, planning and programming, public relations and so on are carried out. In most cases the several managers of the sub-systems, including the town clerk, are united in a central management team, which is held responsible for the total functioning of the organisation and overall coordination. The several sub-systems are each self-supporting and autonomous. These integrated organisations can function as systems, wherein a business-like way of operating is possible, with each held responsible for effective and efficient management and its own budget. At the same time, a very clear structure can be presented to the external customer, the citizen, where he may buy his services and express his demands and questions.

As far as strategy is concerned, there is a growing external orientation: the organisation is concerned with the needs of society and pays more attention to the real effects of policy implementation. Delegation and mandating to lower authorities in the organisation is practised. At these lower levels, self-coordination and trust replaces classical bureaucratic models with their rules and regulations. The organisation becomes less procedure and more result-oriented. Also the management style and management instruments change: the manager promotes more team-work, and has the duty of creating the conditions for organisational work instead of controlling the individual worker. The civil servant becomes more a generalist than a specialist. Organisational culture can be characterised as business driven, directed to the development of corporate identity, less sensitive to status and hierarchy, less formal and more oriented to flexibility and the will to change.

It should be clear that it is no simple task to give form to such abstract demands, but a process to be worked out over a number of years. The demands have a symbolic value as guiding principles more than measurable goals. At the same time, they also indicate that in the case of municipal reorganisation it is not sufficient to change the more concrete items such as structure and systems. The real change begins with the change in attitude of people in the organisation. The existing organisational culture has to be broken through, and it is necessary to encourage this change in attitude in a stimulating way, by continuously holding a mirror in front of people. In many Dutch municipalities this has been attacked in a planned fashion by a series of education programmes. The most important element, however, is to build up an internal support system for change, starting with professional guidance and followed by the guidance and example of senior managers. It is often here that the real obstacles to a cultural breakthrough lie. Another obstruction exists in the rigid legal position and labour conditions of the Dutch civil servant; this deprives management of the right instruments (a flexible personnel and reward policy) to motivate the cultural breakthrough. As a result, more and more civil servants, who do possess flexibility and the urge to succeed, are choosing to go over to the private sector.

Reorganisation cannot only be limited to official departments; the municipal council and its executive board also have to operate differently. The tasks of the governing body and officials have to be more clearly separated to avoid overlap. This means that management has to be given some freedom to decide how to realise politically directed goals. Mutual interests between politicians and officials have to be recognised and a proper framework for communication created, perhaps through regular meetings between the governing body and management to discuss the main points of policy and implementation.

Management by contract is an approach which was initially recommended by central government, and now increasingly by municipalities. Agreements are made between the governing body and officials about the tasks to be executed and the performance to be delivered, leaving management to decide how it will execute the tasks. Early exponents since the beginning of the 1980s have shown promising results, with the following advantages. The contract forms the basis of a clear definition of tasks between officials and politicians; by putting more emphasis on performance, it makes management more aware of the efficient use of resources, while leaving it free to decide how to use them. Moreover, the contract approach breathes new life into official behaviour by reducing to a minimum the burden of regulations and increasing organisational and individual incentives; as the organisation becomes more independent, staff feel more involved in it. There are practical objections to management by contract, but it should be recognised as a means not only of efficient management, but also of changing attitudes in the new municipal organisation.

Contracting out, management by contract and the creation of new integrated functional organisations must also ultimately have an effect on the central support services of a municipality: financial, personnel, computer and maintenance departments. Under the old system, functional departments had to use these support services: bills were not presented so overhead costs remained invisible. With the change, these 'truck systems' are being disposed of and replaced by paying systems where the quality and cost of a support service are taken into consideration. The support services thus also become exposed to competition.

Retrospect

The government is being made increasingly more aware of its changed position in society, of the limitations of its ability to direct society, and even of its capacity to direct itself. Dutch municipalities are now dealing with the question how to withdraw from this situation and to develop a more businesslike approach. It is too early to say how effective they can be, but a number of observations can be made.

The withdrawal of municipalities from direct provision and control has been tackled through developments such as deregulation and privatisation, but there has been no fundamental revaluation of the position of municipalities in society. Deregulation is too much directed to the simple objective of reducing the number of rules, while underlying questions about whether regulation can be an efficient guiding instrument have been left unanswered. Privatisation has not been advanced on fundamental ideological grounds, but purely for reasons of financial stringency.

Much has been accomplished with regard to generating a more businesslike approach in municipalities, in terms of the renewal of organisation and management. Much remains to be done, but it is true that many municipalities have made more progress than central government. It is important for the success of municipal organisational change that one avoids comparison with the private economy, and takes into account the political dimension. Changes in structure and system are not sufficient without well-directed attempts to change attitudes. This requires the will for change and strong management. Concepts such as management by contract can help to bring about cultural breakthroughs by stimulating competition within and between governmental organisation.

All these changing ways of functioning and the revaluation of goals and products will bring local authorities to answer the question of their essential function in local society. Society is also searching for new roles for private initiative and there is a growing disbelief in the steering capacity of national authorities; new opportunities are occurring with the development of cross-national regions within an integrated European Community. Municipalities have new possibilities not in their classical role as monopoly service providers, but as coordinators and stimulators of networks of local firms, organisations, social groups and private initiatives. This will bring them into competition with others, and force them to act in a more effective and efficient way, but will also allow them to play a new role in giving direction to social development.

9 The System of Local Government in Portugal

Armando Pereira

Within the processes of democratisation and decentralisation which have taken place in Portugal since the events following the coup of 25 April 1974, important measures have been taken to reinforce local democracy. Under the new Constitution of 1976, local authorities have been given a constitutional guarantee of autonomy. With respect to the archipelagos of the Azores and Madeira, because of their historical aspirations for autonomy, the Constitution of 1976 made them autonomous regions (Gallagher, 1979; Opello, 1978a; Stevens, 1977; Story, 1976).

Taking into account the traditional centralist features of the Portuguese public administrative apparatus, these decisions to decentralise and strengthen local government were enthusiastically supported by all the political forces in the country (Pereira, 1988). This strategic option therefore constituted one of the few non-controversial political issues. Local democracy in Portugal is both a very recent achievement and a renewal of past experiences of municipal autonomy throughout the country.

As fundamental bases of decentralisation, the Constitution established four important principles relating to local government: the autonomy of local units of administration; the existence of local government as part of the democratic organisation of the state; the financial and patrimonial autonomy of local authorities; and local government's self-regulatory capacity (Opello, 1978b). As a consequence, it can be said that the constitutional provision for local autonomy is in practice a means of counter-balancing the centralist Napoleonic tendencies embedded in the global system.

The Portuguese system of local government

In mainland Portugal and in the autonomous regions of the Azores and Madeira, the main units of local government are the municipalities (275 on the mainland and 305 altogether), which are composed of parishes, the lowest-level units of the system (of which there are more than 4000). In the autonomous regions, the supervision of local governments (also municipalities and parishes) rests with the regional authorities. At the higher level and only in the mainland, administrative regions were to be brought into being by law at a later date, but in fact this has not happened until now. Setting up the administrative regions with agreed delimitation of their boundaries and functions is currently one of the principal issues on the agenda of political and administrative organisation in Portugal.

In the more than eight hundred years of Portuguese history, the municipalities (*municipios*) have had an important place in public administrative life throughout the country. However, for a period of almost fifty years under the pre-1974 autocratic regime, they essentially played a role as units of administration of the state (Opello, 1981 and 1983). As a result of the constitutional reforms of 1976, municipalities were established as democratic local governments, but the pre-1974 municipal boundaries have remained. Unlike the local reforms carried out during the last few decades in some West European countries, no reorganisation of that kind was achieved or even intended in Portugal under the new regime. The present municipal boundaries are essentially the result of a reform introduced in the last century. Two main reasons were taken into account for keeping them: the people's attachment to their municipalities, because of existing historical and traditional links; second, the average size of these units was already large. In fact, Portuguese municipalities, with an average of more than 32000 people (34000 on the mainland) are among the biggest local units of government in Western Europe, despite Portugal's small size. Even if one takes area into consideration as a measure, they are amongst the largest in the West European countries (301 sq. km)

Below the municipal level, parishes (*freguesias*) represent the bottom tier of the Portuguese local government system. There are around 4200 parishes in the country which have an average of

2300 people and an area of less than 22 sq. km. That number includes a group of around 200 new parishes that have been created in recent years by the sub-division of others. The territory of each municipality is thus made up of parishes which are institutionally represented in the organic structure of their respective 'municipal autarchy', as will be seen below. Nevertheless, as the parishes consist of small units, they strongly depend upon each respective municipality. Their range of functions is in practice very narrow, the financial resources at their disposal are, in general, insignificant and their technical and administrative capacity is extremely limited, with the exception of those in the more urban areas. As a consequence, the parishes generally act both as units of self government and as delegated units of service delivery on behalf of the municipality. In the latter case, the municipality delegates some tasks, or even some permanent functions to the parishes and consequently transfers to them the corresponding additional resources, taking advantage of the proximity of those local units to the population.

Concerning local structures within the Portuguese system of local government, the basic feature to keep in mind is a clear separation between two boards which correspond to the executive and the deliberative functions. In the parishes, the executive body (*junta*) is composed of between three and seven members, one of them being the president who is the main representative of the parish. All members of the executive body come from the assembly of the parish, the deliberative board, which is directly elected by the parish voters. Elsewhere, in small parishes, the assembly is replaced by a village meeting (or plenary assembly) which all the registered voters are entitled to attend and take part in.

In the municipalities, the deliberative body (a unicameral municipal assembly) and the executive body (municipal chamber), are elected separately. However, the assembly is composed of two groups: one comprises all the presidents of the executive boards of the parishes existing in the municipality's territory; the other group is formed by an equal number plus one of members directly elected to the municipal assembly. The municipal assembly approves major municipal policies, the annual plan of activities, the budget and major budgetary amendments, as well as the accounts and the yearly financial report. Additionally, the assembly discusses current municipal policies and approves major reforms in internal services. The executive board is normally comprised of between five and eleven members, one of them being the president (president of the chamber) who is a powerful mayor (as in France). In view of their size, Lisbon and Oporto have 17 and 11 members respectively.

The two bodies which rule the municipality therefore have the same political legitimacy. Moreover, according to the decision of the municipality, there may be a third branch, the municipal consultative council. A tripartite subdivision then exists: deliberative, executive and consultative. The consultative board is comprised of appointed representatives from the municipality's economic, social, cultural and professional organisations. Some authors see in this surviving influences of the strong corporatist tradition in Portuguese ideology (Wiarda, 1977 and 1978; and Schmitter, 1975).

Institutional measures for the reinforcement of local autonomy

During the latter years of the 1970s, some regulatory measures were taken in Portugal in order to implement the autonomy which was granted to the local authorities by the new Constitution. A description of these measures will shed light on the Portuguese system of local government, but the wider implications of such changes in the corporatist, Mediterranean countries are discussed further in Kohler (1982) and Wiarda (1973). The first action consisted of drawing up a law regulating local elections (the Local Elections Act) which enabled the first local elections to take place under the new democratic regime in December 1976. Thus, in each constituency coinciding with the parish and the municipal boundaries, the citizens vote simultaneously, but separately, for the parish assembly, municipal assembly and municipal chamber, for a four-year mandate. The elections are held by direct universal suffrage under a list system of proportional representation, seats being allocated in accordance with the Hondt highest average method. This was indeed a remarkable achievement for a country where a few years previously the local mandates were filled primarily by appointment from above. The second major step in order to implement local autonomy was the construction of a basic legal framework for local authorities: the 1977 Local Government Act. This settled the main elements with respect to the local government system. Such elements were, for example, the allocation of functions, the organisation of local units, the relationship between levels of government, the extension and limits of prefectoral tutelage, and the financial framework. In fact, this constituted the practical basis for building local autonomy, or what is called 'the reinforcement of local power'.

Finally, an important parliamentary measure, taken in the late 1970s in order to consolidate local autonomy, was that dealing with the financial autonomy of local government, the 1979 Local Finances Act. This regulated the financial framework of the municipalities: the budgetary principles were settled; the source of local funds was set out in an objective way, concerning both their own revenues and grants from central government; local fiscal policy was defined; the system of municipal borrowing was laid down; finally, the financial ties between municipalities and parishes were also established, in order to guarantee the normal operation of the latter. Consequently, in the early 1980s local authorities had at their disposal the essential instruments for exercising their autonomy. The above-mentioned financial framework is probably the single most important contribution to the aim of decentralisation and reinforcement of local government's role. Nonetheless, the financial field is one of unique difficulty and sensitivity, since this is also the weakest aspect of the system. In fact, the financial resources at the disposal of the local governments are extremely limited. Moreover, the municipalities do not have fiscal capacity, that is they cannot yet impose local taxes. Thus, they remain somewhat dependent upon central government.

Portuguese local financial resources are still too sparse, bearing in mind the Constitution's 'generosity' relating to local autonomy and given the local apparatus of democratic rule and the resulting public expectations. The new local democratic machinery has created in citizens hopes which local officials at times cannot satisfy. Financial restrictions are felt by local authorities, given their natural will to respond to the challenge of pressing local needs in a country with real problems of development. Regarding financial resources, Portuguese local governments depend strikingly upon the centre. They have weak fiscal revenues of their own, with around 50 per cent of their resources coming directly from central government.

However, the above description of financial dependence may erroneously give the idea of a real lack of autonomy on the part of the municipalities. Three points should be made in order to shed further light on this picture of Portuguese local finances. Firstly, the scarcity of local resources is not an isolated phenomenon; rather the contrary, it is a national problem of public finances. This problem has been felt internationally since the 1970s, and has had a particularly great impact on the feeble Portuguese economy. Secondly, another feature of the local financial framework in Portugal is in general its preservation of local independence in decision-making with respect to budgetary considerations and spending. All limiting rules, such as the relation between current and capital expenditure, a borrowing plateau, and minimal transfers to parishes, are expressly established in the Local Finances Act by Parliament, without interference by the current central government. Thirdly, despite the significant dependence on central transfers, financial allocations from the centre are objectively defined by law in Parliament, thus reducing central government's margin for manoeuvre and manipulation. This gives Portugal the position of 'one of the European countries which follows a more neutral policy regarding the financial transfers from the centre to the local authorities' (Council of Europe, 1985).

The status of local authorities and their relationship with central government

Given the recent developments, features and trends in Portuguese local government, it is now possible to comment on its status in relation to central government. It has been emphasised that the present local democratic arrangement in Portugal is a very recent one. It may seem, therefore, that there is little to learn from this incipient system. Nevertheless, although it is still in the process of maturation, Portuguese local government has achieved interesting accomplishments given that, in its modern form, it has been built up from scratch. In a country which experienced a long history of centralisation, the local government system is indeed one of the most successful achievements of Portugal's young democracy. The status and relevance of local government is not a matter of dispute and speculation; instead, there is a clear attachment of the population to municipal services and activities and an increasing responsiveness of political representatives to public accountability. Evidence for the accepted relevance of local government is provided by the fact that national politicians also run as candidates in municipal elections; the leader of the Socialist Party successfully stood as Mayor of Lisbon in December 1989. During the recent years of national economic recovery and of a general effort to bring to the population the benefits of economic and social development, local authorities have played a crucial role. The debate now is essentially centred on ways of improving the system, ameliorating relationships between levels of government, enlarging the scope of local action, and perfecting legal forms of control and tutelage in order to give coherence and public unity to local actions in the field.

Thus, at present the status of local government could be labelled, typically, as one of relative autonomy. In fact, local governments act freely within a legally pre-determined framework. Moreover, the existing national association of municipalities is a well organised and consistently demanding body, an active lobby which is formally consulted in most government decisions about local authorities. The relationships with central government are more or less clearly stated and the two levels of government often share investment policies (lately through a system called the 'contract-programme'). Despite the latest developments of a new framework of control and tutelage, whose consequences still cannot be anticipated, there is no clear perception of arrangements leading to a transition to a less autonomous model. Nevertheless, there is a striking weakness in the present system and in the model, since, as already mentioned, resources are scarce and local authorities cannot raise their revenue through direct taxation. They obtain instead the product of some major national taxes and of several local services, and also transfers from central government previously defined under the Local Finances Act.

Another weakness should be pointed out which is related to deficiencies and shortcomings of internal organisation and staffing in the local government system. This is due essentially to a lack of administrative and managerial training, in addition to the limited political experience of a great number of the new local representatives. Specific programmes of training have been carried out in order to meet these needs. Even so, it is the areas of financial resources and administrative and technical support which have been the main factors limiting more wide-reaching action by the municipalities, in addition to those concerning the interference of central government in the action of local authorities. In view of the absence of technicians and professionals in most of the municipalities, and a consequent lack of technical capacity, mainly in the less developed areas, a system of technical support was created throughout the mainland. The 275 municipalities were arranged into about 50 groups, or 'municipal blocks' and in each block a technical office was set up (known as a GAT or technical support office), with a staff of engineers, architects, topographers, designers and, latterly, planners, economists, sociologists and other professionals. The GATs have played an important role since the middle 1970s, mainly in the more deprived areas.

In this context it is worth considering the relationships between local and central governments brought about by the GATs. This system is in fact a valuable and singular innovation in the classical set-up of intergovernmental relations. The coordination of the GATs is ensured by regional field services, on behalf of central government and, hierarchically, the GATs report to these regional bodies. The personnel working for the GATs hold civil servant status, which has provided a more attractive professional career structure. However, the financial costs are shared by the central government and the municipalities. On an annual basis, the priorities and most activities are defined by the mayors of the municipalities of the respective blocks, who also monitor the projects and make subsequent adjustments. For operational reasons, one of these mayors is appointed by the others as president of the block of municipalities. The GAT system has also been a way of motivating the new and individualist local elites to associate with their neighbours. The habit of dealing with other municipalities stimulates a sense of association and a supra-municipal consciousness. Some of these blocks have become formally associations of municipalities. Moreover, this has led to a means of resolving the problem of rigidities in governmental structure and relationships, a way to bridge the gap between central administration services and the newly autonomous local governments. This is an important aspect, given the decline of the prefectoral role and its services in the Portugal of post-1974. Finally, the central government sees its own influence enlarged, in using these mixed field and local government services, particularly in those matters relating to the local authorities.

The organisation of local service delivery and the political control of local government

In the previous sections, a critical description was attempted, relating to the features and trends of the Portuguese local government system. I then discussed the status of local authorities and their relationships with other levels of government. From the above-mentioned features, trends and relationships, it is worth synthesising the relevant elements concerning the organisation of local services delivery and the political control of local government.

In effect, Portuguese local authorities generally provide services directly by employing their own staff and resources. In specific areas, such as in public investments (roads, housing construction, sanitation networks, etc.) or in the economic field (for example, in the entrepreneurial development of economic activities) they act as contractors-out or enabling authorities as well. However, despite the increasing tendency towards the enabler role, this does not constitute a major alternative to direct provision. Likewise, it is worth noting that those options of contractor-out or enabler depend exclusively on the local authorities' decision, according to their political strategies, priorities and available resources. Thus, the creation of autonomous or semi-autonomous agencies taking functions away from local government is not a real phenomenon in the Portuguese system.

The picture referred to above does not mean, however, that central government is not making an effort to stress competition and effectiveness in the provision of local services to the public. The current central political ideology accentuates competitiveness and the free market and seeks to reduce the role of the state and public enterprises. But the measures leading to this desideratum have had a more clear application at the central level, not having consciously influenced local strategies as a whole. Two main reasons for this dichotomy may be identified. The first is linked to local government autonomy which is protected by constitutional guarantees, by the action of the consistently demanding national association of municipalities, and by the successful performance of the local authorities during recent years. The second reason for functions not having been taken away from the municipalities and for local competition not having been introduced is related to the small amount of activities currently allocated to local government in Portugal. In fact, the existing belief is that the range of local functions should be enlarged and not reduced, inasmuch as financial resources and technical capacity are increased. Services such as schooling, social assistance, local culture and others are still outside municipal jurisdiction, and the next step may be to introduce direct or indirect municipal action in these fields. In the Portuguese system of local government, functions are not limited by the *ultra vires* doctrine but by the fact that general competence can be specifically restricted in ways defined by the law.

A central strategy directed at enlarging municipal capacities, technically and financially, in order to achieve a better provision of local services, is being pursued by stimulating and facilitating forms of municipal association. In the big urban centres, particularly in the large areas of Lisbon and Oporto, efforts have been made to encourage the municipalities to create institutional arrangements for the effective provision of important supra-municipal services. This is the case, for example, with urban transport, housing, water supply, refuse collection and sewage treatment. The creation of two metropolitan areas is presently a particular issue on the central-local government agenda.

Another example in the context of the effort to provide more effective services to the public, is a national programme of 'de-bureaucratisation' of services. This includes the 'modernisation' of administration and the 'personalisation' of the services provided ('The administration has a face'). The programme is intended for application to a large range of activities and agencies, from public enterprises and public offices to local government. In fact, central government envisages the implementation of this programme in the local sphere by negotiating and even financing certain actions through special schemes ('contracts of modernisation'). In conclusion, taking into account local service delivery and political control, it can be added that, in parallel to the initiatives for bringing the whole administration closer to the public, central government has made increasing efforts to persuade local authorities to achieve certain objectives or to pursue given performance standards. This is achieved essentially through negotiation, contract-programmes and other persuasive devices. However, the central-local partnership may be broken in situations of illegality, fraud or corruption. These cases are brought to light through administrative and financial inspections and are widely publicised and prosecuted. The political punishment may mean withdrawal from public office or a judicial action, according to the crime. These inspections, although presumably independent from the government's pressure, are the clearest form of interference by the central administration in the sphere of local authorities. The main current effort of central government is the enactment of legislation to reinforce that role of control and tutelage. However, it is worth noting that this does not take the form of financial control, but has essentially a legal-administrative character.

In fact, local authorities in Portugal are not reliant on central financial controls nor on government discretionary grants. Administrative tutelage is instead a 'tool-kit' at the disposal of central government, essentially for controlling the legality of municipal action. Politically, local executive action relies on the deliberative assembly in the first instance. In the last resort, in their strategies, policy measures and forms of spending resources, municipalities respond to local electors but never to central government. Little academic speculation has been forthcoming on the relevance of local government because its importance has been naturally assumed. It may be an ingenuous posture, but it is generally believed that it is possible to achieve an efficient provision of local services in a political environment of effective local democracy.

References
(restricted to items in English)

Council of Europe (1985) *Report on the Grant Policies of Local Governments*, RM/RL (85)6, Strasbourg.

Gallagher T. (1979) 'Portugal's Atlantic territories: the separatist challenge', *The World Today*, pp.353–60.

Gaspar, J. (1976) 'Regional Planning, decentralisation and popular participation in post-1974 Portugal', *Iberian Studies*, vol. 5, no. 1.

Graham, L. S. (1983) 'Bureaucratic politics and the problem of reform in the state apparatus', in L. S. Graham and D. L. Wheeler (eds) *In Search of Modern Portugal: The Revolution and Its Consequences* (London: Wisconsin Press, 1983)

Kohler, B. (1982) *Political Forces in Spain, Greece and Portugal*, European Centre for Political Studies, Policy Studies Institute, London.

Opello, Jr, W. C. (1978a) 'The Second Portuguese Republic: politico-administrative decentralisation since April 25 1974', *Iberian Studies*, vol. 7, no. 2, pp.43–4.

Opello, Jr, W. C. (1978b) 'The parliament in Portuguese constitutional history', *Iberian Studies*, vol. 7, no. 1, pp.22–9.

Opello, Jr, W. C. (1981) 'Local government and political culture in a Portuguese rural county', *Comparative Politics*, vol. 13, no. 3.

Opello, Jr, W. C. (1983) 'The continuing impact of the old regime on the Portuguese political culture', in L. S. Graham and D. L. Wheeler (eds) *In Search of Modern Portugal: The Revolution and Its Consequences*, Wisconsin Press, London.

Opello. Jr, W. C. (1985) *Portugal's Political Development*, Westview Press, Boulder, Colorado.

Pereira, A. (1988) *Disruptions and Continuities in Portuguese Politics: The Effectiveness of Decentralising a Napoleonic-type State*, Dissertation, 152 pp, University of London School of Economics and Political Science, London.

Schmitter, P. C. (1975) *Corporatism and Public Policy in Authoritarian Portugal*, Sage, Beverly Hills/London.

Stevens, R. M. (1977) 'Asymmetrical federalism: the federal principle and the survival of the small republic', *Plubius*, vol. 7, no. 4, pp.177–203.

Story, J. (1976) 'Portugal's revolution of carnations: patterns of change and continuity', *International Affairs*, vol. 5, no. 3, July, p.425.

Wiarda, H. J. (1973) 'Toward a framework for the study of political change in the Iberic Latin tradition: the corporate model', *World Politics*, vol. 25, pp.206–35.

Wiarda, H. J. (1977) *Corporatism and Development: The Portuguese Experience*, The University of Massachusetts Press.

Wiarda, H. J. (1978) 'Does Europe stop at the Pyrenees? Or does Latin America begin there?', *Occasional Paper Studies*, no. 2, The Centre for Hemispheric Studies, American Enterprise.

10 Improving Access to Administration in Spain

Juan Ferrer Mateo

The regionalisation of the Spanish state

After the death of Franco, public interest which had been germinating for some time overflowed into the streets with the movement for civil rights, political freedom and justice for the historical regions of Spain. The question of 'nationalism' came to the fore. In the subsequent twelve years, Spain has moved towards new forms of state organisation, giving autonomy to different regions by different paths. Regions have obtained self-governing capacities in different degrees and with different levels of responsibility for transferred services.

Regions such as Catalonia, the Basque Country and Galicia, claimed greater autonomy and, above all, wanted to satisfy the strong feelings against central government which had been growing for decades under Franco's rule and former dictatorship. Led by nationalist, independent, socialist or just democratic parties, paramilitary organisations or terrorist groups, no one questioned the right of the Spanish regions and historical kingdoms to decide their new relationships with the Spanish State. This movement produced a new state structure with 17 regions with autonomous governments, 17 regional administrations and an unusual organisation of public business if compared with other European countries. There are overlaps between local, central and regional governments, depending on the number of provinces involved in the autonomous region and the constitutional path taken to self-government. Parallel to the central administration, sometimes against the opposition of local governments, a new administration took shape.

Spain has four tiers of administration:

1. Central government has its own administrative apparatus and 'peripheral' administration in each of the provinces and departments.
2. Regional government has its own administration and territorial services in its provinces and departments.
3. Local government: at this level, mayors may retain their administration intact or delegate it to decentralised units depending on the size of the municipality and its activities.
4. The provincial government previously under the control of a centrally appointed governor, now has its own elected council and indirectly elected president. The provincial administration has the function largely of offering support services to municipalities.

A further kind of local organisation is appearing in some regions, such as Catalonia: *mancomunidades*. These are associations of municipalities and regional governments gathering together in order to obtain scale economies in the supply of services. Without political powers in the strict sense, they are a form of administration fully devoted to the organisation and provision of services.

From the political point of view, only regional governments and administrations are in fact new. Their attributions were at first to do with powers rather than services. Basic services such as cleaning, transportation, public markets, local security, cemeteries, traffic and urban infrastructure were traditionally provided directly by local government or indirectly through monopolistic concessionaries subjected to regulated prices, for instance in water systems. Recently some locally based services (health care, education) hitherto operated by the centre have been transferred to regional governments.

This complex structure has led the Valencian regional government to make an agreement with the local government of Valencia city to promote the simplification of procedures involving both administrations. The intention is to reduce steps and the time taken in administrative action, and to establish the basis for administrative simplification. It is difficult to reach this kind of agreement between levels of government when a hypothetical loss of powers and independence is implied. Despite this, the reorganisation of local and regional administrations is a need strongly felt by those politicians and civil servants who have a broader view of the role that public administration must play. The particular approach adopted is the 'single window' or 'one stop shop' approach, but before we describe this, the nature of the problem of Spanish public administration should be explained.

The Spanish administrative problem

The Spanish conception of public administration is that it exists to administer powers. This classical point of view has been shifting in recent years to the concept of service provision. The old concept of administration still exists, but the construction of regional government has opened a space which allows a bridge to be built between local administration, mainly concerned with providing services, and regional administration, concerned with the administration of power but also increasingly of services. This concern with service also has to take into account the new idea of citizens as clients or customers, a point of view which carries some contradictions:

a) a free market is not possible while there is no choice between administrations, nor between having or not having a license;
b) to talk about citizens as customers implies that they have no rights until they pay taxes;
c) public finance theory suggests different ways of fixing prices for public services (shadow prices or whatever) but there is no system for pricing the administration of power (permissions or controls).

It is not possible to implement sweeping changes unless the cultural conditions for the changes exist. There is resistance to change in an administration inherited from the Franco era and there are interests concerned to retain its incredible independence. The idea of public administration as service provider which may be normal in Northern Europe is strange to us. One question was whether the problem lay in our administrative law, shared in many respects with other continental countries, and developed under the heavy influence of the Roman Catholic Church, which maintained the bureaucratic tradition of the Roman Empire. The French Revolution changed the ownership relations of property on the Continent, but it rebuilt a large bureaucracy which was later used as a model for nearly every continental country. The Prussian, Austrian, Russian and Spanish administrations were reorganised at the same time as Gladstone was developing the quite different machinery of the British State. Differences in administration, law, constitutional systems and the nature of power became entrenched at this time, and remain, even though continental administrations now also see themselves as service providers.

The continental attitude to administration is regulatory, and the real instruments of power are the official gazettes, journals and bulletins since only published regulations have legal character and force. It was Curzio Malaparte who said that the most strategic target in a putsch was the official journal. In Spain there are 52 official provincial journals (*diarios*), 17 official regional journals, one official bulletin of the State, and some cities also have their own means of issuing regulations. Officials use these publications to give general effect to internal rules, because once published, these have the force of law as much as regular laws and decrees. Internal rules, formally concerned with matters of organisation, thus become law and help to extend and protect official power. So one of the first objectives is to prevent organisational matters from being converted into law, and another is to rid the law of the detailed regulation which results from the use of legal dispositions as organisational tools.

Even these two reforms leave untouched the capacity of civil servants to produce arbitrary internal rules in order to make their work easier or keep control of their functions. In fact civil servants are producing, applying, judging and establishing what they think are suitable penalties without any control, overreaching the most basic democratic rules. This is the real core of the Spanish administrative problem.

The experience of reform

One solution is to take legislative action to reduce redundant regulations, rules which could be substituted by internal protocols or simple organisational changes. The advantage of this approach is that it could simplify the whole framework of action, but it also faces problems. Very many regulations involving more than regional or local administrations would have to be redrafted, creating great difficulty in reaching agreements among affected institutions. Differences between autonomous bodies with different practices and approaches to self-government add problems to problems. Such a process initiated by a particular regional administration could require central government to change general regulations relating to regions with different powers and capacities. The most likely reaction would be the appointment of a commission or steering committee which would never produce any conclusion, and would become a central instrument for preventing action. On the other hand, deregulation undertaken by the separate regions could produce differential barriers to economic development, segmenting markets within Spain just at the time that the Single European Market is being created. A defective judicial system would also obstruct the deregulation process.

It was therefore decided that deregulation should remain the target but that it should be achieved through means which were not dependent on others. The only ground where regional and local government can act without the interference of other administrations and special bodies is in their own organisation through their top officials. By not involving central government and its administration, the obstacles to change are limited to officials who see their powers reduced by the simplification of procedures and to possible judicial interventions as a result of individual complaints. This approach also avoids the need to produce new regulations and begins the process of cultural change, thus opening up the possibility of a deeper impact on the administration.

In Valencia, the attempt to make these organisational changes through the 'single window' approach has, indeed, produced opposition from officials whose procedures are affected. Opposition has particularly come from a group of professional intermediaries (the *gestores administrativos*). In Spain, the difficulties of dealing with the administration were traditionally so great that this profession arose to act on behalf of applicants. *Gestorias*, as the firms devoted to these activities are called, were and still are good business. The *gestor* deals with all aspects of the citizen's relationship with the administration, in return for payment: for example, applications for passports, identity cards or a license, or permission to undertake street repairs. The profession is regulated by the state which provides a legal basis for its operations and a strict examination system for entry. It is an open question whether this close relationship with the state has not also led to the creation of procedures to provide work for *gestorias*. They enjoy the privilege of special queues at special windows in nearly every service or licensing activity of the administration. The idea of a 'single window' for all citizens therefore has particular significance in Spain. It is a strategic way of making people feel like real citizens, closing a long era in which the borders between the corporatist and the democratic states are still unclear.

The single window is an important part of the Socialist Party's programme for the renewal of public administration. Its adoption by the regional government of Valencia is a demonstration of a new concern with the provision of services as opposed to the traditional view of government as being about the administration of power. There is also a commitment to provide cost effective services, so as to avoid increased taxation and public borrowing. However, the laws introduced by the new socialist regional government to bring about the reforms led to strong internal opposition by officials of the central government administration, as well as by those transferred to the regional level. The Supreme and the Constitutional Courts have acted to maintain the principles of established administrative law, making a series of unfavourable decisions between 1982 and 1986 to block or reject the reforming initiatives of central and regional governments.

The single window approach

A single window is a working environment in which various organisations come together so as to simplify the relationship between the administration and the citizen.

The actors combining to work together in the same place may be not only local, regional and central government administrators, but also other related organisations such as chambers of commerce or voluntary social service organisations. The idea of bringing them together is both to avoid competition and to stimulate cooperation between them and to facilitate matters for citizens who would otherwise need to deal in different places with multiple administrations with different procedures. This also marks a shift into a more trusting attitude to citizens: first, the system of 'positive administrative silence' has been introduced, meaning that unless the administration makes explicit regulatory requirements, the citizen is assumed to be free of any obligations; secondly, supervision has been made *a posteriori* in place of *a priori*, that is instead of a system which tries to anticipate and prevent any deviation from the rules, we have a system of checks, monitoring and auditing.

The single window also tries to reduce the number of different procedures. For example the licensing procedure for polluting activities is different depending on whether the activity contaminates air or water, whether the pollution is produced by manufacturing or mining, and whether or not it takes place in an industrial area. In future, all these will be considered as different cases of one general procedure instead of having different procedures for the same sort of case. The objective is also to reduce the number of forms, procedural steps, overlapping permissions, certificates and documents.

Finally the single window is being used to reduce the delays which occur in step by step processing through one agency, or part of an agency, and on to another. This sort of consecutive processing of, for example, an application to establish a business, may result in considerable delay and loss of money: the total time taken is, at best, the sum of all the time involved in taking each step. It is possible to save time not only by eliminating steps, but also by allowing steps which do not require consecutive treatment to be dealt with simultaneously.

There were two possible approaches which the regional government of Valencia could have adopted: either to create a single window for all matters, or specific windows for specific activities. The second was chosen partly because it was easier, but also because Valencia was able to learn from similar experience in

Madrid, which was a pioneer in this field. The approach which Madrid adopted was, however, not to coordinate the activities of different agencies and reform their practices, but to offer a set of free citizen advisory services on specific activities. The Barcelona Chamber of Commerce, which is interested in the simplification of procedures for the establishment of new businesses in Catalonia, has looked at the Madrid and the Valencia models, and so far seems to favour the more pro-active, reformist Valencian position.

As in the case of Madrid, Valencia has begun in the field of economic activity, partly because of possible employment generating effects, and partly because the complexity of official relationships in this area makes it a good test case. The fact that citizens who wish to establish economic units are relatively influential also makes this a good area in which to challenge the delaying action of civil servants. An examination of the existing formalities required to get a license to open a factory or any other business showed that there were classifications for 620 different economic activities, 140 different routes to obtain a license, and 59 points at which the applicant would be expected to contact a governmental agency concerned with town planning or pollution issues. Different public bodies and levels of government may use different classification systems; for each, the citizen has to fill in separate application forms because there is no system for transferring information. Computerisation will allow us to transform this situation by identifying the simplest route through the process for the particular applicant.

However, the most immediate steps which could be taken to improve the situation were, firstly, to reduce the number of forms per topic, and secondly, to create a team of official inspectors from each of the agencies concerned. The ultimate objective is to have a single form per topic, and a single inspecting authority, but these immediate coordinating steps have been taken so that we do not appear to be intruding into others', particularly local government's, areas of competence. We are seeking not to intrude, but to reorganise an intricate environment so as to help people and public administration to save time and money.

The short-term effects of the single window are paradoxical: it increases the overlapping and cost of administration. Since it was decided at the outset not to use legislative action to abolish existing agencies and regulations, the single window becomes in effect a competitor with existing administrative units duplicating their personnel and functions. The only way to cut them out is to provide a better service to the citizen who, for the first time, is able to choose between alternative paths.

11 Local Government in Ireland

T. J. Barrington

There is an old joke that an Irishman can never answer a simple question without delving deeply into history; but it is difficult to understand the present predicament of Irish local government without a rapid survey as to how that predicament has come about. The task is not made easier (or more interesting) in that the story has no dramatic climaxes, just the steady working out of the logic of a set of values, implicit and explicit, in what is largely an intellectual vacuum, in conditions not of dialectic but of drift. These values are the acceptance of a substantial role for government in a highly centralised parliamentary democracy, the tolerance of considerable incompetence in the consequential structures and performance, the growth of bureaucracy, and indifference to the place of local democracy in the modern nation state, itself as in many European countries under pressure both from above and below, without and within. In short, as a perceptive present-day critic has put it, there is no real discussion of the nature of the Irish State. Hence the difficulties this commentator has in objectively addressing the general questions with which this book is concerned.

The discussion in this chapter is divided into two main parts. The first provides an account of the development of local government in Ireland which suggests that local government institutions have lost much of their relevance under the weight of strong tendencies for centralisation and bureaucratisation. The second part of the chapter addresses the key questions identified in the introduction to the book. It comments on Irish experience in terms of the status of local government and the changing nature of service delivery and local political management.

Loss of relevance

Ireland was a member of the United Kingdom from 1801 to 1922. Hence its public institutions are mostly based on British models, with some local adaptations. Since 1922 there has been some borrowing of American ideas and now, as a consequence of involvement in European institutions, some minor awakening to the possible relevance of other solutions to institutional problems. This is true of the local government system of what is now the Republic of Ireland – that of Northern Ireland, which remained within the UK after 1922, was to take a separate course touched on below. The striking feature of the local government system in what is now the Republic has been one of progressive and intense centralisation compounded during the past forty years by a lethal mixture of political cynicism and administrative neglect. By a different route the local government system in Northern Ireland has travelled even further along the road of centralisation. In both parts of the island local government is in a bad way.

Nineteenth-century origins

As institutional reforms were introduced in England and Wales in the last three-quarters of the nineteenth century they were extended to Ireland, usually after a gap of some years – e.g. the Poor Law after three years; reform of municipal corporations after five; the great Public Health Act after three; the creation of county councils after ten; and so on. By the turn of the century the structures of the Irish local government system, as far as it went, were very similar to those of England and Wales, county councils; county boroughs; boroughs, urban districts and incorporated towns; poor law unions; and rural districts. Apart from some smaller incorporated towns there were no really small elected local government bodies, urban or rural – no parish councils, for example. Outside the county boroughs most activity was in the hands of district authorities, urban and rural. In the whole island there were close to six hundred local authorities of all kinds. The functions of local authorities were also similar to those in England but were more restricted. Given the widespread discontent about the Union with Britain, policing in Ireland was (and, indeed, remains) wholly a central service; and the sectarian tensions of the early nineteenth century kept the newly developed educational system also as a national service – with, at the end of the century, the minor exception of local structures for 'technical education'.

Twentieth-century concentration

The period from 1886, when the first Irish Home Rule Bill failed, up to 1922 was one of spasmodic disintegration of British rule in Ireland, of increasing confusion, inefficiency and petty corruption, culminating in the breakdown of law and order. In this climate the new revolutionary and puritanical rulers of what is now the Republic were determined to rule effectively and honestly, and with 'efficiency and economy', key words at the time. For a small country with small government the logical way to achieve that 'efficiency and economy' was universally held to be through intense centralisation and general subordination to central government. In consequence some 460 local authorities in the new state were reduced by three-quarters (1923,1925); the draconian tutelage exercised over the poor law authorities was extended to all the survivors (1923); a civil service appointments system and an open competitive promotion system was applied to all local professional and senior administrative posts – believed to be the first of its kind (1926); and the American idea of city managers – but in a rigid form borrowed from Bombay city management in the 1880s – was progressively applied, first to the county boroughs (1929–39) and then to the counties (1940). There was a clear vision – unperturbed by thoughts of developing local autonomy, responsibility or democracy – of a streamlined, efficient, workaday system of local government operating basically as a dispersed agency of central government. That was effectively achieved by the end of the 1940s. But the central controls over local initiative continued to accumulate so that in 1967, the Maud Committee on the Management of Local

Government in Britain, having studied local government in seven countries including Ireland could conclude that, in Ireland, 'central control is the most stringent of all'.

In the heady days of the 1960s Ireland enjoyed one of its rare periods of good government. Following the enactment of the Local Government (Planning and Development) Act, 1963, and the institution at national level of economic and social planning, the idea emerged of turning local authorities into agents of dispersed national development. They were to become 'development corporations'. To translate such fine words into action would have involved dismantling the vast array of central controls; instituting major financial reform, accompanied by real leadership central and local; the dissemination of responsibility, and the freeing of initiative. But for this arteries had grown too hard and bureaucratic sclerosis had become too far advanced.

The function and structure of local government

The principal functions discharged by local authorities, in what is now the Republic, have been roads; water and sewerage; fire-fighting; housing, urban and rural; income maintenance; and health. A few local authorities had electricity and/or gas undertakings. The electricity undertakings were in the 1920s incorporated in the new national electricity authority; more recently those gas undertakings that survived have been, in effect, nationalised. From the 1950s income maintenance activities were progressively incorporated in a central government department and, as will be seen, health seems to be headed in a somewhat similar direction. Nowadays, the Irish local government system proper is almost wholly concerned with environmental infrastructure plus limited cultural activities.

The chief victims of the drastic reductions in the number of local authorities in the 1920s were the rural ones. First, the poor law unions (and with them the concept that a town and its hinterland were bound up in common interests) in 1923 had their functions concentrated in the county councils. Then the rural districts were incorporated in the counties in 1925. Attempts on the urban districts were postponed until the 1970s, but sustained neglect of their problems in the meantime had reduced most of them to impotence and irrelevance.

Increasingly the counties became the key bodies. But, steadily the belief grew that they, too, were too small and, their boundaries stretching back to the twelfth century, therefore archaic. Hence a vogue for regionalism in the late 1960s and the early 1970s. Regional structures were set up for tourist development, for planning, for health, even (of a sort) within centralised national bodies such as government departments and state sponsored bodies. There are no historical or cultural 'regions' in Ireland – apart from four vestigial 'provinces' (of which two-thirds of one – Ulster – is in Northern Ireland); but nothing like Bavaria, Catalonia, Tuscany; so region-building became an exercise in creativity. Nearly every national body with local operations has its own set of regions, and some have two or three. Where 'regions' have been established as distinct organisations they tend to have two characteristics – they have some representation from the county councils and county boroughs in the region and, usually but not invariably and now to a diminishing extent, are made up of whole counties. Regional planning and coordination, where they have been briefly attempted, in practice become impossible where regional boundaries are not standardised and all effective decision-making remains concentrated in Dublin. The overall result has been one of minimal democratic legitimacy and maximum collective confusion. Central government has steadfastly refused to give the 'regions' legal legitimacy and to standardise and coordinate their roles and structures.

The major exception has been the eight statutory health regions; but these now present the most striking example of the ebbing tide of regionalism: moves are afoot to incorporate them into one national body. Health illustrates centripetalism at its more insatiable – the absorption of the districts by the counties, of the counties by the regions and, now apparently, of the regions by a national body, the transition from local democracy to central bureaucracy.

Democracy, parliamentary and local

There is a striking contrast between the Republic as a deeply-rooted *parliamentary* democracy and its weakness as a *local* one. On its face local democracy has considerable democratic legitimacy. Voting, both in parliamentary and in local elections, is voluntary. In the seven local elections held between 1950 and 1985 turn-out ranged between 54 per cent and 67 per cent with an average of 60 per cent. This compares with an average turn-out in parliamentary elections held over much the same period of close to 75 per cent. The national parties have almost completely colonised the local councils and subjected the councillors to the iron party discipline characteristic of Irish politics. There is nothing in Irish local government comparable to the 'notables' in France. Certainly, since the mid-1970s central government has been untrammelled in what it has wanted to do, or to neglect, in relation to local government. Untrammelled, that is, from the periphery while the problems of actually governing at the centre have greatly grown. That is, of course, the nemesis of centripetalism.

Reform

In 1971 a White Paper proposed a number of changes in the local government system, notably to relax the controls on local discretion and, failing to think through the roles of small towns in a rapidly urbanising and modernising society, proposed to abolish local government in about half of them. This latter provoked strong dissent from local representatives – until recent months their last discernible sound. But the idea was dropped. It is too soon to say whether the organisational restlessness in the latter part of 1989 of those local councillors who belong to the largest political party, Fianna Fail, represents the beginning of an awakening or some form of death-pang.

During the 1970s there were big problems of local finance, exacerbated by the rapid growth of the health services, partly financed by local rates, and the failure to modernise an archaic system of valuation for rates. In a disgraceful auction between the two main national political parties, rates on domestic dwellings were abolished in 1977, on the promise of meeting the cost from the Exchequer, itself in heavy and rapidly increasing deficit. This promise was kept only in part. Shortly afterwards the system of agricultural rating also fell apart behind its patches. In consequence Irish local government has been living financially from hand to mouth exacerbated by the imposing by central government of stringent controls, unilaterally applied, on total local expenditures, partly as an anti-inflationary measure. This at a time when central expenditures themselves were seriously out of control.

As a footnote, modest attempts by local councillors to open up contacts with European local authorities were firmly stamped upon by central government. Even this was tamely acquiesced in.

Members of county councils and of county borough councils have one significant political card in their hands: they constitute a good part of the limited electorate for the Senate, the upper house of the Oireachtas (Parliament); but despite small stirrings of discontent, no effective use has been made of that power. Between the tiny bureaucracies of the political parties and the major bureaucracy of central government Irish local government is being steadily squeezed to death.

In 1985 it looked as if a new dawn might be breaking, that the tide of centripetalism might be turned back. The government announced a major programme of devolution to local authorities and, for other services, their appointment as agencies for central departments. This programme manifestly evoked no enthusiasm in the central bodies and, when that government went out of office in early 1987, just one function had been transferred – the licensing of dogs! Even central government was not now strong enough to cope with the entrenched centralisers of the central bureaucracy. Since 1987 centripetalism has evolved a new, unrestrained vitality.

Northern Ireland

In Northern Ireland, which remained part of the UK with its own parliament and government from 1920, the local government system was left substantially undisturbed until the early 1970s. There the local councils were significant pitches for the sectarian conflicts that led to the existence of the Province – as it came to be called – in the first place. The institutional changes in Britain after the Second World War had significant effects on the administration of education, health and welfare; but housing, in particular the location and allocation of houses, because of the effects on the sectarian balances of voters, remained a continual source of dispute. It was the allocation in 1968 of a house to an unmarried Protestant girl rather than to a Catholic family that set in train the 'Troubles', that, 22 years later, still continue. In the early 1970s the whole existing system was swept away. The social services – education and library; health and welfare services – were given, respectively, to five and four nominated regional bodies on which local authorities are represented. Virtually all the other functions – e.g. planning, sanitary services, roads, housing – were given to government departments and state appointed bodies.

Twenty-six newly-formed single-tier local authorities, each based on popular election and constituting a significant town and its hinterland, were created with sharply circumscribed functions confined largely, as the slogan has it, to 'dust-bins and burial grounds'.

Big government

From the mid-1970s there has been in the Republic a major surge in public expenditure so that Irish government has become, relative to its resources of men and money, very big. In relation to GDP, public expenditure in 1987 was just over 50 per cent, ranking in that year fifth highest of the European OECD countries, after Sweden, Denmark, the Netherlands and Belgium, in that order. Since 1987 there has been some contraction of Irish public expenditure. The 'market share' of local government in the business of government has also been slipping, from 20 per cent of total public expenditure in 1977 to 15 per cent in 1987. (In Northern Ireland local expenditure comes to some 7 to 8 per cent of public expenditure). The Council of Europe has published a comparative table of local grants and taxes as a percentage of GDP in 16 countries in 1981. Table 11.1, derived from that study, shows Ireland's comparative position. While Irish government spending as a whole ranked with the big spenders, Denmark, Sweden and the Netherlands, in terms of resources for local government it ranked at the bottom of the list, the three lower countries in 1981 then only recovering from the crushing of their democracies, central and local.

TABLE 11.1 Local grants and taxes as a percentage of GDP in 16 European countries, 1981

4 highest	%	ranking	4 lowest	%	ranking
Denmark	31.0	1	Ireland	4.5	13
Sweden	22.8	2	Portugal	2.9	14
Norway	15.2	3	Spain	2.7	15
Netherlands	11.3	4	Greece	1.7	16

Source: Council of Europe (1986) *Policies with Regard to Grants to Local Authorities*, Report No. 36, p.6.

The growth in the size of Irish government has been accompanied by a sharp decline in its quality, but there are few signs – apart from a virtual state of emergency in relation to the public finances – that the underlying causes are being tackled, certainly none – other than that brief fantasy of 1985–7 – that serious thought has been given to sharing the load with a reformed system of local government as has been done elsewhere in Europe. In 1985 the Council of Europe adopted a European Charter of Local Self-Government, so far signed by some two-thirds of the members of the Council, including all the members of the European Community, except Ireland and the UK. The Irish reason for not signing is reported to be that to do so would pre-empt the terms of the 'impending' local government reform, a false pregnancy that has lasted since 1971 at least.

Restructuring local democracy

The agenda for restructuring Irish local democracy is long and lengthening – local taxation and finance as part of a no less urgent reform of national taxation and finance; local democratic freedom and initiative; rationalisation of local representative and administrative structures, district, county and regional; urbanisation, urban boundaries and 'rurbanisation'; electoral equality; task sharing with central government; and, generally, a programme for local democratic development. But neither the intellectual nor the political conditions exist for any such programme and there is no present sign that these conditions will emerge, although the new government formed in July 1989, has promised to institute an inquiry into 'the whole question of local authority funding, structures and functions'.

The Irish State was set up in 1922 with a small stock of ideas so far as government was concerned. Central to these was, and remains, an intense belief in democratic centralism. As this took firmer and firmer shape concern for tackling the problems of local government seemed irrelevant and the pattern of choosing the centralised, rather than the decentralised, solutions to national problems became increasingly the norm. Given the panoply of central controls that frustrate local initiatives and the corresponding lack of challenge for potential local leaders, elected councillors survive by adopting protective colouring from the adverse environment, so becoming in practice increasingly irrelevant to the problems of modern living.

Lessons?

It will be obvious from this brief account of the sorry history of Irish local government that it is a long time since it became the object of the interplay of ideas or ideologies. In effect, for just two generations local government has remained largely immune to ideas whether native or imported, slowly losing relevance and gradually silting up like some city lost in the desert. The period since the 1960s at least has been one of considerable experimentation and change in European local government but the changes, some dramatic, have been viewed in Ireland, when noticed at all, with either a polite incuriosity or, as in the case of the European Charter of Local Self-Government, a degree of hostility. In the constitutional and jurisprudential areas generally the impact of American ideas, over a somewhat longer period, has been dramatic, but nothing has penetrated about local democracy apart from a bureaucratised aspect of the managerial revolution: it is as if de Tocqueville had never laid bare the roots of American democracy and the soil that nourished it. British ideas, although more accessible, have also made little impact, except to reinforce the trend to ever more intense democratic centralism and the belief in the efficiency of bigness. So, it is, as noted, difficult to address, from an Irish perspective, the general issues posed by this book.

The overall lesson is clear enough. In the great and increasing range of the responsibilities of government in modern society there is primary need to mobilise all available institutional resources at its disposal, not least those of local democracy. This on Al Smith's principle that 'All the ills of democracy can be cured by more democracy'. Even in a small country – perhaps particularly in a small country where outstanding human abilities are absolutely scarce – local democracy can be a significant contributor to the health of the democracy as a whole and as a developing partner in sharing the great and increasing burdens of modern government. So to confine local initiatives as to deprive them even of the autonomy for self-renewal and responsibility is for the governmental system in particular and the democracy as a whole to emphasise the gap, pointed out by Gramsci, between the state and the civil society. Irish experience would suggest that, beyond a certain point, centripetalism and the increasing bur-eaucratisation it nourishes each develop a major momentum of their own that becomes extraordinarily difficult to overcome before there is a major breakdown. That is to say, local democracy and local government demand to be seen in the context of national democracy and national government as a whole and to have their respective roles defined accordingly. There is nothing esoteric about this. For example, a number of the members of the European Community have been tackling these issues for a generation or more. But in Ireland we have a gift for transmuting our problems from the critical to the chronic so that we can live with them with relative comfort. In this way we can avoid or postpone the need for institutional change.

The specific lessons are more difficult to draw with assurance.

1. Current changes in the status of local government

It will be apparent from what has been described above that Irish local government is faced not with positive change or remodelling but a steady process of decay, occasionally hastened by acts of omission and commission by a central government largely inspired by expediency. For example, the removal of rates on domestic houses and the degree to which they were replaced by central grants decrease the responsibility of local councils, replacing the discipline of local taxation by a 'handout mentality', providing as excuse for poor services the failure by central government to honour the promises when rates were removed. Some, rather pathetic, attempts to aid local finances by making charges for water, library and other services have led to significant pockets of local resistance but not to any degree of user control.

As to contracting out, this is being used extensively for major road works and house building and to some degree for scavenging (i.e. refuse and waste disposal). Otherwise the 'market', democratic or otherwise, has made little impact on direct provision of services other than highly specialised ones.

So far as Irish local government is concerned, therefore,

- in general there are no principles governing its status, apart from the brief flirtation with devolution in 1985 to 1987, and little sign that any will emerge on which possible reforms could be based;
- the sole consistent theme in such limited public discussion of the future of local government as has emerged is that it should be, piece by piece, dismantled.

This is not acceptable to all commentators, but amongst effective decision-makers the consensus is striking.

The dominant model of central-local relations is the agency model. There are, however, some elements of the inter-action model. This is most apparent in relation to economic, especially industrial and tourist, development where there is a good degree of cooperation between national bodies, such as the Industrial Development Authority and the Tourist Board, in relation to the provision by local authorities of local infrastructural services, and serviced industrial estates. But, overall, the trend is towards the sidelining of local government away from local responsibility and autonomy.

2. Changes in service delivery

It is difficult to discern any conscious policies in relation to changing the delivery of services. The imposition of service charges, especially for water and scavenging, as a result of the abolition of domestic rates, has caused considerable local discontent and deterioration of relations between local citizens and their local authorities.

But there is also the factor of organic change, for example in relation to enablement. There has been a longstanding tradition of local authorities working with, and at least partially funding, voluntary bodies, of which there are very many. In this context most of them operate in relation to health and welfare, and as these functions were removed from the local government sphere, this side of local authority activity is much reduced. Against this, in recent years there has been a rapid growth of community and environmental groups impacting on the remaining activities of local authorities resulting in a decisive local authority commitment to community development and renewal. So far as relations between local authorities and community bodies are concerned there does not seem to be any coherent philosophy. For example, the two leading cities, Dublin and Cork, are much involved in this work. Dublin is committed to paternalism – a grant for a street party, for example. Cork tries to underpin community groups in programmes for community renewal and development, for example, in deprived housing estates or semi-derelict inner city areas. In addition, there are the usual incentives to private developers to build on local authority land made available to them, assisted by grants and facilities under the Town Planning Acts. This in the hope of stimulating life in decayed inner cities.

The question of user choice has not become an issue. Neither user control nor the market sphere figures significantly. The general trend – in a wholly pragmatic way – is to enhance central bureaucracies, at the price of less responsiveness and flexibility.

Against this must be put the extraordinary degree of Irish clientelism which engulfs both national and local politicians. Whatever its failings – and they are many – it does have the effect of keeping public representatives well informed about public sentiments and grievances and the representatives' survival depends on their being able to 'service' their constituents in this way. This is an abuse, but a necessary counterweight to increasing bureaucratisation.

3. Political management

The Irish experience is not of a separate political executive. The explicit model for local government has been an adapted form of the business firm – a board of directors and a separate executive. The problems of adaptation were to reconcile the business model of a small board with significant popular representation, on the one hand, and, on the other, to adapt the system of appointing officers to a civil service model. So, when city and county management were applied the sizes of councils were reduced: most county councils now have between 20 to 30 members. This was a necessary compromise to provide reasonably widespread representation. The role of the councillors is, formally, to decide on policy matters, but individual representatives are always straining at the leash to get involved in the detailed problems of their constituents. This is exacerbated by the fact that they are elected in multi-member constituencies. An individual councillor who neglects his constituents will find himself replaced by a new, more active councillor, often from his own party. Hence the intense personal rivalry and concentration on the special, rather than the general.

The special is formally the concern of the county or city manager, a permanent career official selected by a national selection agency, the Local Appointments Commission, with secure tenure. Hence, there is potentially a very strong bureaucratic system, usually moderated in practice by good sense on both sides. On the whole this system has worked well, but contrasts with modern developments, such as the fall of the prefect in France. The system can be criticised for separating real responsibility from election, whereas the development of local democracy would seem to lie in uniting them through some less bureaucratic mechanism, for example the directly elected chairman or mayor, of which there has been no Irish experience. However, the major bureaucratic threat to local democracy is the shift of functions and responsibilities not to local bureaucracy but to the national one, with all the impenetrabilities that involves.

On electoral systems, there is a rising consensus that multi-member constituencies are a bad mistake, nationally and locally. Nationally, they are deeply entrenched in the Constitution, but this barrier does not exist in relation to local government. There are no structures for direct democracy or local referenda, but active local communities have no difficulty in making their views felt to councillors individually, at council meetings, and to local officials.

Perhaps one can close with a big general question. Is it possible to maintain a national, popular parliamentary democracy while local democracy dies of inanition? If not, what exactly is the necessary connection between the two levels of democracy? If so, what is the likely impact on the movement for a *Europe des Régions*?

Postscript

A Committee of Ministers was set up in the summer of 1990, assisted by an expert group chaired by T. J. Barrington, to promote rapid reform of the Irish local government system.

12 The Changing Local Government and Politics of Sweden

Agne Gustafsson

The structure of local government

Local self-government is one of the cornerstones of the Swedish Constitution. It operates on the same constitutional basis at both local and regional level through municipalities and county councils respectively. The Local Government Ordinances of 1862 laid the foundations of modern local self-government in Sweden, and it is still in many ways applicable. Sweden has like all the Scandinavian countries, with the exception of Finland, a two-tier system of local government with presently 284 municipalities (*kommuner*) and 23 county councils.

The 284 municipalities are responsible for most of the functions directly concerning the individual, above all in the social and school sectors. But they have also important tasks concerning planning, housing allowances, communications, utilities and industrial enterprises, emergency services, environment and health protection, waste regulation, and leisure and cultural activities. The county councils are mainly concerned with health and medical services, public dental care, education and training for mentally retarded persons, but have also increasing duties in, for example, the educational, cultural and social sectors as well as shared responsibility with municipalities for public transport. The county councils – the decision-making bodies of the counties – have always been directly elected in special elections. Both the municipalities and the county councils have the same general competence.

The creation of the current 23 county councils established the particular structure of regional administration which is so typical of Sweden. The state county administrative board and the county council both cover essentially the same geographical area but have different duties. The existence of both national and local government authorities at county level has not precluded integration and cooperation between the two. The state county administrative boards have the main responsibility for state administration at county level, and it is their task to coordinate social regional planning with reference to the state and local government sectors alike. On the other hand all 14 laymen of the state county administrative board are appointed by the county council for a period of three years. Only the county governor, the head of the board, is appointed by the government for a period of six years. The lay members of the board decide certain important issues of general policy where the governor, who chairs the board, has a casting vote. This arrangement, primarily introduced in 1971, involves elements of decentralisation within the state administration, since previously the administration had been unequivocally led by the county governor.

The great and the consistent tendency in Sweden has been that of decentralisation from central state to regional or local level. This decentralisation process and expansion of the local government sector began in the early years of the 1930s, but the major expansion started after the Second World War. The division of responsibilities between the three levels – central state, the county councils and the municipalities – has not been immutable (see Figure 12.1). Changes have occurred in various directions. Some duties have been transferred to the state (road maintenance, labour market affairs, police), while others have been taken over by local and regional statutory competence.

The 1977 Local Government Act declares, equally and uniformly for municipalities and county councils, that municipalities and county councils shall conduct their own affairs. The meaning of 'their own affairs' is not directly explained in the Act, and it is to a great extent determined by precedents. Each member of the municipality or county council – and nobody else – is entitled to contest decisions by a municipal or county council and its

FIGURE 12.1 The division of responsibilities between state, county council and municipal agencies in Sweden

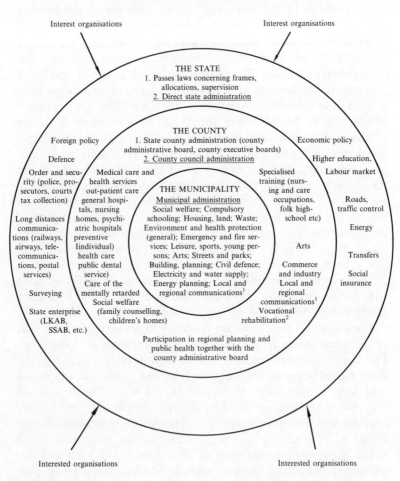

Notes:
This figure illustrates the integration of national and local authorities, but it also reflects the mutual independence of municipalities and county councils.

1. Operated jointly by municipalities and state councils.
2. Operated jointly by the state and the county councils.

Source: Gustafsson, 1988.

committees by appeal. The Swedish local appeal is mainly a way of controlling the legality of a decision of a municipal or county council or an optional committee concerning its non-regulated 'own affairs'. This process results in a flexible system which can be adjusted smoothly in response to social developments. Decisions by the administrative courts of appeal and the Supreme Administrative Court are primarily based on the principle that the decision must concern a matter of public interest.

The most important sectors covered by general competence are leisure, cultural activities, public utilities, and industrial enterprises, traffic water and sewerage, electricity, heating, technical services, streets and parks, the environment, commerce and industry. General competence gives the municipalities and county councils, within the general or unregulated sector, extensive powers of initiative and decision-making.

Of special interest is the entitlement of municipal authorities to subsidise private enterprise locally. This has been a debated point. In order to stimulate local economic development, the municipalities have to undertake general measures on behalf of commerce and industry as a whole rather than benefiting one single undertaking, for example by laying out industrial estates and providing industrial facilities. In principle, subsidies to a particular private undertaking are not allowed, but individual firms have received financial support in various forms. For example, municipal authorities can legally support a particular enterprise if closure or cutbacks would mean heavy unemployment in the locality.

The growth of municipal and, to some extent, county council activity in the field of enterprise during the 1970s and 1980s has been an important supplement to the efforts of national labour market agencies. National municipal temporary employment projects are organised in conjunction with the labour market authorities, one reason for the permanent low unemployment in Sweden, today about 1.6 per cent.

Special powers emanate from about 20 enactments, together with their associated statutes and instructions. These include social tasks which in many countries are the direct administrative responsibility of the state. Laws of this kind include the Education Act, the Planning and Building Act, the Social Services Act, the Environment Protection Act, and the Health and Medical Care Act. It is, for example, the duty of a municipality to ensure that social assistance is given to all needy persons staying in the municipality. Similarly, it is the duty of a county council to ensure that sick persons are cared for, irrespective of where they live. Some of this legislation is detailed, as for example in the Education Act, and some is of a more general nature, merely laying down guidelines for the activities concerned, as for example in the Social Services Act and the Health and Medical Care Act. As a guarantee that every municipality and county council can live up to the aims defined in legislation, the state pays grants-in-aid to municipalities and county councils for certain purposes, such as teachers' salaries and medical care.

A municipality or a county council can decide on measures going beyond the statutory minimum. Therefore a municipal or county council decision can be based on specially defined statutory competence and general competence at one and the same time.

To clarify the legal situation which may sometimes be unclear, a number of enabling acts have been passed to empower a municipality or county council desiring to make a decision concerning a particular matter, as for example in the act concerning grants to political parties by local authorities and in the act entitling municipal authorities to levy charges in public places (car parks, streets, markets, kiosks, etc.).

The power of taxation and local government finance

The principal sources of local government finances are local income tax, state grants-in-aid, charges for services and some trading income, as well as loans. The local income tax is the most important source followed by the charges and state grants. Charges and reimbursements for services and benefits could in principle cover costs but may not yield a profit. There are no special restrictions concerning the right of local authorities to raise short-term or long-term loans, not even abroad.

Due to the relations between the state and local government, the local income tax and state grants are the most interesting forms of financing. Both municipalities and county councils (and also parishes) are entitled to levy direct local income tax. These extensive local powers of taxation, enshrined in the constitution, have been a vital ingredient of local autonomy, explaining in many cases the great expansion of municipal and county council activities. The combination of extensive competence, including the powers of general competence, and of the extensive independent power of taxation makes Swedish local autonomy unique by international standards and imparts genuine substance to decentralisation.

The overwhelming proportion of municipal and county council revenues derives from direct local income tax, over 40 per cent of municipal and over 60 per cent of county council revenues. The framework for the power of taxation is given by law. Neither the constitution, nor the present law, dictate limits or ceilings for local taxation rates. The councils of the municipalities and the county councils are free to levy as high a rate of taxation as they find necessary. However, since 1970 the steep rise in local taxation – especially in the county councils – has led most of the municipalities and county councils on three occasions to impose voluntary limits on their rates of taxation in response to recommendations made by their representative associations, together with the government.[1] For many years the taxation rate has stabilised but that is due to the growing resistance of residents to paying high taxes. Local income tax is paid by all earners in the municipalities and the county councils. Tax assessment is based on the annual tax returns submitted by all taxpayers, but the local income tax rate can vary considerably from one municipality or county to another.

Legal entities ceased to be taxed locally in 1985 and this tax is now a state privilege as is the taxation of private property. Owing to their economic difficulties the three largest municipalities, Stockholm, Gothenburg and Malmö, recently demanded the return of tax revenues from legal entities.

The main purpose of the state-grants-in-aid is to ensure that every municipality and county council, irrespective of size and financial circumstances, will be able to discharge its obligations enshrined in special enactments. The aim is to encourage the expansion and maintenance of particular local government services and level out differences in their costs. In spite of the fact that the municipalities have been enlarged there are still important differences between them concerning their economic status and service to residents.

State grants may take the form of special grants, which constitute the largest part, or general grants. Together they accounted for about 26 per cent of municipal and 18 per cent of county council revenue in 1986. Special state grants, which are earmarked, have sometimes been accompanied by quite detailed state control. For reasons of national government finance and in order to decrease this state control the number of special grants has been reduced and funds have been transferred to the tax equalisation grant instead. Current government policy is to limit the automatic increases and detailed regulation in order to improve the effectiveness of services and to adapt them more closely to local conditions. Special grants for childcare, home helps and medical care have been revised with this aim in mind.

The general state grants are dominated by the tax equalisation grant which takes the form of a general grant computed according to average taxation resources in the country. The aim of tax equalisation grants is to reduce differences in the tax potential and costs of local authorities in different parts of the country, and to help the municipalities and county councils to maintain a fairly even standard of local government activities irrespective of the income status of their residents, their geographical location and some other factors. In 1988 ordinary tax equalisation grants were paid to 253 municipalities and to all county councils except Stockholm's. In addition to ordinary grants the government can award extra tax equalisation grants in special cases to municipalities and county councils in financial difficulties. The largest tax equalisation grants are paid to the Island of Gotland and municipalities and county councils in the sparsely populated rural areas in the northern part of Sweden. Municipalities which do not receive ordinary tax equalisation grants are for instance in the three metropolitan areas: Stockholm, Gothenburg and Malmö. But, on the other hand, these municipalities demand support according to their very high level of service and higher costs as a result of, for example, their social structure and traffic problems.

Some important changes in the way of financing the tax equalisation may be observed. Previously all costs of tax equalisation were financed by the state; however, increases in the period after 1986 have been financed by a special charge on the total base of all municipalities and county councils. For 1989 this charge was 0.47 per cent for municipalities and 0.34 per cent for county councils. Furthermore since 1986 municipalities with the largest tax bases (for example Danderyd and Lidingö in the Stockholm area) have been subjected to an additional progressive charge in order to reduce the most extreme differences in local tax rates as an additional means of equalising taxation rates by means of transfers to the poorest municipalities from the richest.

The whole system of state grants is a matter of continuing debate. A consequence of the special earmarked state grants is that the largest contributions are given to municipalities with a good economic position, large taxbase and well developed services. Reformers therefore demand that all special earmarked grants should be abolished and superseded by general state grants without any provisions.

The state grants are one important reason for the clear trend in recent years towards greater similarity in service standards between municipalities concerning social welfare, especially child care, care of the elderly and medical and health services. In general the Swedish municipalities are by international standards relatively equal. However in regard to services provided under general powers, there are still in many cases great differences.

The expansion of local government

The expansion of local government activities, coinciding with an era of ongoing industrialisation, migration and urbanisation, has accelerated since the Second World War. This interaction is to some extent automatic. Firstly, the rapid growth of the largest cities and towns led to the need for increased housing and heavy investments: streets, water supply, sewerage and electricity. Secondly, the increasing employment participation rate of women led to increased municipal measures in the child-care sector. Thirdly, the general rise in living standards led to heavier municipal expenditure on leisure amenities. Fourthly, the development of motor transport required further investments in local government facilities.

Certain other tendencies have led to greater demands being made on the local government sector to expand and develop particularly its social and welfare services (Slunge, 1986). The importance of the home has diminished leaving local government to take on further responsibilities. The care of children, the sick, the handicapped and the elderly previously and mostly provided by women in the home is no longer available there. The proportion of women gainfully employed has increased to about 80 per cent. The cost of services has increased more rapidly than the cost of goods in Sweden as in other countries. Productivity does not increase in the same proportion in the service sector as it does in manufacturing. However employees in the service sector do not accept that their wages should increase at a slower rate than those in the manufacturing sector. The employees in the local government sector are many, they are also electors and highly unionised. Up to the middle of the 1970s the gross domestic product (GDP) in all Western European countries grew at a steady pace and this facilitated a continuing development of public services. Since then the growth of GDP has been declining in Europe, and Sweden is no exception; there is therefore no longer scope for both increased real wages and increased taxes. As a result of these economic difficulties, demands have been made on local authorities to find new forms of organisations for carrying out their local activities.

Today municipalities and county councils account for more than two thirds of all consumption and investments in the public sector. In 1986 state and local government accounted for roughly 8 and 22 per cent respectively of GDP (Gustafsson, 1986). The greater part of the increase occurring since the 1960s has come within the county council sector, because of the heavy expansion of health and medical care and the transfer in 1963 of the responsibility for primary care and in 1967 the psychiatric service from the state to the county councils. Activities in the local government sector as a whole expanded in real terms by over 5 per cent per annum in the 1950s, and by about 8 per cent per annum at the end of the 1960s. The growth rate of local government activities began to decline somewhat in the 1970s, a process which has continued during the 1980s, levelling out at about one per cent per annum. Even during 1976–82, when non-socialist governments ruled the country, the local government sector expanded to some extent. Since 1982 – with a socialist government in power – the public sector as a whole has reduced, although by very little.

National and local government still employ roughly one third of working people in Sweden; the personnel strength of the public sector today exceeds that of industry. Roughly a quarter of the total persons in employment are employed directly in local government. If national administration and state utilities and national and local government enterprises are also included, the figure rises to about 40 per cent (see Figure 12.2).

FIGURE 12.2 The growth of the public sector in Sweden: personnel strength (in percentages) in the public sector and in commerce and industry, 1965, 1970, 1977 and 1985.

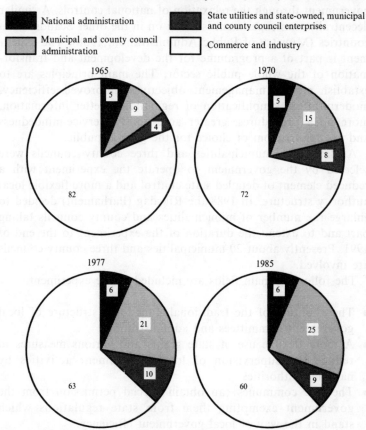

Source: Gustafsson, 1988.

The need to constrain the growth of local government consumption is now accentuated by labour shortages and by the risk that large wage increases are being used as an instrument for local government recruitment. The government is keen to encourage efforts to utilise existing local government personnel more productively and to reduce staff turnover.

The free local commune experiment

The main purpose of the free commune experiment in Sweden, which was launched in 1984, was to test new departures in local government through the relaxation of national controls. A similar decentralisation experiment is going on in the other Scandinavian countries (Ministry of Public Administration, 1988). The experiment is part of a programme for the development and transformation of the whole public sector. The main principles are to establish clearer management objectives, improved efficiency, modernisation, simplification of regulations, better information, more open procedures, greater accessibility, service-mindedness and greater freedom of choice for the general public.

At first nine municipalities and three county councils were selected by the government to operate the experiment with a reduced element of detailed state control and a more flexible local authority structure. In 1988 the Riksdag (Parliament) decided to enlarge the number of municipalities and county councils taking part and to extend the duration of the experiment to the end of 1991. Presently about 20 municipalities and three county councils are involved.

The following main fields are included in the experiment:

- The abolition of the traditional, functional structure of local government committees and administration.
- A more flexible use of state grants and various measures to reduce the supervision of local government activities by national authorities.
- The free communes can obtain special permission from the government exempting them from state regulations which stand in the way of local government efficiency.
- The improvement of cooperation between national and local authorities.

The Riksdag retains certain restrictions on the experiment. Exemptions are not to be awarded where there would be neglect of fundamental considerations of: fair distribution of social services, protection of the lives and health of the general public, legal safeguards and the general economy.

At present there are only preliminary evaluations, but some results seem clear. The wishes presented by the free communes have in general been accommodated by the government. About two thirds of the proposed changes relate to planning and building development, to schools and the labour market. Certain experiments have been found sufficiently beneficial that they have led to the introduction of amendments applying to all municipalities in the country; some parts of the new Planning and Building Act are one result.

The experimental activities include, for example, municipal and county council organisations with full liberty to introduce or refrain from introducing special statutory committees of various kinds, except for the Executive Committee and Election Committee, which are still mandatory. Ale, Bräcke, Sandviken and Örebro municipalities have for example substituted an area-based political organisation covering the entire municipality for a functional one.

The free communes have been given the opportunity of transferring operational responsibility for primary health care from county councils to the municipalities (Örebro, Gnosjö). In the school sector and on housing policy certain decisions which are normally made by the appropriate state regional agencies are now instead being entrusted to the experimental free communes. The municipalities have shown a great interest in taking over responsibilities from state agencies in order to augment the local influence on labour market policy or to eliminate administrative obstacles to cooperation between distinct but closely related activities. Within some participating communes the process of review has also resulted in the discovery that the obstacles to more practical working routines lie in the systems created by the commune itself!

Local employment committees have been set up (with both state and municipal representatives) with a view to cooperation between the state authorities and municipalities, and to encourage municipal activity in the framing of labour market policy.

However, the competence of these committees has been limited as the national labour market authorities and the free communes have not always been able to agree. The former will stand up for labour market policy as a national task, while the municipalities have promoted local activity and local responsibility on employment.

Given the position of Swedish local government, in some respects the free commune experiment is limited. It has to be seen as a reaction against the often detailed form of some special enactments which lay duties upon local authorities. But it also has to be remembered that general competence and the special legislation give the Swedish municipalities and county councils as a whole great liberty of action. The term 'free communes' should not be taken to imply that all other communes are unfree.

The most important effect of the free communes experiment has been a will to check effectiveness and reconsider the form of relations between the state and local government. It is a strong indication that the state and the Swedish system is moving towards greater decentralisation and the augmentation of local autonomy. The experiences gained as a result of the experiment will undoubtedly be of great value for further discussion and development. The dialogue between the state and local authorities has developed and acquired a partly new content.

There is now an element of concern that the political will of the government and Riksdag may become ineffective as a result of decentralisation from the central level. The economic difficulties caused by a growing concentration of investments and resources in the metropolitan areas (Stockholm, Gothenburg, Malmö) and the difficulties of the municipalities and the county councils in performing their service duties to residents, has intensified the debate on decentralisation. The issue is one of balancing demands for local self-determination and decentralisation against the need for a co-ordination of public administration, the rule of law and, particularly, of equal access to social services whatever one's residential location

However the decentralisation process goes on and there are no propositions for transferring any tasks from the local government to the national sector. Rather a debate has started concerning the division of responsibilities between county council and municipal agencies. Some part of the health services to the elderly are going to be transferred from the county councils to the municipalities; discussion is also under way about the transfer of primary health care and the care and assistance of some groups of mentally retarded persons.

Local government expansion has mostly occurred within the sector regulated by the special enactments, but the sector regulated by the Local Government Act has also expanded. The result is an increasing interdependence between state and local authorities so that it is very difficult to distinguish between questions of national and local politics because they are integral parts of the same political culture. The relationship between the state and the local authorities was manifested in the 1974 revision of the constitution and the institution of a common polling day for national and local elections. Partly as a consequence thereof the electoral turnout is nearly as high in the local as in the national elections. In 1988 the turnout in the national election was 86.0 per cent, in the county council elections 84.2 per cent, and in the municipal elections 84 per cent. The slightly lower turnout in the local elections is partly explained by the much lower turnout among foreign nationals (1988: 43 per cent) who have been entitled to vote in local elections since 1976 if they have been registered residents for the three years preceding the election.

Political organisation in local government

Sweden has no mayors or separate political executive. The whole organisation is run through a system of committees with the full councils being the supreme decision-making bodies. Business is drafted and decisions are implemented by executive bodies, the committees, headed by the executive committee in both municipalities and in county councils. The committees have their own administrative offices and staff at their disposal. The municipal council and the county council are the only bodies directly elected by the residents. The councils in turn then elect the members of their respective executive committee, the members of the various other committees, the chairmen of the committees, and the municipal and county council commissioners. All municipalities and county councils elect full-time or part-time commissioners, usually one in smaller and three or four in the larger municipalities. The councils can also appoint local bodies in geographically defined parts of the municipality or county, investing them with independent decision-making powers on certain matters. The members of these bodies are always appointed by the councils on a political basis involving proportional representation.

A municipal or county council may to a limited extent delegate to the executive committee or another committee certain matters on its behalf, but decisions on matters of principle or other important issues may not be delegated in this way. In order to increase efficiency through management by objectives, the municipal and county council are permitted, through a recent addition of the Local Government Act, to give the executive committee or another committee general appropriations which they are allowed to dispose of in a free manner. However, the council must lay down clear guiding principles on the activities which are to be followed.

A distinctive feature of Swedish local government is the existence of many committees to draft business to be decided by the council, to implement the decisions by the council and to attend to certain administrative business. Some committees are optional, while others are statutory, coming under special legislation. Every municipal and county council must have an executive committee comprising the foremost representatives of the political parties. Usually a municipality will have between 9 and 14 committees, in the largest up to 30, each with 11 or 12 members and the same number of deputy members. Some county councils have 5 or 6 committees, while others have up to 13. The policy decisions of the executive committee and the other committees are made by the elected representatives, who have at their disposal salaried officials for technical and administrative work. The elected representatives participate directly at all levels, from drafting to decision-making and implementation. Urgent matters are delegated in various forms to the chairman, a small group of politicians or to an official, acting on the committee's behalf.

Management of financial administration and the drawing up of the budget are among the most important duties of the executive committee. It also leads and coordinates the administration and supervises the activities of other committees whose business has to pass through the executive committee on its way to the council. In supervising the activities of other committees, the executive may not interfere in the performance of duties for which a committee is responsible under special legislation; nor can the council interfere in such matters. Another restraint is that a council may not restrict the allocation of funds in such a way as to prevent a committee from performing obligatory duties. Unlike council meetings the meetings of the committees are held in camera.

Reforms of the local political system

Four main paths of reform have been discussed as a means to strengthen both the efficiency and the democracy of local self-government.

The most important path has been the improvement of conditions for the political parties and better contacts with voluntary organisations and opinion groups. There have also been reforms of local government in order to define political responsibility more clearly. A degree of majority rule has been accomplished in almost all municipalities and county councils by the majority party or parties appointing the chairman of all committees and appointing all municipal and county council commissioners. Next, the establishment of local bodies (district and sub-municipal committees) has been a most important type of reform. Local bodies of various kinds can be set up, by decision of the municipal council, in sub-municipal areas to supplement and even in some cases to deputise for the central committees. These local bodies can also be introduced on a sectoral basis: for example district committees might be set up for the leisure or school sectors, or on an area basis, to cover two or more sectors taking over the administrative and executive duties of several central committees. The municipal council decides the duties of the sub-municipal committee and appoints their members and deputy members. In some cases local bodies constitute an alternative to the partition of recently amalgamated municipalities where things have not gone very well.

The most common and the most interesting alternative is the rise of the sub-municipal committee with administrative duties across several sectors. These committees can if the municipal

council so decides, include both general competence responsibilities (for example, culture and leisure), and special enactments (for
example schools and social welfare). In this way an inter- sectoral
sub-municipal committee can assume general responsibility for a
large proportion of the main municipal tasks within its geographical area. As part of the free commune experiment a
number of municipalities have been given special permission to
abolish the majority of the central committees and to organise
their committees in keeping with local conditions. County
councils are also free to set up local committees at sub-county
level.

Local bodies represent an opportunity of direct local influence
and decision-making in matters affecting the sub-municipal level.
Many argue that the political parties and voluntary organisations
will thus acquire a natural local forum, and many hope for better
opportunities for personal contact between residents and their
representatives. Local bodies should also give more opportunities
for more residents from presently under-represented groups to
play a part in public affairs. However, the sceptics argue that
local bodies, especially sub-municipal committees, may result in a
reversion to the structure of small municipalities, which existed
before the amalgamations. They are sceptical of the hopes of less
expensive administration, greater efficiency and closer contact.

The trade unions have in many cases been unsure of the
implication of these experiments for the personnel. Evaluations
indicate both positive and negative effects, but they are not yet
complete. It seems, however, that sub-municipal committees have
not yet implied any democratic revolution as they are not directly
elected by the residents of the area and their political composition
is not based on the state of the parties there.

The fourth main reform measure has been the local referenda
which were allowed under the 1977 Local Government Act. Now
a straight majority of municipal or county councillors may decide
to hold an opinion poll or some form of consultative referendum
during the drafting of a matter to be discussed by the council. A
number of municipal and county council referenda have been
held under the new provisions, mostly concerning municipal
partitions. Many of the referenda have been held at the same
time as the ordinary elections, and the turnout has been between
60 and 70 per cent.

User control is an alternative model which has been given very little attention until now. By an addition to the Local Government Act the Riksdag has recently decided that the executive committee and other committees should encourage consultations with those who are using their services. Users in this connection are, for example, pensioners, parents of school children or children at day nurseries. Another new clause declares that an official, who has been empowered to decide certain matters on behalf of the committee, cannot decide without having the agreement of the users' representatives. These new statutes have not yet been applied.

Local government employees

The existence of such a large employment sector (one quarter of the working population) has many consequences concerning economy efficiency and democracy. Local government personnel represent a very wide variety of occupations, educational qualifications and pay levels. Half of all municipal employees are to be found in the social services, and about 85 per cent of county council employees in 1986 were employed in the health and medical services. There is also a striking segregation of the sexes: women in 1986 constituted 78 per cent of municipal employees and 85 per cent of county employees, as compared with 48 per cent of the entire working population. In 1986, 55 per cent of municipal employees were employed part-time or paid by the hour, and 93 per cent of these were women. About 90 per cent of these municipal and county council employees are unionised. By international standards Sweden has a very high rate of union membership, particularly in the public sector.

Since 1966 the conditions of employment of all public servants have in principle been fixed by collective agreements. Thereafter it has also been possible for the trade union organisations and the public employers to resort to certain forms of direct action (strikes or lockouts respectively). The Swedish Association of Local Authorities and the Federation of County Councils represent the municipalities and the county councils as their central negotiators with the main trade union organisations.

A delicate problem connected with pay talks and collective agreements in recent years has been the relationship between the private and the public employment sectors. Is private industry or public administration to lead pay levels? The debate on 'level pegging' has provoked serious conflicts in recent years within the public sector, both in national and in local government. Sweden has experienced frequent and extensive labour disputes which have been detrimental to the beneficiaries of social services, health and medical care, and education. Recently, efforts have been made to decentralise the existing very centralised pay negotiation procedures and to give the administrative authorities greater discretion. The rising wage costs of the public sector cause attention to focus on the need for greater efficiency and rationalisation in that sector (Gustafsson, 1986).

Concluding remarks: the continuing influence of politics

In Sweden local party politics is an important factor in a markedly politicised system of local government. The parties have important tasks of integration between national, regional and local politics. In general they are the same parties at each level. In the 1988 municipal council elections the small local parties only gained 243 seats out of a national total of 13 564 seats. From 1970 the polling day has been in common for both national and local elections.

The parties nominate candidates for elective political appointments, supervise the management of affairs and decide whether or not the elected representatives should be re-elected. In both national and local elections voting is based on party lists and candidates are elected on a proportional basis. Proportional representation gives voters little chance of directly exacting political accountability from an individual local politician, but surveys have suggested a steady increase in split voting between local and national candidates. In the 1988 elections 17 per cent of national voters supported a different party in municipal elections and 12 per cent did so in the county council elections.

The state has facilitated the integration between national and local politics by empowering municipalities and county councils through an enabling act to give financial support to parties which are represented at local level. Local party subsidies are the most important source of income for all political parties, and are paid to each party at a uniform rate per seat. The local and regional party organisations have most to say in the nomination of candidates for municipal and county council elections, and the party organisation is also consulted when party groups in municipal council and county councils nominate members to the executive committee and other committees.

The representatives of each party in a municipal or county council form a party group, which usually assembles before each council meeting to discuss the agenda as well as general long-term issues. Group meetings are also held by the representatives before their various committee meetings. The decisions or recommendations reached by the party groups or the party organisations are not legally binding on the individual councillor, but they are usually complied with. A person who votes against the party line too often may risk being passed over next time candidates are nominated.

At present the political parties undoubtedly have some problems. They are finding it difficult to recruit new active members especially among young people, and the turnover rate among politicians has increased, in general due to voluntary resignation. In recent years a noticeable decline can be observed in public confidence in politicians and political parties. For the future these developing tendencies may prove to be the weakest point in the Swedish system of local self-government.

Note[1] Since this chapter was written an important new measure has been adopted by the Swedish government. In order to protect wider tax reform plans and curb public spending, the Swedish Parliament in June 1990 approved a proposal for a temporary local tax freeze for 1991 and 1992. This unusual measure cuts across the tradition of local government autonomy in Sweden.

References

Gustafsson, Agne (1986) 'Rise and decline of nations, Sweden (On Mancur Olson, Rise and decline of nations)', *Scandinavian Political Studies*, vol. 9, no. 1, pp.35–50.

Gustafsson, Agne (1988) *Local Government in Sweden*, 2nd rev. edn, 1988, the Swedish Institute, Stockholm.

Magnusson, T. and Lane J.-E. (1987) 'Sweden', in Page, E.C. and Goldsmith, M.J. (eds) *Central and Local Government Relations*, Sage, London, pp.12–28.

Ministry of Public Administration (1988), 'Free local government experiments in Sweden', SPL/Loc/Ost (88) 12, Council of Europe, Strasbourg.

Slunge, W. (1986) 'Reorganisation of Local Government in Europe: Modern-isation and Adaption', *Report to the Standing Conference of Local and Regional Authorities of Europe*, Strasbourg, 14–16 October 1986.

13 Key Issues in the Local Government Debate in Denmark

Ove Nissen

Functions and finance

Denmark has five million inhabitants and three administrative levels: central government, 14 counties (*amter*) and 275 municipalities (*kommuner*). Unlike Germany for example, cities are incorporated into the counties with the exception of the two boroughs forming the central part of the capital, Copenhagen. These two boroughs carry out both local and county functions.

Municipalities vary in size from 2528 inhabitants in the island and municipality of Laesoe in the Kattegat, to 259 493 inhabitants in Aarhus, the main city of Jutland. About a half of municipalities have less than 10 000 inhabitants, while only 14, or 5 per cent, have a population of more than 50,000. All counties have more than 200 000 inhabitants, with the exception of the island and county of Bornholm in the Baltic, which despite its only 47 000 inhabitants has been given county status because of its isolated geographical position. The last comprehensive local and regional boundary reform was carried out in 1970.

The main municipal functions are: local (town) planning, primary schools, social services, care for the elderly, water supply, sewage and waste water treatment, solid waste and local roads. County functions include: regional planning, hospitals, primary health services, care for the handicapped and disabled, secondary schools, environmental quality, protection of nature and natural resources, major roads and public transport. This leaves central government with all those functions concerned with national sovereignty, but very few domestic services: police, post and telecommunications, universities and certain types of specialised education.

All three levels of government levy their own taxes, the main sources of income for both municipalities and counties being taxes on income and land. These are levied on the basis of one income and property declaration. All income taxes on wages and salaries are retained by the employer and paid into the account of the National Tax Agency, which administers their further repartition. Block, general purpose grants exist, but make up a decreasing part of local and regional income (see Table 13.1).

TABLE 13.1   Sources of income as a proportion of total income in Denmark

	1976(%)	1980(%)	1988(%)
Counties			
Taxes on personal income and land	59	59	81
Block grants	36	37	18
Interest on assets	4	4	1
Consumption of assets, loans, etc.	1	–	–
Municipalities			
Taxes on personal income and land	58	64	70
Block grants	20	18	14
Consumption of assets, loans, etc.	9	2	4
Reimbursements	13	16	12

There are considerable differences in the tax base between and within counties. There are those with more elderly people and others with more children, and there are counties with long distances and few people and counties with a small and very densely populated area. Average declared taxable income per person varies from DKK 62 324 (£5 798) in Bornholm County to DKK 108 367 (£10 081) in Copenhagen County, with an average in all counties of DKK 78 577 (£7 309). This would lead to significant differences in actual tax rates unless there were some kind of money flow from richer to poorer counties and municipalities. In fact the differences are partly levelled out in complicated intercounty and intermunicipal redistribution schemes. Between the counties 85 per cent of the deviation from the average is paid or received, taking into account both the deviation from the income average (tax revenue per person) and the expense average: the 'ideal' expense budget of a county being calculated on the basis of the number of old people, school children, lengths of roads, etc., in a complicated calculation. At municipal level the redistribution percentage is only 52 per cent of the income and 35 per cent of the expense deviation. In spite of the redistribution, the differences in taxation are considerable (Table 13.2).

TABLE 13.2   Personal income tax as percentage of declared income in Denmark

	1976 (%)	1980(%)	1988(%)
Average county	6.3	6.9	9.4
Lowest county	5.5	5.2	8.5
Highest county	7.8	8.7	10.1
Average municipality	15.4	17.4	20.6
Lowest municipality	10.4	11.5	13.5
Highest municipality	18.9	21.4	22.5

The differences can be explained partly by demography in the widest sense of the term and by different service levels, but land policy and investment sequences are often of equal or more importance. Service levels also vary with the highest providers spending between 20 and 40 per cent more on hospitals, primary health and secondary schools than the lowest.

The growth and control of local expenditure

Between 1970 and 1984 municipal and county employment exploded (see Table 13.3). In the years before the economic crisis of the mid-1970s this was probably partly due to a demand for higher service and willingness to pay for it. But the main reason has been the massive decentralisation of tasks from central government to municipalities and, more often, to counties. The municipal and county budgets have grown but corresponding reductions in central budgets can hardly be traced.

TABLE 13.3   Changes in levels of expenditure and employment in Denmark

	1976	1980	1988
Indexed expenditure			
Municipalities	100	131	131
Counties	100	163	183
Number of full-time employees			
Counties	73 443	108 090	127 676
Municipalities	231 232	310 826	350 982
Total labour force	2 514 000	2 626 866	2 857 143
Employees as % of total labour force			
Counties	2.9	4.1	4.5
Municipalities	9.2	11.8	12.3
Total counties and municipalities	12.1	15.9	16.8

By 1979 it was realised that there was no easy way out of the problems caused by the oil crisis depression. Deficits in central budgets were booming, mainly the costs of unemployment benefits and the ever increasing amount of interest to be paid on domestic and foreign borrowing. Counties and municipalities, for their part, had become responsible for 70 per cent of public expenditure (excluding income transfers such as pensions and unemployment benefits), with 23 per cent accounted for by the counties and 47 per cent by the municipalities. In principle, there are no limits on the right of local and regional authorities to levy taxes, as long as they are used for legal purposes. Municipalities may bind every book in public libraries in the finest leather, and counties may equip every hospital bedroom with a private pool and sauna. Many came close to that in the first merry years of the 1970s! But by 1979 it was commonly realised that the problems of public finance in Denmark were the responsibility of all levels of government, and that they must be tackled in common.

As Denmark is a unitary state, there is no constitutional body to represent the interests of the regions (or municipalities) in Copenhagen. There is no Ständerat as in Switzerland or Bundesrat as in Germany to voice officially the attitudes of the *Kantone* or *Länder*. There are local and regional government organisations, but they are in no position to enter into legally binding agreements on behalf of their members, unless each and every one of the members has duly asked them to do so. In spite of that, 'agreements' have been made every year since 1979 between the government and the National Union of Local Authorities and the Association of County Councils respectively. The inverted commas signify firstly that the two organisations are unable to do more than recommend an 'agreement' to be followed, secondly that they could hardly be expected to be enthusiastic about agreements which they had been forced to enter.

At first, agreements with the then Social Democratic Government were aimed at curbing the growth rates in local and regional spending. Between 1979 and 1982 agreements were made to reduce budgeted growth in real terms from 3 per cent per annum to zero. Between 1983 and 1985 control of spending was accompanied by drastic cuts in the block grants.

In 1986 penalties were introduced for the first time. If total spending in that year exceeded the 1984 total, the difference was to be paid into the Treasury as a fine. Although the conformity of this penalisation with the constitution can at least be doubted, it was never challenged. However, it was applied only once. Instead, in 1987 and 1988 an amount corresponding to the excess in spending compared to the 1985 total had to be deposited for four years in the Treasury, interest being paid only from the second year onwards. From 1989 new agreements switched attention to halting increases in income. For 1990 county taxes have to be kept at least unchanged, and municipal taxes have to be reduced by at least 0.2 per cent.

The local and regional government organisations have had limited choice but to appease and to attempt to avoid threats of centralisation and of abolishing the right of taxation altogether. It might be asked whether, after ten years of control by agreement, there is any reason to defend this right. However, the control has never been so absolute as to eliminate differences in service and tax levels.

The negotiations have also been used to force the state to expose the contradiction in its expectations. The government has succeeded in balancing its own budget, but decentralisation has continued over the period and new tasks in the field of health and the environment have been defined for local and regional authorities. Demographic developments (especially in the growth in the proportion of old people) have also increased the demands on service budgets. The declared intention to reduce public expenditure has thus not been accompanied by a corresponding will to contain demand for public services. The government emphasises its role in controlling local and regional expenditure, but councillors now also expect more support from government and parliament in explaining the corresponding necessity to restrain service levels. The Danish public sector is too big both for the taxpayer's purse and also for the national economy.

An abortive attempt at local and regional government reform

Does a small and coherent country like Denmark with only five million inhabitants need three levels of government? This question was raised by the Conservative Prime Minister Poul Schluter in a Copenhagen tabloid daily in July 1988. The ever-expanding public sector is easy game at all times of the year; headlines on this topic can always sell a few thousand copies to the tax-haunted citizens.

As some kind of central government cannot be avoided, and as some kind of local organisation is needed to run the schools and remove the rubbish, the debate focused on the counties. At first the idea of abolishing the counties, transferring their tasks to the municipalities and the centre, was universally hailed. Why was that?

The taxpayer and reader of tabloid dailies does not like to pay taxes nor does he like bureaucracy: a civil servant behind a desk is a natural enemy. The citizen understands the need to pay taxes to obtain health services and a solid education for his children; the county hospital system has high public approval; but few will link the county administration to the county hospital or understand the need to pay for proper management. County councillors find themselves close to the bottom of the popularity list with journalists and members of parliament.

The chairman and members of the board of the National Union of Local Authorities are in their vast majority recruited from the bigger municipalities. The mayor of a city with 50 000 to 100 000 inhabitants and an effective administration sees no need for a county to run secondary schools and public transport. The mayor of a rural municipality with 8 000 inhabitants, on the other hand, is overloaded with problems and finds it natural to seek advice in County Hall. The local authority voices in the debate reflect these different attitudes, but it took some time for the 'smaller' mayors to gain access to the media. Consequently, in the first months of the debate the counties seemed to be squeezed from both sides.

Denmark has learnt to live with minority governments, a product not only of the proportional representation system but also of a longing for compromise, rather than clear-cut solutions. With just 2 per cent of the vote the way is opened to parliament. The present tripartite centre-right government of Conservatives, Liberals and Social Democrats disposes of only 35 per cent of the seats in parliament. The Conservatives are by far the strongest party among the three with close to 20 per cent of parliamentary seats. In town and county halls, however, they have only a marginal influence with no more than two dozen mayors. The municipalities and the counties are firmly in the hands of Liberals and Social Democrats. They have a roughly equal number of mayors but the Social Democrats command the bigger cities and counties. Abolition of the counties would not only create considerable problems for the smaller, Liberal municipalities but if, in consequence, the municipalities were made bigger, they would probably be lost to the Social Democrats. The Liberal ministers in the cabinet, in fact, did not respond very positively to the suggestions of the Prime Minister. Moreover, the Social Democrats, who for decades have been rather centralistic, are becoming increasingly aware of their local and regional roots after eight years of parliamentary opposition.

The central administration favoured the Prime Minister's proposal, seeing well-functioning local and county administrations as threats to its powers and ultimately to its existence. State administration at regional level disappeared in the 1970s or rather it was transferred to the counties and to the political responsibility of the county councils. The Prime Minister's suggestions seemed to open the way to the re-establishment of vertical organisation for roads, for energy and for the environment under the supervision of the national agencies and departments in Copenhagen. The prospect of 1992 and the internal market was seen as a further justification for national integration. However, these ideas met with little support. Nobody wanted the traditional departmental feuds and strifes repeated at regional level.

Before 1970 the counties were only responsible for hospitals in rural areas and for roads; all other functions were transferred to the counties in the decade between 1970 and 1980. Since then, effective and coherent county administrations have been created to tackle these new tasks. But the basic weakness of the counties still is that they are not and have never been demographic necessities in Denmark. There has never been any popular demand for regionalisation. A Dane identifies himself with his town or village and with the nation, but not with any region. Denmark as a nation is very coherent: everybody speaks the same language and shares the same religion. This gives the county little basis as a political entity, unlike the canton in Switzerland and more like the county in England and Wales. Denmark might well do without a regional level of government, but then it would need municipalities of the English size with a population of at least 75 000 to 100 000. At present, no voices are heard in the public debate advocating bigger municipalities. It is generally felt that they should never be so big that the citizen loses his or her feeling of belonging and responsibility to the local community.

Another reform of local government may eventually be successful but this one was abortive because it focused on administrative structures and not on functions and services. Until then county councils will be necessary to secure democratic influence on specialised community services, which the municipality is too small to provide, and which the central departments are too far from and too split up to make available in a coherent and unbureaucratic way.

14 The 'Free Local Government' Experiment in Norway

Petter Lodden

In this chapter a brief outline and analysis of the Norwegian experiment with 'free local government' will be given. The focus will be on the experimental approach of the programme, on certain characteristics of the process and on the value of evaluation and learning built into the reform programme.

The context

By way of an introduction a few points will be made on the context in which this experimental programme is taking place.

Norway has a two-tier system of local government, with 448 municipalities (varying greatly in size and population) and 18 counties. Although Norwegian local authorities have a general competence, many of their activities are carried out on the basis of legislation and regulations which lay duties upon local authorities (in some cases there are quite specific demands as to organisation and task-solving within local government, accompanying these duties). To a large extent the post-war expansion of the Norwegian welfare services has been implemented through local government which employs two-thirds of all public officials.

There has been an ongoing trend towards decentralisation over the last 10 to 15 years in Norway, accompanied by active local government reform measures. The 1980s were marked by a number of initiatives by the government aimed at public service reform in Norway. These took various forms: from campaigns directed towards improvement of the service-mindedness of the authorities, via programmes for the simplification of rules and regulations, to the present Programme for the Renewal of Public Administration (put forward by the former Labour government in May 1987).

The idea of a 'free local government' scheme was first introduced in Norway (drawing on Swedish experience) in a report to Parliament presenting a Programme for Simplification of Rules and Regulations. Thus it finds its place as one amongst a number of instruments for public administrative reform in general, as well as one amongst a number of decentralising measures and specific 'modernising' initiatives in local government. From the start the scheme has been given broad political support. There have been some conflicts between the political parties on specific matters (for instance on the question of privatisation), but nothing has threatened the overall legitimacy of the project. Indeed the programme was introduced by a Conservative government but implemented with Labour in office, roughly along the same lines.

The launch of the 'free local government' experiment: origins and objectives

The provisional Act relating to the 'free local government' experiment was passed in Spring 1986. It invested the government with the authority to grant up to 20 municipalities and 4 counties special 'free' status upon application. Later it was decided to include 2 more counties and to run the experiment to the end of 1991 rather than 1990, which will make it consistent with the election period for the local councils. About 50 local councils applied for 'free' status. The winners were selected by the government in December 1986, about two months after the applications were sent in. It was an explicit goal to minimise the time spent in the selection process, because it was considered of crucial importance to maintain the locally generated motivation to carry through the projects proposed.

The special free status allows for pilot projects and experiments with the following objectives:

- better adaptation of local government to local conditions
- improved service for the general public
- better and more efficient use of the available resources.

The special status municipalities and counties may be exempted from existing legislation and regulations (within certain limitations), which govern how tasks are to be solved and activities organised. Instead the councils can determine their own by-laws, subject to approval by the Ministry of Local Government on authority delegated by the King.

The Act describe in general terms the areas in which experimentation was to be encouraged. These included: organisation, reallocation of functions between tiers of government, and some loosening of central government control measures. However, the Act does not permit projects which may weaken the legal protection of the individual by curtailing the rights or extending the duties of the individual in relation to existing legislation.

The free local government experiment differs substantially from other Norwegian pilot project programmes. In the first place, it encompasses the entire range of activities at the local level, not just one (service) sector. Moreover, the fact that the experimental programme is based on a (legal) method that is tied neither to sectoral or professional interests nor to legislation regulating specific fields of service, focuses attention on the municipalities and counties as territorial authorities.

In the second place, the experiment is based on a bottom-up strategy. The alternative models of working are *not* designed by central government or state agencies. Nor is the programme backed up by central funding, a method which has often been used to stimulate local government to innovate along lines indicated 'from above'. On the contrary, this programme calls for the local councils themselves to propose alternative ways of service production, delivery, organisation and management, based on a local perception of tasks and conditions. The entire responsibility for the initial ideas, the design of concrete proposals and the ultimate implementation and conducting of the experiment rests with the local authorities. The 'resource' offered by the central government is liberation; the opportunity to adapt solutions to local conditions.

A primary objective of the programme is the evaluation of whether this opportunity to adapt solutions to local conditions produces better results than standardisation through central government regulation. The design of the scheme also aims at stimulating innovative processes in local government in general. The experimental method, characterised by the limitation in time and number of units involved, is considered to have some important advantages:

- it allows for a regular and thorough evaluation of effects since as a reform measure it is based on learning through doing and experience. It remains to be seen whether the process of transforming project-experience to general reform measures will in fact take place, as the method actually foresees and prescribes.
- it gives valuable freedom of action in the process of change, as it is based on an explicit dynamic way of working. Thus projects can be altered when under way and new projects and perspectives can be brought into being.
- it allows for greater audacity by constituting a prime argument for testing out more radical alternatives, despite the resistance that might be raised from certain authorities or organisations. Thus it might demonstrate that solutions, thought not 'realistic', can work. It provides a mechanism to spread enthusiasm for change.

The emerging experience of the project

The applications for free status from local authorities gave the first indication of their desired reforms. In general the material submitted showed that local government, beyond focusing on its own organisation and problem solving, was even more concerned about the division of responsibilities between the governmental tiers and sectors. Local councils also expressed their concern about the conditions established by central government to facilitate coordinated local problem-solving. The project proposals are characterised by a variety of perspectives and levels of ambition. At one end of the project scale we find proposed small changes in one sector of local government and marginal adjustments in methods of central control over local government activities. At the other end, we find proposals involving far-reaching changes in the structure of local government and comprehensive delegation of authority and responsibility from the central to the local tier of government.

The proposals may be said to fall into one of the following three categories:

(a) Some projects were related to local government administration, organisation and financial management. Common motivating factors were the desire to increase the political control of local government activities and to clarify relations within and between the political and the professional or administrative spheres. A principal aim was to 'modernise' the division of responsibilities between the local council, the executive board, the principal standing committees and the administration. Increased delegation was seen as the key to more efficient management.

(b) Other projects involved a request for the termination or simplification of some of the central government control and approval routines, which are conducted by the county governor or by special central government agencies at the county level.

(c) A third element in proposals was the desire from the applicants to assume responsibility for tasks previously performed by the central authorities and to establish more integrated service-solutions within the framework of local government. Briefly, these proposals were aimed at facilitating fairly comprehensive restructuring of tasks across sector boundaries and between agencies in different tiers of government. Such projects would enable local authorities to coordinate activities related to the same client-groups.

Interestingly the applications showed that many of the projects could be carried out without exemptions under the free status provisions, as existing regulations constituted no barriers to the solutions proposed. In quite a few of the projects actually approved and launched, the necessary exemptions represent minor, but important, elements of the whole measure. The invitation to apply for free status may have met with and perhaps strengthened local processes of change and adaptation already underway. The evidence may be that in some cases the local authorities operate under some self-imposed restrictions on action, under the assumption that they are the requirements of central government. On the other hand there are cases of central government activities where voluntary guidelines have been presented in a form that invites local authorities to perceive them as regulations.

When the free status municipalities and counties were selected (December 1986), they also received governmental reaction to the project proposals put forward, as guidelines for the next steps to be taken locally. At this stage some proposals met such resistance that they were stopped, primarily because they fell (or could be said to fall) outside the scope of the Act. In some few cases the reason for 'closing the door' was ongoing reform processes in the same field. In retrospect this was a somewhat dubious argument, because such reform-measures may not prove to be in accordance with the local expectations at all.

The applications varied a lot in form and substance, but none contained precise project designs nor corresponding by-laws. Nor was this to be expected. It was recognised by all that substantial work remained to be done locally after the assignment of the free status.

Of the 50 by-laws approved up until Autumn 1989 only 7 were approved in 1987 (covering 5 municipalities and one county), 32 in 1988 and the rest in 1989. Thus, the implementation of the free commune experiments has been a more time-consuming process than probably many of the parties involved had expected. In some cases the delay occurred in obtaining central approval. It other cases the design of the projects had been a rather lengthy process at the local level. Central approval has been most time-consuming in connection with projects aimed at a change in the division of responsibilities between the tiers of government. This feature probably reflects the complexity of the inter-agency negotiation involved. Further it is worth noting that we are still receiving projects and by-laws for approval and completely new project concepts are still being introduced.

With regard to progress, as well as to ambition and scale, the situation varies a lot between the local participants. An important factor in the process seems to have been the strength of local commitment, and the degree of original support given by the political and administrative leadership in the free communes. The degree of initial involvement is probably of crucial importance for understanding the implementation and further local progress of the free commune activities.

The role of the Ministry of Local Government

The Ministry of Local Government has the responsibility for coordinating the activities of the free local government programme. To perform this task a small secretariat has been established within the Ministry, for the programme period. It is obvious that all the ministries concerned with the project proposals of the free communes have an obligation to contribute to the fulfilment of the intentions of the programme. All the same it is natural that the responsible Ministry, through its secretariat, has become the central focal point of activities and the centre of communication between local and central government and within central government.

To the free communes the secretariat has offered guidance as to the process – for instance, when and how to communicate with other parties involved (public institutions, agencies and unions) – and in legal or technical matters especially concerning the elaboration of by-laws. Once projects are established some local authorities have taken the opportunity to discuss matters of concern with the secretariat, other have trusted to their own abilities and judgment. Local demand has decided the form of support given by the secretariat, ranging from advice over the phone, through written comments on project drafts, to visits and meetings with the local authorities. The prime task of working out the actual alternative solution has stayed at the local level. In no case has the secretariat undertaken the role of actual 'project-maker' for a free commune, but we have been partners in a dialogue when invited. Early in the process, some short, written guidelines were developed to support the local elaboration of by-laws, but, beside the requirements of the Act, no statutory demands have been made with regard to local project planning. This non-interventionist role of the central government springs from the basic idea of the programme: to give local government, for a limited period of time and through selected representatives, the opportunity and responsibility to formulate the agenda and direction of renewal activities.

Central government has not met the local initiatives in a uniform way; on the contrary, the reactions have varied between the ministries and agencies involved, and a negative response has emerged in a number of cases. This is mainly the result of project proposals which have not been in complete accordance with provisions of the Act, but to a certain degree it is also a matter of the attitude of central departments. Indeed where central departments have identified positive benefits for their own views in the project proposals, the basis is laid for a more liberal interpretation of the legal restrictions in question.

It has become the role of the secretariat to function as advocates for the free communes within central government. It has become spokesman for the local (territorial) 'rationality' presented in the projects. In the process the professional and administrative rationality of central government agencies, their demand for unified solutions and equal treatment of individual cases has been challenged. The secretariat has continuously been arguing for the expansion of the room for experimentation allowed to local authorities.

With the general political support for the experimental scheme, there has been an overall movement towards a somewhat more positive handling of and reaction to the initiatives of the free communes during the process. The fact that this scheme in many ways represents a definite new and alternative strategy for change may help to explain the initial resistance as well as the eventual movement towards a less restrictive attitude on the part of some of the departments and agencies involved. A lot of information was needed within central government and its agencies, probably more than foreseen initially, and it takes time and effort to overcome scepticism towards unfamiliar ways of doing things.

The role of consultation

The Norwegian scheme brought the organisations and unions of local government employees into the free commune process, and close cooperation with the Association of Local Authorities was also encouraged. They were represented on a central consultation group which has played an active part in the process from the selection of the free communes to the offering of advice to the Ministry on project proposals, by-laws and the process in general. The consultation group has become a valuable tool within the scheme providing an arena for solving or overcoming conflicts that might otherwise have brought processes to a halt; to some extent it has also brought new perspectives into the programme. Some of the applications from free communes have proposed changes in local government labour agreements. Such adaptations cannot be brought about by means of the free commune Act alone but, of course, are a matter for the parties involved. However, the consultation group has made it possible to include such elements in the projects in question, after specific negotiations between the responsible unions and local authorities and their associations.

In general the local government unions have not been wholly satisfied with their opportunities for partaking in the elaboration and operation of the projects at the local level. The situation has varied between the various free communes. Some projects more than others affect the interests of the employees or call on their ideas for better organisation and working methods. It took some time for the unions to get used to the idea of directing their demands and expectations towards the responsible local authorities rather than towards central government.

The evaluation of the programme

A core idea behind the free local government scheme in Norway is that the wealth of experience gained from the pilot projects should provide the basis for general reforms of existing legislation and regulations. The scheme is intended as a strategy for change, adaptation and renewal of local government and the framework within which it operates. Thus learning and learning processes become the crucial matter.

If the experience gained from the projects is to function as the basis for considering wider measures, it must be documented. The free communes thus have a strong impetus to formulate and report their own conclusions from the projects. This will be of benefit to themselves in deciding further steps, and to the rest of local government, which can learn from good ideas. For central government it will be a necessity, if the scheme is to function as a relevant basis for evaluating the framework within which local government operates. In line with the basic idea of the scheme, the free communes will remain free to choose the design and manner of summing up their own results and perspectives. The Ministry has produced some general guidelines for this process of evaluation which they may use as a starting-point, while the Association of Local Authorities has organised seminars on the subject to stimulate locally based evaluation processes.

The activities of the scheme are also being evaluated through a research programme under the auspices of the Norwegian Research Council for Applied Social Sciences, NORAS. Different conclusions will probably be drawn from the experience gained throughout the process, not least depending on the observer's position, for example within a free commune or within a central government agency. There is, therefore, a need for a professional, research-based evaluation of project results as a supplement to the locally defined or interested party conclusions. This research programme was initiated during the Spring of 1987 and was established by the end of the year, that is, a year after the selection of the free communes. This time-lag was intended to avoid researchers becoming the actual project-planners for the free communes thus weakening local ownership and responsibility for the projects. Otherwise the research activities are intended to involve and be organised for the users both locally and centrally.

The government is to make a report to the Parliament on the free commune experiment in the spring of 1991. At the time of writing most of the projects have been in operation for so short a period that it is difficult to make specific guesses as to what kind of recommendations will come out of the process. However, some preliminary thoughts follow.

Firstly, it is hoped that experience from the various free commune experiments will be absorbed into current reform activities in their respective fields. Traces of this are already to be seen, especially within departments with an open and positive mind to the scheme. The very fact that an alternative model has been introduced has evoked substantial interest in a number of cases, even if definite conclusions from operational experience still lie some time ahead. The challenge is to stimulate such a positive curiosity even in departments that have only reluctantly accepted experiments. Secondly, in some cases it will probably take considerable time and elaboration to transform successful project experience within specific fields to general reform measures. In a number of experiments, success has been the result of local adaptation to local conditions. Such cases show that it would be unwise to replace one model or set of statutory demands with new ones, on a standard basis for all local authorities. The issue seems more to be one of deciding on an expansion of the area for local definition of solutions – a shift in the framework within which local government is to operate. Such basic matters may prove difficult to get changed and a period of slow adaption and change may be required. Thirdly, we have registered that some of the projects have already had positive consequences by stimulating other local governments and central government agencies to try to establish similar solutions on a cooperative basis, in which case there is no need for change in the formal structures involved.

Eventually, it will be an important matter to evaluate the experimental programme in itself. Will the results meet with the initial expectations and justify the resources spent? Has it proved itself to be a good method for the 'renewal' of local government and its relationship to the central level of the public sector? If so, how can it be continued, taking into account the important trademarks of experiments – limitations in time and space – which legitimise the possible radical nature of alternatives to be tested out? If a new set of local government units is picked out every four years, what would happen to the motivation for modernisation and learning, stimulated in the earlier free communes?

Concluding remarks

One of the parallel reform measures to the free commune scheme, is an ongoing, complete revision of the Local Government Act (the principal features of which date back to 1938). A revised Act is to be operative from 1992, the beginning of the next local government election period. It is a fair guess that many of the elements in free commune experiments concerning political control, management, organisation and administration within local government will be absorbed or integrated into the new legal framework.

There remain, however, the many projects directed at the restructuring of tasks and responsibilities between the tiers of government or across sector boundaries. These show that the challenge for the future may lie not so much in opening up further experimentation within local government itself as in creating arenas for testing out alternative divisions of labour within the public sector as a whole. This demands a responsive central government which is searching for improved solutions and a mutual confidence between the levels of government. It is hoped that the outcome of the present experiments will influence this setting in a positive and constructive manner.

15 Comparisons and Lessons

Richard Batley

Introduction

One of the purposes of this book has been to introduce new ideas into the debate about the future of British local government. Historically, Britain has tended to see itself as a model of local government and therefore to pursue its many reforms in a rather parochial way. If there has been a reference point, until recently it has often been the United States of America rather than other European countries. Given this relative insulation from continental practice, it is surprising that several earlier chapters show that many of the issues to do with the role of local government and the search for new relationships with citizens are in common, though usually less urgently than in Britain. Many of the solutions are shared, and in some respects it could be said that Britain is coming nearer to continental practice; but in general it is clear that Britain is an extreme case of commitment to principles of marketisation, and exceptional in the conflict which surrounds its reforms. The broadest conclusion of this book must be that there are alternative and viable ways of doing things. Even if they cannot or should not be simply adopted, these other trends and practices do throw a cold light on ideological certainties.

Besides the possibility of learning from others' practices and responses there is the case that policy-makers and practitioners need to learn about 'rival' systems. As national boundaries decline in importance within and perhaps beyond the EEC, choices of locality by investors, workers and consumers become freer. A wider collaboration also implies a wider competition between localities to supply the infrastructure and quality of life which will be attractive. National local government systems will be a part of the competition to provide adequate services, environment and local identity, and to respond flexibly to the needs of investors and residents. It will become increasingly important for the city authorities of Birmingham or Bremen to know the advantages of Barcelona or Bordeaux, and for national authorities to allow them freedom to respond.

In the following sections we will identify some broad conclusions on the book's themes, comparing Britain with the other countries represented and comparing our findings with other recent cross-national studies. It is important to note that our business was not to compare national systems and their merits but to identify the main directions of change and lessons for the Britain debate on the future of local government.

Current changes in the status of local government

Chapter 1 identified some broad principles of reform being pursued by the British central government – financial accountability, competitive efficiency, user control (as opposed to across the board representative democracy) and enablement (as opposed to direct provision). A trend was indicated from a relatively autonomous form of local government to an agency role with regard to the centre.

In all of the countries studied, except for Ireland, reform programmes are being or have recently been undertaken. Together with Britain, these are currently most radical in the Scandinavian and Iberian countries where, in different ways, the relationships between both central and local (or regional) governments and between local government and citizens are being changed. Earlier radical French reforms creating elected regional government and restricting central supervision are being consolidated. In the Federal Republic of Germany, the Netherlands and Italy, current reforms are more narrowly directed to new forms of service delivery often in response to financial cuts. It is striking that much of the language of reform is universal: elsewhere as in

Britain, the phrases which recur are against monopoly and bureaucratic uniformity and in favour of deregulation, accessibility, responsiveness, choice and efficiency. The means by which these ideals are to be realised vary and Britain is clearly at one end of the spectrum in the degree to which they are taken to require a challenge to the role of local government. Reform elsewhere is not a matter requiring the *imposition* of legislation or new practices on local government, although financial leverage may be used as a means of encouraging change in the Netherlands and West Germany. The impression is of changes being worked out by a more incremental adjustment between levels of government, with changes in practice often affecting all levels. In Sweden, Norway, Denmark and Portugal there is a clear presumption in favour of local (as opposed to central or regional) government, that its role in policy choice and service delivery should be enhanced rather than changed.

The most substantial recent or current reform programmes – in Sweden, Norway, Denmark, Spain, Portugal and France – have been advanced in the name of decentralisation. This has involved allocating wider functions to local or regional levels and increasing the amount of financial discretion and freedom from central regulation. This is not just a question of starting points, that is the idea that centralised systems like Spain and Portugal (and perhaps France) had only one direction to go. The Scandinavian countries are adding powers and discretion to communes which already enjoy a relatively high degree of both. In some cases, however, there is room for scepticism about whether the local level really is acquiring the power to exercise extended discretion: the decentralisation of functions may coincide with financial cuts (Germany); the municipal level may find itself subject to even more expansive regional government (Spain and perhaps France). Moreover, it could be argued that the ultimate decentralisation is not political but to the citizen as a consumer choosing between service providers on lines which the British government purports to pursue.

British local government has often been seen as multi-functional compared with most other European systems, in respect of the range of activities which it organises and finances (Page and Goldsmith, 1987, p.156). Evidence to the Widdicombe Committee of Inquiry into the conduct of local authority business suggested that Britain was a special case in its wide range of functions (Goldsmith and Newton, 1986, p.134). We would wish to qualify this in several respects. Some of these direct functions have since been removed – higher education and airports; in several others there is now only a tenuous relationship with local government – police, justice and road transport are areas of local government influence rather than direct functions. Some other functions which are important for example in Sweden, Norway and France are ignored in the evidence to the Widdicombe Committee – social transfer payments, communication systems, sewerage. Regional levels of administration which are unelected in Britain, on the Continent are regional governments which have important functions, are elected and are frequently of similar size to British counties. Most importantly, a distinction should be made between direct *spending functions* and the usually wider range of *responsibilities*. The responsibility may be shared with regional and national government agencies but in most cases it involves a stake in such basic services as water supply, sewage disposal, personal health and hospitals, and (in Sweden and Norway) energy, as well as in the services with which British local government is familiar. The British post-war pattern by which basic infrastructure, health and utility services have been nationalised and then in some cases privatised, leaving local authorities essentially with social and maintenance services, is not the general rule.

The wide spread of responsibilities can be attributed to the underlying constitutional principle of 'general competence' which is prevalent in continental Europe. While general competence may have little more than a symbolic meaning in terms of what local government can really do on its own in situations of extreme financial constraint and competition or restriction by higher levels (Page and Goldsmith, 1987, p.158), it does mean that local government in Scandinavia, Germany and France has been able to retain wide spheres of legitimate responsibility and influence even though often sharing these responsibilities with other communes, elected regional governments or the voluntary sector.

The British principle of *ultra vires*, on the other hand, has led to the statutory allocation of specified spending functions to local government. This has given British local government some clear and protected spheres of operation and real professional capacity in for example education and housing. However, it follows that the weakening of local government's direct providing role in these spheres in favour of competition and collaboration is a profound challenge to the role of local government, having a quite different significance to the evolutionary development of shared responsibility across a broad range of functions on the continental pattern. The question of who does what is particularly important in the British context.

This may explain why continental contributors to this book found almost unanimously that the British debate was dominated by a view of local authorities as agents for the provision of public services. In contrast they emphasised their view of local government as a system by which a community governs itself, chooses its own leaders and direction and acts as a local forum. Service delivery is important (and newly important in the case of Spain and Portugal) but there is a wider role of representing the views and interests of a locality and making policy choices in its name (Stewart, 1989). In that case local government is not made or broken on whether it runs a particular service, nor is it simply one among other possible service providers which can be dispensed with if it is found to be relatively inefficient (Dawson, 1985, p.47). A utilitarian or instrumental view of the status of local government is challenged by a constitutionalist posture which in Britain used to be represented by an operating code of respect for the 'dual polity' (Rhodes, 1987, p.21). Lodden points out that the 'free commune' experiment is intended partly to restore this idea of the commune as a territorial authority and not just as a service provider.

Changes in service delivery

In Chapter 1, we identified the attempt to shift local government in Britain from the self-sufficient provider to the enabling role in which it would be dealing with a wide network of public and private agencies on a contracted, arms-length or partnership basis. Choice and user control are to be encouraged within the public sector and competition encouraged from the private and voluntary sectors.

As we have indicated, the language of reform has much in common in the countries studied including Britain. In different ways the issues of choice, proximity to the citizen (or customer) and reduction of bureaucratic control, complexity and uniformity are being addressed. In some cases these reforms are being pursued in the context of an ideology of the efficiency of competition, market and business – most clearly in Britain but also the Netherlands, Germany and perhaps Italy. In other cases the ideology is more to do with the citizen's access to a democratic state (Sweden, Norway, Spain, Portugal). Most have elements of both sorts of reform; in the other countries, ideological postures are less clear-cut, and the argument for change is more consensual and therefore less confrontational than in Britain. Incremental change rather than a shock to the system is sought, and in most respects local government is seen as a willing partner in and even beneficiary of change; in Scandinavia, it could be said to be the leader in change. Two explanations for this difference emerge. One is that the monopoly provision of certain, defined, mainly social services by British local government has been unusual. Combined with a central government which is both anti-statist and concerned with welfare dependency, this makes British local government the object of challenge on the one hand and determined to defend its provider role on the other. The other side of the argument is that in every other European state there has been a long history of partnership in the provision of services between levels of local government, between communes and between the private and voluntary sectors; the question who does what is neither new nor a threat.

Even the Scandinavian local government systems, with a larger share of public expenditure than in Britain, share a large number of their activities with neighbourhood councils, non-profit companies, cooperatives and joint federations of local authorities. In less well resourced systems, where responsibilities are wide ranging and where basic local government units are small there is a clear impossibility for local government to be sole provider. The Italian case shows a variety of institutional relationships in the provision of different services in different regions, involving partnership between levels of government, semi-autonomous organisations, private concessionaries and voluntary organisations financed by government, fees and private sponsors. French communes often cooperate in water, sewerage, transport and refuse services, either managing these services directly or effectively franchising or leasing them to independent companies.

Three main types of reform measure can be identified. One is to expand the role of local government and to free it from restrictions: examples are the shift to general grants in the Netherlands and Norway; more dramatic are the deregulation and free commune experiments in Scandinavia where central government offers the 'resource of liberation' (Lodden), or the constitutional changes in Portugal which release local government from its role as representative of the centre at local level. The second type of reform relates to the improvement of public service practices: the simplification of the complexity which often results from responsibilities shared between levels of government (Germany and Spain), the setting of performance standards (Portugal), staff training for greater responsiveness to clients (Germany), and strengthening user influence and neighbourhood decentralisation (Sweden). Third, there is the incorporation of business methods and competitive practices into the public sector through, for example, the devolution of budget responsibilities to service operators, deregulation and contracting out in the Netherlands, and the charging of fees for services in Italy. 'Privatisation' is spoken about (particularly in the Netherlands, Germany and Italy) but generally taken to signify something short of a full severing of (local) government's operational and financial responsibility, whether by contracting, leasing or charging fees.

A clear distinction is made, for example in Sweden and France, between the services for which contracting out, franchising and business methods are appropriate and those which should remain under direct administration or with the voluntary sector. In the Swedish case a distinction is made between on the one hand, technical services including, for example, refuse, road maintenance, energy supply and property administration which can be contracted out to commercial operators or undertaken by municipal enterprises and, on the other hand, social, health and educational services which cannot be contracted out but where choice and user influence should be encouraged within a 'renewed' public sector. The term 'franchise' has been used to describe the relationship between French communes and technical service operators because the public interest is secured not by

detailed and specific contractual requirements, but through a
more political process of mayoral negotiation and public complaints backed up by global regulation by the state. The French
(and probably any other) commune is drawn much less than the
British district council into managerial questions of value for
money and competitive efficiency.

The British system which was peculiarly dominated by direct
public service provision is being pushed into a wider web of
relationships with other providers as is the case in most European
countries. However, a new peculiarity has developed which is the
emphasis on competition between providers and the imposition of
competitive practices by central government. Has this been the
necessary 'shock to the system' to bring about the change in
organisational culture which Bekke, Grunow and Dente see as
the prerequisite for changes in management practice? Or, as
Riberdahl (1989) suggests, is municipal government being com-
pelled to adopt a culture which is alien to its ideological and legal
character?

Political control and local democracy

The British reforms are concerned with depoliticising the control
of services and increasing the role of managers, users and the
private sector. A completely inelastic form of local taxation is
intended to make local councils more sensitive to taxpayer
resistance and certainly makes them more dependent on central
grant and vulnerable to changes in method of grant calculation.
Other factors reduce the scope for local political control – the
loss of some areas of activity, the increasing importance at local
level of centrally appointed bodies, compulsory competitive
tendering, the strengthening of managerial control of specific
services and the consequent weakening of the cross-service
political and strategic role of local government.

In Britain, the stream of central interventions in local practice
marks the culmination of a shift from a tradition by which local
politics have remained more separate from national politics than
in any other country (Bulpitt, 1983, p.134). In this 'dual polity'
local government's constitutionally subordinate position was
combined 'with a considerable degree of discretion in decision-

making on local services' (Rhodes, 1987, p.21). We are still in a transitional stage and it is not clear what forms of integration between the two polities are to replace their relative insulation from each other. Earlier forms of representation by professional interests to central spending departments and by politicians through local government associations are now seen by the centre as self-serving; more detailed financial controls and regulation of local administrative practices are taking their place.

In the other European countries presented in this book there are well established but changing systems for the integration of local into national politics. They are complex and interactive and it is therefore difficult to discern the balance of power which they imply, because at the same time they may limit local discretion and give local government access to influence at higher levels. On the whole, the pattern of change is towards a reduction of detailed control but from a starting point often involving higher degrees of regulation than in the British case. It is here that the 'language of reform' most clearly is not in common – the enhancement of local political control is not on the British government's agenda.

We may distinguish between *political* integration and forms of *administration* which lock local government into a subordinated or a negotiating relationship with the centre. The relative weakness of these two mechanisms in the British case may at the same time be a sign of its relative autonomy and also of the absence of a protecting network of established and respected procedures. Goldsmith and Page (1987, p.87) argue paradoxically that the higher degree of local control of services in Britain contributed to local politicians' insulation from and therefore political ineffectiveness on the national stage.

The clearest case of centralised political control is Ireland with a combination of national party discipline imposed at local level, the reduction of local politics to a vehicle of clientelistic access to the centre and the accumulation of local political posts by national parliamentarians. But this same *cumul des mandats* and interpenetration of national and local political careers may work in France not so much to subordinate local politics as to lift local values and interests 'right to the core of the central government' (Mény, 1987, p.88). The French national Senate is itself composed of local authority representatives. In Italy, a broadly centralising party system operates at all levels to bind together a myriad of public organisations as well as levels of government, but this structure also makes central government open to a two-way traffic of local influence through the careers and pressures of professional politicians (Sanantonio, 1987, p.126). In Scandinavia, the political interrelationship depends less on personal careers and territorial advocacy through the party system and more on the building of consensus through arrangements familiar but weaker in British local government – the pressure of councillors speaking on behalf of local government through the political parties and negotiation by local authority associations with central government over legislation and policy. Nowhere, except perhaps the Netherlands, is the interaction of local and central politicians as weak as it is in Britain (Rhodes and Wright, 1987, p.9).

The administrative solution to the integration of local and central government lies in instruments of financial control, obligatory duties imposed by the state, supervision and regulation of local activity and influence on executive appointments. Once again the clearest case of control must be Ireland with the appointment of city and county managers on the recommendation of a national board and the fragmentation of functions between appointed special purpose boards. Similarly in the Netherlands, the burgemeester (mayor) is appointed by the Crown, on the recommendation of a provincial commissioner, as chairman of the municipal council and executive. In both these countries and in Italy and Portugal, local government is extremely or absolutely dependent for finance on central grants. But Pereira and Berg show that an apparently dependent structure can be counterbalanced by other factors – the lobbying power and high legitimacy of local government in the Portuguese case, party coalitions which cross the centre-local divide and ministerial divisions which disunite the centre in the Dutch case.

In the apparently decentralised systems of Scandinavia, nevertheless, four sorts of administrative limitation on local discretion apply: the fact that the majority of their expenditure is accounted for by mandated services imposed as duties by the centre, detailed regulations about how activities are to be performed, central participation in the budgeting process, and supervision by the state through regional or county boards both on general issues of legality and accounts and on specific policy issues. The 'free commune' experiment and other reforms are primarily directed at transforming this central-local relationship from regulation and supervision to advice and support.

In this respect there is a convergence between Britain and Continental Europe. As they, especially Scandinavia but also France, Spain and Portugal, try to reduce the degree of regulation, Britain is moving from a system which allowed discretion in service provision towards detailed central control. The risk, as Page and Goldsmith (1987, p.86) note, is that effective control will require the sort of bureaucratic, prefectoral supervision which other governments have found to be costly and stultifying.

Even when tightly controlled, most local government systems have enjoyed a degree of legitimacy and electoral support which affords protection. Low electoral turnouts are a simple reflection of British local government's comparative position but the issue involves not only local electors' judgements but legitimacy within the wider governmental system. Several factors relating to local government's wider legitimacy in continental countries can be identified – status in written constitutions, general competence or at least comprehensiveness of responsibility, the intermingling of national and local political careers, the perception of local government as representative of a community and not just a service provider, the interpenetration of central and local government in national administration. The majority vote system in Britain may be another factor which by polarising party positions leads central government to call into question local government where it is represented by opposition parties; whatever the disadvantages of proportional representation it is coalitional in nature and therefore likely to soften attitudes between the centre and locality.

There are other factors which have more to do with local identity. Firstly scale and continuity: Britain has by far the largest local authority units and probably has gone through more reorganisations of scale and boundary, leaving local identity confused and amorphous. Most countries went through attempts to achieve agglomeration in the 1960s and 1970s but the Latin countries' communes were able to resist change while in others the reorganisation was less drastic. Basic units of government in other European countries generally have populations little larger than parish councils which in Britain are practically functionless, where they exist. The commune persists with a historical identity. Secondly, and as a consequence, smaller scale allows a greater proximity between representatives and electors: in Britain not only is the town hall more distant but also fewer councillors represent larger numbers of constituents.[1] Thirdly, there seems to be a greater tendency in the British case for national and local governments and representatives to overlap in their claims to represent local interests. Members of Parliament may often compete with councillors to take up complaints related to local government affairs,[2] while central governments may 'hi-jack' parochial issues (for example, litter) into the national arena. In the other countries studied, the local politician or mayor is more often seen as the first resort for electors even where the issue is not purely local. There can be no easy explanation but possibilities are that the party list voting system combined with very large constituencies reduces the national politicians' need to cultivate a very local electorate, that tighter party pyramids more clearly integrate and maintain functional distinctions between levels, and that the strong executive mayor system (of the Latin countries and Southern Germany) gives local government a clear public persona and political importance.

This is not to say that other local government systems have all the virtues. The same qualities which make for local identity may generate personalistic or clientelistic politics and coalitional conservatism in place of Britain's collective style of leadership and clear choice between parties. The 'price' of retaining small communes in France, Italy and Spain may have been that they were considered too small to take on many of the decentralised powers which were instead allocated to elected regional government (Page and Goldsmith, 1987, p.166). The more interactive style of many continental systems may confuse accountability between levels of government.

Common trends and explanations

Our comparison shows a fairly high degree of commonality in the trends affecting West European local government. The expansion of the role of local government which all countries saw up until the 1980s has continued for most. The language of reform is almost universal, expressing concern to decentralise, debureaucratise and deregulate and to improve efficiency, responsiveness and access. No simple distinction can be made between Britain and other countries: most share some elements of their reform programme. Even in Britain a market version of the concern with decentralisation is apparent, although in most European countries this matter is clearly about the decentralisation of political control as well as the administration of service delivery. Reform in service delivery methods for some countries (especially the Netherlands and Britain) involves the introduction of business practices and competition but it is more often about decentralising, encouraging flexibility, reducing central regulation and developing user control and client responsiveness; privatisation on British lines is not a major issue. While forms of political and administrative integration are more elaborate in other European countries, there is a tendency in most for the reduction of supervision and regulation.

Britain is approximating continental practice in two main respects. The first is the shift from monopoly provision by the government sector to a wider involvement of parastatals, private agencies and the voluntary sector; the second is the shift of central government into a more supervisory and regulatory mode. There are, however, some distinctive aspects of the British case. Firstly, the reforms are imposed from the centre; in the absence of a written constitution, the old constitutional code (mutual insulation within a dual polity) has been upset. Secondly, the reforms' intent is to depoliticise service delivery in favour of market processes. Their emphasis is on the development of a variety of competitive rather than collaborative providers. 'Decentralisation' is then to do with the extension of consumer choice or user control rather than the enhancement of the role of local politicians. Thirdly, and partly as a result of the first two points, the process of reform in Britain has been peculiarly politicised and conflict-laden.Various explanations for this conflict have already been suggested: a long tradition of political and administrative insulation between centre and locality leading to an absence of routines for conflict resolution; the high degree of local government involvement in direct service provision; the consequent shock to local government's role of the centre's interventionist yet anti-statist reforms; the effect of the majority vote system in creating uncompromising divisions between the centre and oppositional local government. What is more, the reforms were not only challenges to the established local government system as such but also party political assaults by a Conservative government on bastions of the Labour Party in local councils and public service unions (Gyford, 1985).

The fact that there is nevertheless something in common in the trends observable in the different countries raises the questions why and why now? It should be noted first that the trend towards the decentralisation of public expenditure to sub-national levels of government is not new. Sharpe (1988) shows that for most Western democracies, while total government expenditure grew between 1950 and 1982, central government accounted for a declining proportionate share. This leaves aside the finer questions of the degree of local level dependence on central government grants, control and regulation which many national governments are now seeking to reduce. Sharpe offers as possible explanations that urbanisation has generated demands for local services and that the centre has off-loaded the growing tax burden and associated public disenchantment to the local level. Rhodes and Wright (1987, p.15) add that the expansion of the welfare state at the local level then creates its own political and professional interests against central control and financial restraint. While the British government has tried to assert both control and restraint, several others (notably the Danish) have tried to achieve financial restraint without centralisation.

Several writers in this book and elsewhere refer to current developments in society and economy to explain the reforms which are not only concerned with the allocation of functions to local level but also with local control and more flexible and responsive forms of service delivery. At one level it is possible that a certain discourse about desirable ideals and directions of reform spreads by international exchange, but these writers identify more substantial motives for change within their own countries. Gustaffson comments on the difficulty of maintaining Swedish public services in a situation of labour shortage and declining economic growth: the efficient use of resources, less bureaucracy and the mobilisation of local resources are ways forward. Grunow refers to the motivating power of the fiscal

crisis as higher levels attempt to shift responsibilities without
resources to lower levels; local government in Germany becomes
the agency chosen to 'administer scarcity'. Moreover, the old
parties have to demonstrate some response to the demands for 'a
revival of politics from below' (Hesse, 1987, p.81) emanating
from new social movements and especially the Greens which
were active first at local level. For Berg (1989), with increasing
specialisation of organisations and individuals in the Netherlands,
there is a growing individualisation of demands which cannot be
satisfied by the old collective forms of public provision. Torrani
(1989) argues that the technological revolution creates both the
conditions for and a possible response to change. In Italy it has
generated a flourishing of small businesses linked with 'auto-
nomist' movements arguing for decentralisation; big firms, mass
labour and standardised, large-scale public service providers lose
their advantage to small-scale units capable of responding flexibly
to more specialised demands.

A possible synthesis of these views exists in Stoker's (1989)
application of regulationist theory to British local government.
Briefly, the argument is that patterns of public sector intervention
and regulation grew up to support the form of economic
organisation which was pre-eminent in Western countries between 1930 and 1970. Mass production in the leading sectors
based on large-scale plants and routine assembly line operations
generated a mass work force and standardised patterns of
consumption. These 'Fordist' conditions of production and
consumption were sustained by the extension of the state's role
in collective provision; moreover state organisation was influenced by the dominant Fordist organisational form (scale,
centralism, hierarchy and standardisation). This was the era in
which local government was developed as the primary agent of
mass collective provision in housing, social services, public health,
education, transport and physical infrastructure. The post-Fordist
economy emerges out of changed technical conditions of production and more discriminating consumer demand in a wealthier
market; it is associated with shorter runs of more specialist
production, higher market segmentation and more flexible forms
of organisation. This represents a threat to the traditional form
and content of state intervention: public sector provision becomes
less necessary and bureaucratic uniformity less appropriate.

Local government as the main agent of collective provision is at the forefront of such change, but, as we have seen from the countries studied, change may go in more than one direction. It may either favour the marketisation of public services and the weakening of local government's role, or the reform of public services and the decentralisation of government so as to create the conditions for more diverse, flexible and responsive decision-making.

Lessons for Britain?

Practices cannot be simply transferred and, in any case, there should be no suggestion that the Holy Grail can be found in any of the other countries studied. Nevertheless the comparison suggests ideas which can be introduced into the British debate-about the future of local government. Many such ideas are available in earlier chapters: below we summarise some leading points. The implications of several of these points for British local government are elaborated in Stewart and Stoker (1988 and 1989).

There is an almost universal concern with finding ways towards more flexible, responsive and efficient administration. Change is normal but the emphasis given in Britain to market-oriented solutions is unusual in its intensity; in most countries the enhancement of local democracy and political discretion is a major element of reform, and none would share the British government's commitment to the central imposition of competitive practice. On the other hand, partnership between a whole variety of service providers and levels of government is the normal practice in most other West European countries. The degree to which British local government used to be a monopoly provider for example of education, social housing and social services was unusual and the tendency to its adoption of a coordinating and enabling role within a wide network of providers brings it into line with European practice. Withdrawal from direct provision is not intrinsically a threat to the integrity of local government; indeed, it might allow the development of a more wide-ranging role.

However, pushes and shifts in this direction *are* a threat when at the same time the status of local government is ignored, derided and under challenge. The concept and recognition of local government as a territorial authority, forum and representative of a community is missing in the British debate.

Centralist intervention and destabilising reforms are facilitated where British local government lacks legitimacy in the eyes of central government and identity in the eyes of local electors. What lessons from Europe might help to redress this situation? Local government in the other countries has a constitutional status which is more formal than the operating code which in Britain perhaps served more to maintain a gulf rather than respect between levels of government. As part of that constitutional status, the concept of general competence is important at least symbolically but also as a statement of local government's wider community responsibility, if not always of wide spending functions. Potentially at least, this wide responsibility allows local government to adopt a strategic role, reinforcing its nature as government rather than only as provider of specific services. Local identity and understanding of local government may be enhanced by the strong executive mayoral system although effective local government in Scandinavia manages without this. Perhaps more important are the smaller scale of local government in all other countries, the higher density of representatives and the historical continuity of local units (especially in the Latin countries). Local government then has a more secure and respected base from which it can connect with the centre through personal political careers, party structures, joint lobbying and professional interaction. Britain, by comparison, lacks effective platforms for local government at national level (whether for example through noted politicians or through representation, as in France, in the second house of parliament) and lacks clear working understandings, even within parties, between politicians at different levels; the result is the appropriation of local issues by national politicians and government. The party list voting system in most European countries may also serve to reserve local issues for local government by detaching the central politician from specific localities.

The history of the relative insulation of British local government from national government has been replaced by increasing financial control, regulation and supervision. The rules of this new game are constantly changing as central government intervenes in specific issues, crises and conflicts (for example over the community charge, the sale of council estates, 'opting out' of schools). Unless there is a return to the traditional insulation, it seems likely that crisis intervention must give way to a more routinised and generalised relationship as precedents and practices become established. The European experience suggests that the routines could be of two sorts: either the close financial control and prefectoral supervision (under a central government agent at local level) from which most countries are seeking to move; or a more mutual arrangement worked out between levels of government, based on new codes of understanding (constitutional, party political or legal) about spheres of influence, and creating forums for routine contact between central and local politicians and officials whether through party or governmental frameworks.

Conflict is inevitable at a time of reform when interests vested in established practice are being challenged, but it seems a peculiarly endemic feature of the British central-local relationship. Deep partisan divisions colour the relationship and obstruct the development of a working partnership; local government is at the centre of what seem, by comparison with other countries, to be often totemic struggles between the parties. Proportional representation may or may not be the cause but it is certainly associated with a more pragmatic and open-minded style elsewhere.

Notes

1. Research for the Widdicombe Committee (vol. iv, 1986, p.140) reports that the average population size of British local authorities is four times that of the Swedish which are the next largest in Western Europe. The ratio of councillors to citizens is 1:1800 in England and Wales against an average ratio among Western nations of somewhere between 1:250 and 1:450 (Norton, 1987). A counter-argument is that in Britain, unlike many continental systems, the councillor is identified with a particular ward rather than the municipality as a whole.
2. Research for the Widdicombe Committee (vol. iii, 1986, p.54) found that 47 per cent of electors would turn to their MP to influence their local council if they felt that it had made a wrong decision.

References

Berg, E. (1989) 'The Dutch experience: lessons for the UK?' Conference on European Local Government, INLOGOV, Birmingham.

Bulpitt, J. (1983) *Territory and Power in the United Kingdom*, Manchester University Press, Manchester.

Goldsmith, M. J. and Newton, K. (1986) 'Local government abroad' in Widdicombe Committee, vol. IV.

Goldsmith, M. J. and Page, E. C. (1987) 'Britain' in Page and Goldsmith (eds), pp.68–87.

Dawson, D. A. (1985) 'Economic change and the changing role of local government' in Loughlin, Gelford, Young (eds), pp.26–49.

Gyford, J. (1985) 'The politicisation of local government' in Loughlin, Gelford and Young (eds), pp.77–97.

Hesse, J. J. (1987) 'The Federal Republic of Germany: from cooperative federalism to joint policy-making', in Rhodes and Wright (eds), pp.70–87.

Loughlin, M., Gelford, M. D. and Young, K. (eds) (1985) *Half a Century of Municipal Decline*, George Allen and Unwin, London.

Mény, Y. (1987) 'France' in Page and Goldsmith (eds), pp.88–106.

Norton, A. L. (1987) 'Local government in other Western democracies', INLOGOV, Birmingham.

Page, E. C. and Goldsmith, M. J. (eds) (1987) *Central and Local Government Relations A Comparative Analysis of West European Unitary States*, Sage, London.

Page, E. C. and Goldsmith, M. J. (1987) 'Centre and locality: explaining cross-national variations' in Page and Goldsmith (eds), pp.156–168.

Rhodes, R. A. W. and Wright, V. (eds) (1987) *Tensions in the Territorial Politics of Western Europe*, Frank Cass, London.

Riberdahl, C. (1989) 'Changes in municipal service delivery and management: the trends in Sweden', Conference on European Local Government, INLOGOV, Birmingham.

Sanantonio, E. (1987) 'Italy' in Page and Goldsmith (eds), pp.107–129.

Widdicombe Committee (1986) Committee of Inquiry into the Conduct of Local Authority Business, Research vol. III, *The Local Government Elector*, and Research vol. IV, *Aspects of Local Democracy*, HMSO, London.

Sharpe, L. J. (1988) 'The growth and decentralisation of the modern democratic state', *European Journal of Political Research* 16, pp.365–80.

Stewart, J. D. (1989) 'A future for local authorities as community government' in Stewart and Stoker (eds).

Stewart, J. D. and Stoker, G. (1988) 'From local administration to community government', *Fabian Research Series* 351, Fabian Society, London.

Stewart, J. D. and Stoker, G. (1989) (eds) *The Future of Local Government*, Macmillan.

Stoker, G. (1989) 'Creating a local government for a post-fordist society' in Stewart and Stoker (eds).

Torrani, P. (1989) 'Italian local government and the organisation of local services', Conference on European Local Government, INLOGOV, Birmingham.

Index